PROPHETIC WARFARE
MANUAL

THE
PROPHETIC
WAR
OF WORDS

Scripture quotations are taken from the Holy Bible, King James Version. The King James Version is public domain in the United States of America. All bolding and emphasis are added by the author.

Cover Illustration and Design by: Guy Manzur

Formatting by: Deborah Ling and Emmanuel Okpeniku

Printed in the United States of America

Dedication

I dedicate this book to God the Father, Jesus His Son, and the Holy Spirit. I attribute all that I am and anything I have accomplished to the Godhead. All three of the Godhead have played an integral part in my life. You revealed yourselves to me when I was young and have always been there for me throughout my whole life. I love you with all my heart, mind, soul, body, and strength. I will never forget what you have done for me. I THANK YOU from the bottom of my heart!

I also dedicate this book to my wonderful wife, Eunice. The way you love me and take care of me does not go unnoticed. You also played a significant role in getting this book out. Thank you for always supporting me, my walk with God, and the ministry God has given me. You are not only my wife, but you are my companion and friend.

TABLE OF CONTENTS

DEDICATION III

INTRODUCTION I

CHAPTER 1

THE BEGINNING OF THE WAR 5

CHAPTER 2

SONS OF GOD 17

CHAPTER 3

ALL OF YOUR WORDS COME TO PASS 33

CHAPTER 4

THE HAND OF THE LORD 49

CHAPTER 5

DOUBLE PORTION OF HIS SPIRIT 61

CHAPTER 6

LAW OF FAITH 71

CHAPTER 7

LAW #1: SPEAK DIRECTLY TO THE MOUNTAIN 85

CHAPTER 8

LAW #2: BELIEVE WHAT YOU SAY WILL COME TO PASS 99

CHAPTER 9

LAW #3: BELIEVE YOU HAVE RECEIVED 115

CHAPTER 10

LAW #4: NO DOUBT IN YOUR HEART 131

CHAPTER 11

LAW #5: CALL THINGS THAT BE NOT AS THOUGH THEY WERE 143

CHAPTER 12

    LAW #6: The Will of God 157

CHAPTER 13

    LAW #7: Forgive Everyone from the Heart 167

CHAPTER 14

    LAW #8: A Pure Conscience 175

CHAPTER 15

    LAW #9: Keep the Commandments of God 191

CHAPTER 16

    LAW #10: Faith Without Works is Dead 205

CHAPTER 17

    LAW #11: Meditation + Confession = Possession 213

CHAPTER 18

    LAW #12: Patience and Faith Inherits the Promises 225

CHAPTER 19

    LAW #13: Prayer and Fasting 235

CHAPTER 20

    LAW #14: Faith Works By Love 247

CHAPTER 21

    LAW #15: The Name of Jesus Christ of Nazareth 259

CHAPTER 22

    LAW #16: Thanksgiving 271

CHAPTER 23

    Speak No Evil 283

CHAPTER 24

    David's Words vs. Goliath's Words 297

CHAPTER 25

SOLOMON THE KING OF PEACE 307

CHAPTER 26

JEZEBELIC HIT 321

CHAPTER 27

THE LOST ART OF REBUKING 335

CHAPTER 28

THE POWER OF PROPHECY 347

CHAPTER 29

PRAISE AND WORSHIP 357

CHAPTER 30

SPEAKING THE BLESSING AND THE BENEDICTION 369

CHAPTER 31

THE END TIME BATTLE OF WORDS 379

CHAPTER 32

MANIFESTING GOD WITH YOUR MOUTH 393

CHAPTER 33

FINAL WORDS 403

ABOUT THE AUTHOR 409

INTRODUCTION

I became a Christian at the age of seventeen after a powerful encounter with God. At the beginning of my walk with God, He started teaching me about the power of words and faith. As a young Christian, I was reading the passage where Jesus appeared to the apostles after His resurrection. It says He opened the eyes of their understanding to comprehend the Scriptures. Let's look at this verse together from the Book of Luke.

Luke 24:44-48 (KJV)

*44 And he said unto them, These are the words which I spake unto you, while I was yet with you, that all things must be fulfilled, which were written in the law of Moses, and in the prophets, and in the psalms, concerning me. 45 **Then opened he their understanding, that they might understand the Scriptures,** 46 And said unto them, Thus it is written, and thus it behooved Christ to suffer, and to rise from the dead the third day: 47 And that repentance and remission of sins should be preached in his name among all nations, beginning at Jerusalem. 48 And ye are witnesses of these things.*

I knew that I could miss great revelations from this verse if God did not open my understanding. The Pharisees and the Jews studied the Bible regularly, and even with all this reading and studying, they still missed God being in their midst when Jesus, the Son of God, came on the scene.

The apostles themselves walked with Jesus for over three years and still missed many things Jesus was trying to reveal to them about His death and resurrection. To avoid the possibility of *me* missing God, I repeatedly prayed that God would open the eyes of my understanding to comprehend the Scriptures. I can now say that God has done just that. This book has many of the revelations and secrets God has shown me over the years. I pray these Divine truths will change your life as they have changed mine.

A few years back, I had another life-changing experience with God. I asked myself why the Ark of the Covenant, the most sacred relic in the Holy Temple, is not mentioned once by Jesus. If He did speak of it, it was not recorded. It is also not mentioned much in the New Testament. It is noted once in the Book of Hebrews, but it says we can't speak much about it in that passage. It is also mentioned in the Book of Revelation. After some thought, I let the subject go and just thought I may never know the answer. But, it was a Divine question worth asking.

A few weeks after I let this question go, I spent time with God one night confessing Scriptures. Then, when I least expected it, the Holy Ghost fell on me, and I mean He fell on me. You know what I am saying if you have ever had this happen to you because that is precisely how it felt. I immediately went into a vision, and I saw four people carrying the Ark of the Covenant up the steps of the alter to a large Church. As I saw this in my vision, the Holy Spirit spoke to me and said, "Wherever you read Ark of the Covenant in the Old Testament think Holy Spirit, and wherever you read Holy Spirit in the New Testament think Ark of the Covenant. Put the two together, and you will understand Me."

I immediately came out of that experience shocked. It was a precious experience, and I felt closer to God. But, it was also similar to the experience the prophet Isaiah had when he saw the Lord high and lifted up, and it left me feeling undone. I went into a week of deep repentance. I couldn't stop crying as God cleansed my heart. After all my repentance and cleansing, I began to study the Ark of the Covenant. I looked up the Ark of the Covenant in every place I could find it in the Old Testament and copied each Scripture into a word document. Then I moved to the New Testament; I looked up Holy Spirit everywhere and copied it into a word document. It was very enlightening to look up a subject everywhere it is found in the Scriptures. It took some time to study the Bible this way, but the revelations I learned about the Ark of the Covenant and the Holy Spirit were priceless.

I am telling this story because I received mysteries of the Ark of the Covenant, but something much more incredible occured, I was shown how to study the Bible. The Holy Spirit had shown me a way to study the Bible. From that point on, the Holy Spirit began leading me to different subjects, and I would look those subjects up in every place in the Bible. It could be on faith, grace, peace, relying on the Lord, being strong in the Lord, the oils of the Bible, the Lord is with you, and so on. I have done over 400 of these studies and copied them into word docs.

When you look at a subject everywhere it is found in the Scriptures, as led by the Holy Spirit; your mind gets opened to the full counsel of God. These studies and spending time with the Holy Spirit have changed my life. Some of the studies have taken a month or more to accomplish, while some were quicker. I never tried to hurry through any word studies because I wanted to get as much truth and revelation as possible from the Holy Spirit. The Holy Spirit is the best teacher anyone can have.

Having said all of that, I decided to write this book by the leading of the Lord on two of the most important subjects I believe you will ever learn about: your mouth and the power of faith. The Lord also showed me that this book would help many people. There is a war raging between evil words and good words. This subject reaches into the very heart of God, who created all things by His Word, and He will come back and fight the devil and the antichrist with the Sword coming out of His mouth. This Sword is the Word of God that defeats all the enemies of God. Jesus, Himself is called THE WORD OF GOD, and He is the *Author* and *Finisher* of our Faith. I pray that whoever reads this book is enlightened, blessed, inspired, and challenged. May the Holy Spirit open your understanding to comprehend the scriptural truths found in His Word the same way He opened my spiritual understanding.

CHAPTER 1

THE BEGINNING OF THE WAR

In the beginning, God created the Heavens and the earth with His spoken Word. Everything we see, hear, smell, taste, and feel in this world was created in six days by God's spoken Word. These first six days reveal the majesty of God and the creative power of His voice. Through His wisdom as a masterbuilder, He created and ordered a perfect world and universe by the creative power of His voice.

The first thing God created on day one was light. God then divided the light from the darkness, calling the light Day and the darkness Night.

> *Genesis 1:3-5 (KJV)*
> *3 And God said, Let there be light: and there was light. 4 And God saw the light, that it was good: **and God divided the light from the darkness. 5 And God called the light Day, and the darkness he called Night.** And the evening and the morning were the first day.*

Most people believe that the light created on the first day of creation was the sun; however, this is not the case. The sun and stars were not created until the fourth day. You can see this truth when you read a little further in the first chapter of Genesis, which gives the recorded account of God creating the world.

Genesis 1:14-19 (KJV)

*14 And God said, Let there be lights in the firmament of the Heaven to divide the day from the night; and let them be for signs, and for seasons, and for days, and years: 15 And let them be for lights in the firmament of the Heaven to give light upon the earth: and it was so. 16 **And God made two great lights; the greater light to rule the day, and the lesser light to rule the night: he made the stars also.** 17 And God set them in the firmament of the Heaven to give light upon the earth, 18 **And to rule over the day and over the night, and to divide the light from the darkness: and God saw that it was good. 19 And the evening and the morning were the fourth day.***

Since the natural light of the sun and stars was created on the fourth day, we need to find out the mystery behind the light and darkness created on the first day of creation. The light and darkness created on the first day had to do with good versus evil. The light represented the very glory of God, and the darkness represented evil. Let's look at some New Testament Scriptures to prove this point.

2 Corinthians 4:6 (KJV)

*6 **For God, who commanded the light to shine out of darkness,** hath shined in our hearts, **to give the light of the knowledge of the glory of God in the face of Jesus Christ.***

In the Bible, light represents good, and darkness represents evil.

Ephesians 5:8-14 (KJV)

*8 **For ye were sometimes darkness, but now are ye light in the Lord: walk as children of light:** 9 (For the fruit of the Spirit is in* *all goodness and righteousness and truth;) 10 Proving what is acceptable unto the Lord. 11 **And have no fellowship with the unfruitful works of darkness, but rather reprove them.** 12 For it is a shame even to speak of those things which are done of them in secret. 13 **But all things that are reproved are made manifest by the light: for whatsoever doth make manifest is light.** 14 Wherefore he saith, Awake thou that sleepest, and arise from the dead, **and Christ shall give thee light.***

In the teachings of Jesus, He revealed that light was symbolic of good, and darkness was symbolic of evil. So, let's look at what Jesus had to say about light and darkness in the Book of John.

John 3:19-21 (KJV)

*19 **And this is the condemnation, that light is come into the world, and men loved darkness rather than light, because their deeds were evil.** 20 **For every one that doeth evil hateth the light, neither cometh to the light, lest his deeds should be reproved.** 21 **But he that doeth truth cometh to the light,** that his deeds may be made manifest, that they are wrought in God.*

I am revealing this truth for you to see that there was a divide between good and evil right from the beginning. In the beginning, God divided between light and darkness and good and evil. The Scripture is clear that light is good, and darkness is evil.

Now that we can see this truth of light and darkness let's go back to the first days of creation. When God created man and woman, He placed them in the Garden of Eden. Adam and Eve were made in the likeness and image of God. They were also given dominion over all of God's creation.

Genesis 1:26-27 (KJV)
26 And God said, Let us make man in our image, after our
likeness: and let them have dominion over the fish of the sea,
and over the fowl of the air, and over the cattle, and over all the
earth, and over every creeping thing that creepeth upon the earth.
27 So God created man in his own image, in the image of God
created he him; male and female created he them.

Everything was perfect and good when God created humankind and all of creation. God, however, wanted to test Adam and Eve to see if they would do good or evil, so He placed two trees in the Garden of Eden. One tree was the Tree of Life, and the other was the Tree of the Knowledge of Good and Evil. God told Adam he could eat of any tree, but not to eat of the Tree of the Knowledge of Good and Evil. God told Adam that he would die if he ate of this tree.

Genesis 2:15-17 (KJV)
15 And the Lord God took the man, and put him into the garden
of Eden to dress it and to keep it. 16 And the Lord God
commanded the man, saying, Of every tree of the garden thou
mayest freely eat: 17 But of the tree of the knowledge of good
and evil, thou shalt not eat of it: for in the day that thou eatest
thereof thou shalt surely die.

God gave Adam only one commandment and that commandment was to not eat of this one tree. It is interesting to note that it was years later that God gave the Ten Commandments and the whole Law of Moses, but most of the laws were on how people would treat God and other people. For example, thou shalt not commit adultery, but how could Adam commit adultery if there was no other woman besides Eve? Or thou shalt not have any other gods before me; Adam wasn't even aware of any other gods than the God who created him. Who was Adam going to steal from, his wife? There was only one commandment: not to eat of the Tree of Knowledge of Good and Evil because Adam didn't have other opportunities to sin against God.

Now, let's look into the details of what happened right here at the beginning with the devil's temptation of Adam and Eve. We can learn a lot about the history of the world and the war to come throughout all the ages of humanity by what happened in the Garden of Eden. This war has everything to do with God's Word and the war of words. This war is also a war of light versus darkness and good versus evil—a conflict of good words versus evil words.

The devil first comes to Eve, which is how this war begins. So let's look at the beginning of this war in the Scriptures together.

Genesis 3:1-13 (KJV)

*1 Now the serpent was more subtil than any beast of the field which the Lord God had made. And he said unto the woman, **Yea, hath God said, Ye shall not eat of every tree of the garden?** 2 And the woman said unto the serpent, We may eat of the fruit of the trees of the garden: 3 **But of the fruit of the tree which is in the midst of the garden, God hath said, Ye shall not eat of it, neither shall ye touch it, lest ye die.** 4 And the serpent said unto the woman, Ye shall not surely die: 5 **For God doth know that in the day ye eat thereof, then your eyes shall be opened, and ye shall be as gods, knowing good and evil.** 6 And when the woman saw that the tree was good for food, and that it was pleasant to the eyes, and a tree to be desired to make one wise, she took of the fruit thereof, and did eat, and gave also unto her husband with her; and he did eat. 7 And the eyes of them both were opened, and they knew that they were naked; and they sewed fig leaves together, and made themselves aprons. 8 And they heard the voice* *of the Lord God walking in the garden in the cool of the day: and Adam and his wife hid themselves from the presence of the Lord God amongst the trees of the garden. 9 And the Lord God called unto Adam, and said unto him, Where art thou? 10 And he said, I heard thy voice in the garden, and I was afraid, because I was naked; and I hid myself. 11 And he said, Who told thee that thou wast naked?* **Hast thou eaten of the tree, whereof I commanded thee that thou shouldest not eat?** *12 And the man said, The woman whom thou gavest to be with me, she gave me of the tree, and I did eat. 13 And the Lord God said unto the woman, What is this that thou hast done? And the woman said, The serpent beguiled me, and I did eat.*

We can see that the devil first challenged what God said about not eating from the Tree of Knowledge of Good and Evil. Eve responded by saying they were not to eat it or touch it. Eve added, *not touching* to God's Word. The devil then challenged God's Word by saying He was keeping them from becoming like gods, and they would know good and evil. The attack on Eve had everything to do with what God said.

You notice that the separation of God's Word came down to two trees. For the attack to make more sense, you must understand that trees represent people and tongues in the Bible. Fruit in the Bible represents what people say and do. Let's look at some verses to prove this point.

Proverbs 15:4 (KJV)
*4 **A wholesome tongue is a tree of life:** but perverseness therein is a breach in the spirit.*

Psalm 1:1-3 (KJV)
1 Blessed is the man that walketh not in the counsel of the ungodly, nor standeth in the way of sinners, nor sitteth in the seat

*of the scornful. 2 But his delight is in the law of the Lord; and in his law doth he meditate day and night. 3 **And he shall be like a tree planted by the rivers of water, that bringeth forth his fruit in his season**; his leaf also shall not wither; and whatsoever he doeth shall prosper.*

Matthew 3:10 (KJV)
*10 **And now also the axe is laid unto the root of the trees: therefore every tree which bringeth not forth good fruit is hewn down, and cast into the fire.***

Matthew 7:15-20 (KJV)
*15 Beware of false prophets, which come to you in sheep's clothing, but inwardly they are ravening wolves. 16 **Ye shall know them by their fruits.** Do men gather grapes of thorns, or figs of thistles? 17 **Even so every good tree bringeth forth good fruit; but a corrupt tree bringeth forth evil fruit. 18 A good tree cannot bring forth evil fruit, neither can a corrupt tree bring forth good fruit.** 19 Every tree that bringeth not forth good fruit is hewn down, and cast into the fire. 20 **Wherefore by their fruits ye shall know them.***

Matthew 12:33-37 (KJV)
*33 **Either make the tree good, and his fruit good; or else make the tree corrupt, and his fruit corrupt: for the tree is known by his fruit.** 34 **O generation of vipers, how can ye, being evil, speak good things?** for out of the abundance of the heart the mouth speaketh. 35 **A good man out of the good treasure of the heart bringeth forth good things: and an evil man out of the evil treasure bringeth forth evil things.** 36 But I say unto you, That every idle word that men shall speak, they shall give account*

thereof in the day of judgment. 37 For by thy words thou shalt be justified, and by thy words thou shalt be condemned.

The two trees found in the Garden of Eden represented God and the devil. God used the Tree of Life to secretly reveal Himself and His Words. If they only ate of the Tree of Life, they would live forever. If you listen to and obey God's Word, you will live forever. However, if you eat of the Tree of the Knowledge of Good and Evil or listen to the words of the devil, you will die. Later in the Scriptures, we read that man does not live by bread alone but by every Word that proceeds out of the mouth of God.

Deuteronomy 8:3 (KJV)

3 And he humbled thee, and suffered thee to hunger, and fed thee with manna, which thou knewest not, neither did thy fathers know; **that he might make thee know that man doth not live by bread only, but by every word that proceedeth out of the mouth of the Lord doth man live.**

When the devil was tempting Jesus to turn the stones into bread, He brought it right back to obeying God's Word. So the issue has everything to do with obeying God's Word or the devil's words.

Matthew 4:2-4 (KJV)

2 And when he had fasted forty days and forty nights, he was afterward an hungred. 3 **And when the tempter came to him,** *he said, If thou be the Son of God, command that these stones be made bread. 4 But he answered and said,* **It is written, Man shall not live by bread alone, but by every word that proceedeth out of the mouth of God.**

The devil has been challenging man over this issue of obeying God's Word from the beginning, and the war is still raging on. The war is over humankind obeying God's Word or the devil's words. Everyone born is given a choice to decide to obey God or not. The world was created for humankind to live in and choose who they wanted to obey. Man was created in God's image, and God spoke all of creation into existence by His Words.

Being created in God's likeness, Adam also had the power to speak to God's creation, and it obeyed him. Adam's words had power, *as do yours* because you are created in God's likeness. The devil has tried to hide this truth from all of humanity. The biggest weapon of the devil is lies. He loves to lie to people and make them feel weak and powerless. The fact is you were made in God's image, and your words have power. The devil knows this and tries to get you to speak evil things into existence, and this is where the war is at. The war of words has everything to do with who will control your life and mouth. In this book, we will see how the devil has waged war with God's Word and the words that come out of men's and women's mouths.

I now want to turn your attention to a secret about words hidden in the curse God put on Adam for eating the Tree of the Knowledge of Good and Evil. First, let's read the passage where this curse is found, and then I will get into the hidden secret.

Genesis 3:17-19 (KJV)
17 And unto Adam he said, Because thou hast hearkened unto the voice of thy wife, and hast eaten of the tree, of which I commanded thee, saying, Thou shalt not eat of it: cursed is the ground for thy sake; in sorrow shalt thou eat of it all the days of thy life; 18 Thorns also and thistles shall it bring forth to thee;

*and thou shalt eat the herb of the field; 19 **In the sweat of thy face shalt thou eat bread, till thou return unto the ground;** for out of it wast thou taken: for dust thou art, and unto dust shalt thou return.*

This passage is interesting because it reveals a secret about what was going on with Adam from the beginning of creation. Adam was cursed with eating bread by the sweat of his face, and the ground was cursed because of what he did. Adam was not cursed with work. Work is not a curse because we know God worked six days and rested on the Seventh Day. If work were a curse, God would be cursed because God just worked six days, but we know that God cannot be cursed.

So how was Adam working before the fall? He was working just like God, in whose image he was created. Adam worked and tended to the Garden of Eden with his words, just like God works with His Words. The curse God placed upon him was that he now would have to work by the sweat of his brow, with his hands and not his Words. It wasn't until Jesus came on the earth as the second Adam that He empowered people to start working with their words again. When Jesus came on the scene, we read about Him speaking to mountains, storms, devils, fevers, trees, and more. He also taught His disciples to do the same.

Mark 11:20-24 (KJV)

*20 **And in the morning, as they passed by, they saw the fig tree dried up from the roots.** 21 And Peter calling to remembrance saith unto him, Master, **behold, the fig tree which thou cursedst is withered away.** 22 **And Jesus answering saith unto them, Have faith in God.** 23 **For verily I say unto you, That whosoever shall say unto this mountain,** Be thou removed, and be thou cast into the sea; and shall not doubt in his heart, but shall believe that those things which he saith shall come to pass; he shall have* *whatsoever he saith. 24 Therefore I say unto you, What things soever ye desire, when ye pray, believe that ye receive them, and ye shall have them.*

Jesus came to save and restore humanity from the fall of Adam. A big part of this restoration would be to teach His disciples the lost art of speaking to creation once again. The devil has been lying to humankind for centuries and keeping them from knowing their true power. We were originally made in the image of God, who creates and has power with His Words. The devil doesn't want you to know this and wants to deceive you to use your mouth to speak and create evil things to come to pass. While he is doing this, he keeps everyone in darkness to the power of their own words.

The devil has consistently attacked the Word of God and won't stop until he is defeated by the very WORD of God Himself, the Lord Jesus Christ when He returns.

Revelation 19:11-16 (KJV)

*11 And I saw Heaven opened, and behold a white horse; and he that sat upon him was called Faithful and True, and in righteousness he doth judge and make war. 12 His eyes were as a flame of fire, and on his head were many crowns; and he had a name written, that no man knew, but he himself. 13 And he was clothed with a vesture dipped in blood: **and his name is called The Word of God.** 14 And the armies which were in Heaven followed him upon white horses, clothed in fine linen, white and clean. 15 **And out of his mouth goeth a sharp sword, that with it he should smite the nations:** and he shall rule them with a rod of iron: and he treadeth the winepress of the fierceness and wrath of Almighty God. 16 And he hath on his vesture and on his thigh a name written, King Of Kings, And Lord Of Lords.*

Jesus Christ is the Word of God that was made flesh and dwelt among us.

John 1:1 (KJV)
1 In the beginning was the Word, and the Word was with God, and the Word was God.

John 1:14 (KJV)
*14 **And the Word was made flesh,** and dwelt among us, (and we beheld his glory, the glory as of the only begotten of the Father,) full of grace and truth.*

God, and His Word, has waged a war against the words of the devil since the beginning of time. All of humanity is in the middle of this war. God's greatest desire for humanity is that they would repent, come back to Him, and obey His Word. The devil desires to keep everyone in disobedience to God's Word and remain ignorant. The devil does not want you to know the power of obeying God's Word and speaking God's Word. If the devil can keep you ignorant and use your own words against you, he wins. You have power with your words because you were made in the image of God, who has power with His Words.

We will explore the Holy Scriptures together in this book and see how this war has raged throughout Biblical history. We will also explore the laws that govern your words, life, and faith. The *Law of Faith* is very misunderstood. Your words were given to you to work and fight with, not merely for the sake of holding conversations. You were created to communicate, work, and fight with your words just like God communicates, works, and fights with His Words. God intended humankind to work by faith and fight off the devil with the sword of His Word coming out of their mouth. Be ready to be enlightened as we explore the power of God's Word and the war of words in this book.

CHAPTER 2

———•❖•———

SONS OF GOD

When Adam was created, he was made in the image of God, which made him a son of God. However, when he fell through disobedience to God's Word, he lost his position as a son of God. He lost his relationship with God because he did not win the war of words. A true son of God always obeys God and His Word. The Bible says that the sons of God are led by the Spirit of God, which means they obey the Holy Spirit when it comes to the direction of their life. This chapter explores what it means to be a son of God and how Jesus restored humankind as sons in relationship with God the Father, if they believed in Him. You must be restored as a son of God to win the war of words.

Did you notice how I started by saying sons of God and not sons and daughters of God? I referred to the gender in the male terminology because this is the only gender used throughout the Bible when referring to someone being born again as a son of God. When someone is reborn into God's Kingdom, the Bible refers to them as the male gender because that is the only gender in Heaven. When someone gets born again, they are restored as a son of God, including women. You cannot find the term daughter of God anywhere in the Bible.

In the resurrection, we will be like the angels of God, and we will neither marry nor be given in marriage.

Matthew 22:30 (KJV)
30 For in the resurrection they neither marry, nor are given in marriage, but are as the angels of God in Heaven.

Now that we are on the same page regarding God's terminology let's dig into this exciting subject of men and women being restored as sons to God once again. To start with, we have to look at Jesus, who is **The** Son of God. Jesus was declared to be **The** Son of God by the Father Himself with an audible voice at His baptism by John the Baptist.

Matthew 3:16-17 (KJV)
16 And Jesus, when he was baptized, went up straightway out of the water: and, lo, the Heavens were opened unto him, **and he saw the Spirit of God descending like a dove, and lighting upon him:** *17 And lo a voice from Heaven, saying, This is my beloved Son, in whom I am well pleased.*

Two crucial things occurred at the baptism of Jesus. First, the Spirit of God descended upon Jesus like a dove. Secondly, the Father spoke from Heaven and declared Jesus to be **The** Son of God, and He was well pleased with Him. Right after this extraordinary event in the history of all of humanity, Jesus is led by the Spirit into the wilderness to be tempted by the devil.

Matthew 4:1 (KJV)
1 **Then was Jesus led up of the Spirit into the wilderness to be tempted of the devil.**

Before Jesus could start His ministry, the Spirit led Him to be tempted by the devil about God's Word, just like the first Adam was tempted. Jesus is called the last Adam in the Bible.

1 Corinthians 15:45 (KJV)

*45 And so it is written, **The first man Adam** was made a living soul; **the last Adam** was made a quickening spirit.*

Let's see how the devil tries to tempt Jesus, **The** Son of God.

Matthew 4:2-4 (KJV)

*2 And when he had fasted forty days and forty nights, he was afterward an hungred. 3 And when the tempter came to him, he said, **If thou be the Son of God,** command that these stones be made bread. 4 But he answered and said, **It is written, Man shall not live by bread alone, but by every word that proceedeth out of the mouth of God.***

Do you notice how the devil challenged the fact of Jesus being **The** Son of God? Then the devil tried to get Him to do a miracle of changing stones into bread at his command. God, the Father, audibly spoke over Jesus that He was **The** Son of God, which is the first thing the devil challenged. The devil also challenged Him to be led by him and not the Holy Spirit. The devil tried to get Jesus to operate from his command and not the command of God. Jesus responded perfectly by saying, *"It is written"*. Jesus stayed obedient to God the Father and the Holy Spirit by quoting the Scriptures back to the devil. Jesus won the war of words. Now let's look at the next temptation of Christ.

Matthew 4:5-7 (KJV)

*5 Then the devil taketh him up into the holy city, and setteth him on a pinnacle of the temple, 6 And saith unto him, **If thou be the Son of God, cast thyself down: for it is written, He shall give his angels charge concerning thee: and in their hands they shall bear thee up, lest at any time thou dash thy foot against a stone. 7 Jesus said unto him, It is written again, Thou shalt not tempt the Lord thy God.***

In this temptation, the devil challenges Jesus being **The** Son of God again. Then, he quotes a verse to see if Jesus will obey and be led by him and not God. The devil used God's Word against Him. Jesus, however, stayed obedient to the Father and the Holy Spirit and said, "*It is written,*" again.

Now, let's look at the final temptation of Christ in the wilderness.

> ### Matthew 4:8-10 (KJV)
> *8 Again, the devil taketh him up into an exceeding high mountain, and sheweth him all the kingdoms of the world, and the glory of them; 9 And saith unto him, All these things will I give thee, if thou wilt fall down and worship me. 10 Then saith Jesus unto him, Get thee hence, Satan:* **for it is written, Thou shalt worship the Lord thy God, and him only shalt thou serve.**

In this final temptation, the devil knows he can't challenge Jesus being **The** Son of God anymore, so he tries to offer Him the kingdoms and glory of the world. The devil said he would give all these things to Jesus if He would fall down and worship him. Jesus once again quotes the Scriptures and stays in obedience to the Father, the Holy Spirit, and God's written Word.

From these passages of Scripture, we can see the attack on Jesus was about His identity as being **The** Son of God and if He would obey and be led by God or the devil. Jesus passed all three tests and remained faithful to God. Jesus was continually led by the Holy Spirit and obeyed the written Word of God. Jesus was our example of how we should be led by God's Spirit and obey the written Word of God. This is the only way we can defeat the devil in our lives and be a true son of God.

Since the beginning of time with Adam, the devil has been attacking and tempting the sons of God to lose their position with God. The devil knows if he can get the sons of God to disobey God's Word and not be led by His Spirit, he can destroy their lives by breaking their relationship to their Heavenly Father. God is our Father, and we are His sons if we obey His written Word and are led by His Spirit.

The way the devil tempts humankind is by keeping them in sin by obeying the lust of the flesh. The only way you will not fulfill the lust of the flesh is by *Walking in the Spirit*. If you obey the lust of the flesh, you will not inherit the Kingdom of God.

Galatians 5:16-21 (KJV)
*16 **This I say then, Walk in the Spirit, and ye shall not fulfil the lust of the flesh.** 17 **For the flesh lusteth against the Spirit, and the Spirit against the flesh:** and these are contrary the one to the other: so that ye cannot do the things that ye would. 18 **But if ye be led of the Spirit, ye are not under the law.** 19 Now the works of the flesh are manifest, which are these; Adultery, fornication, uncleanness, lasciviousness, 20 Idolatry, witchcraft, hatred, variance, emulations, wrath, strife, seditions, heresies, 21 Envyings, murders, drunkenness, revellings, and such like: of the which I tell you before, **as I have also told you in time past, that they which do such things shall not inherit the kingdom of God.***

When you walk in the Spirit, you will bear the fruit of the Spirit.

Galatians 5:22-25 (KJV)
*22 **But the fruit of the Spirit is** love, joy, peace, longsuffering, gentleness, goodness, faith, 23 Meekness, temperance: against such there is no law. 24 And they that are Christ's have crucified*

*the flesh with the affections and lusts. 25 **If we live in the Spirit, let us also walk in the Spirit.***

The Spirit of God always leads a son of God, and this is how they know they are a true son of God. A true son of God does not live after the flesh.

Romans 8:12-14 (KJV)

*12 Therefore, brethren, we are debtors, not to the flesh, to live after the flesh. 13 For if ye live after the flesh, ye shall die: but if ye through the Spirit do mortify the deeds of the body, ye shall live. 14 **For as many as are led by the Spirit of God, they are the sons of God.***

One of the primary purposes of the ministry of Jesus was to restore those who believed in Him to the relationship of sons of God again.

John 1:12-13 (KJV)

*12 **But as many as received him, to them gave he power to become the sons of God,** even to them that believe on his name: 13 Which were born, not of blood, nor of the will of the flesh, nor of the will of man, but of God.*

Being born again meant that you were reborn as a son of God. You could only become a son of God again by believing that Jesus was the Christ. Jesus tried to explain this new birth to Nicodemus. Let's read what Jesus had to say.

John 3:1-9 (KJV)

1 There was a man of the Pharisees, named Nicodemus, a ruler of the Jews: 2 The same came to Jesus by night, and said unto him, Rabbi, we know that thou art a teacher come from God: for no man can do these miracles that thou doest, except God be with *him. 3 Jesus answered and said unto him, Verily, verily, I say unto thee, **Except a man be born again, he cannot see the kingdom of God.** 4 Nicodemus saith unto him, **How can a man be born when he is old? can he enter the second time into his mother's womb, and be born?** 5 Jesus answered, Verily, verily, I say unto thee, **Except a man be born of water and of the Spirit, he cannot enter into the kingdom of God. 6 That which is born of the flesh is flesh; and that which is born of the Spirit is spirit. 7 Marvel not that I said unto thee, Ye must be born again. 8 The wind bloweth where it listeth, and thou hearest the sound thereof, but canst not tell whence it cometh, and whither it goeth: so is every one that is born of the Spirit.** 9 Nicodemus answered and said unto him, How can these things be?*

We know from reading the Scriptures that no one was restored to the Father as a son of God until Jesus rose from the dead. We can see this truth so beautifully displayed in how Jesus answered Mary at His tomb before He ascended to the Father after His resurrection.

John 20:16-17 (KJV)

*16 Jesus saith unto her, Mary. She turned herself, and saith unto him, Rabboni; which is to say, Master. 17 Jesus saith unto her, **Touch me not; for I am not yet ascended to my Father:** but go to my brethren, and say unto them, **I ascend unto my Father, and your Father; and to my God, and your God.***

When Jesus rose from the dead and ascended to the Father, He restored His believers to the status as sons of God. Father God could now be called our Father and our God, making us sons of God again. Jesus made it possible for us to be sons of God. Jesus restored us to God, making us what the Bible calls a new creature.

2 Corinthians 5:17 (KJV)
17 Therefore if any man be in Christ, he is a new creature: old things
are passed away; behold, all things are become new.

Do you notice here how it says, new creature? When you become a son
of God by believing in Christ, you are made into something new. The
newly created sons of God are not made into the original image of
Adam. Adam was made in the image of God but had an earthly body.
The newly created sons of God will have a Heavenly body.

1 Corinthians 15:45-49 (KJV)
*45 And so it is written, **The first man Adam was made a living**
soul; the last Adam was made a quickening spirit. 46 Howbeit*
that was not first which is spiritual, but that which is natural;
and afterward that which is spiritual. 47 The first man is of the
earth, earthy; the second man is the Lord from Heaven. 48 As is
the earthy, such are they also that are earthy: and as is the
*Heavenly, such are they also that are Heavenly. 49 **And as we***
have borne the image of the earthy, we shall also bear the image
of the Heavenly.

Our newly created spirit as a son of God will bear the new image of Jesus.
When Jesus died and rose again, He was made into something new. He
rose again in a Heavenly image and body. This new body of Jesus could
walk through walls and ascend into Heaven. When you accept Christ as
your Saviour, your spirit is reborn, and when you see Christ, your body
will be transformed into the same image of Christ.

1 John 3:1-2 (KJV)
*1 **Behold, what manner of love the Father hath bestowed***
***upon us, that we should be called the sons of God:** therefore the*
*world knoweth us not, because it knew him not. 2 **Beloved, now***
are we the sons of God, and it doth not yet appear what we shall

be: but we know that, when he shall appear, we shall be like him; for we shall see him as he is.

When Christ appears, and you see Him, you will be made just like Him. You will receive a Heavenly body that can live forever with Christ, the Father, and the Holy Spirit. We can learn more about the celestial body of Christ when we read the Book of Revelation. Let's read what Jesus looks like.

Revelation 1:12-16 (KJV)
*12 And I turned to see the voice that spake with me. And being turned, I saw seven golden candlesticks; 13 And in the midst of the seven candlesticks one like unto the Son of man, clothed with a garment down to the foot, and girt about the paps with a golden girdle. 14 **His head and his hairs were white like wool, as white as snow; and his eyes were as a flame of fire; 15 And his feet like unto fine brass, as if they burned in a furnace; and his voice as the sound of many waters.** 16 And he had in his right hand seven stars: and out of his mouth went a sharp twoedged sword: **and his countenance was as the sun shineth in his strength.***

When you read this depiction of Christ, you are reading a future depiction of yourself if you believe in Jesus. When we see Jesus, we will be just like Him. God, the Father, has been looking for those who will take on this image of Christ as obedient sons of God. This is your future inheritance as a son of God if you believe in Jesus and are led by the Holy Spirit. Those who overcome, God will be your God, and you will be His son.

Revelation 21:7 (KJV)
*7 **He that overcometh shall inherit all things; and I will be his God, and he shall be my son.***

Jesus taught His disciples while He was on the earth that the righteous would shine like the sun in the Kingdom of their Father.

> *Matthew 13:43 (KJV)*
> *43 **Then shall the righteous shine forth as the sun in the kingdom of their Father.** Who hath ears to hear, let him hear.*

From the beginning, the whole destiny of all humanity is that God's Spirit would lead them as sons of God. These sons of God would obey God's Word and overcome the devil. The devil has fought hard to keep humankind from coming into its destiny. The devil wages war against God and His Word. The devil knows if he can win the war of words, he can keep people from becoming sons of God. The secret to winning the war of words against the devil is to claim your right as a son of God by believing in Jesus, being led by the Spirit, and obeying the Word of God.

This whole teaching on sons of God is amazing. God, the Father, has offered humankind an incredible opportunity. The relationship of being a son of God is worth giving your whole life over to Him. There is nothing more important on this earth than your relationship with God, which is the entire reason Jesus died and rose again. Being a son of God is the most incredible destiny of humankind.

Before I end this chapter, I want to teach some practical ways of being led by the Spirit. If sons of God are led by His Spirit, it is important to know how He leads by His Spirit. From Divine revelation and the Scriptures, I have learned how God leads by His Spirit.

To start with, let's go back to how Jesus answered the devil when being tempted by him. Jesus responded by saying, *"It is written."*

Matthew 4:4 (KJV)

*4 **But he answered and said, It is written,** Man shall not live by bread alone, but by every word that proceedeth out of the mouth of God.*

Whenever we are being challenged or tempted by the devil, we must always go back to the Word of God. God's Spirit will never violate the written Word of God. So, if the devil or anyone else, for that matter, tries to get you to do something contrary to the written Word of God, do not listen to or obey them. Holy men of God wrote the Scriptures as the Spirit of God moved upon them. Therefore, the Holy Spirit will never violate what He had men write down as the Word of God.

2 Peter 1:19-21 (KJV)

*19 **We have also a more sure word of prophecy;** whereunto ye do well that ye take heed, as unto a light that shineth in a dark place, until the day dawn, and the day star arise in your hearts: 20 **Knowing this first, that no prophecy of the Scripture is of any private interpretation. 21 For the prophecy came not in old time by the will of man: but holy men of God spake as they were moved by the Holy Ghost.***

2 Timothy 3:16 (KJV)

*16 **All Scripture is given by inspiration of God,** and is profitable for doctrine, for reproof, for correction, for instruction in righteousness:*

All Scripture is God-breathed, and God will never violate His Scriptures. The Holy Spirit inspired holy men of God to write them, and they were written to guide us in doctrine, reproof, correction, and instruction of righteousness. We must read and study the Scriptures so the devil will not deceive us. The Holy Spirit, by the anointing, will teach us the truth from the Scriptures.

1 John 2:27 (KJV)
27 But the anointing which ye have received of him abideth in you, and ye need not that any man teach you: but as the same anointing teacheth you of all things, and is truth, and is no lie, and even as it hath taught you, ye shall abide in him.

The Holy Spirit will also lead you by a still small voice. The still small voice was revealed to the prophet Elijah.

1 Kings 19:11-12 (KJV)
*11 And he said, Go forth, and stand upon the mount before the Lord. And, behold, the Lord passed by, and a great and strong wind rent the mountains, and brake in pieces the rocks before the Lord; but the Lord was not in the wind: and after the wind an earthquake; but the Lord was not in the earthquake: 12 And after the earthquake a fire; but the Lord was not in the fire: **and after the fire a still small voice.***

When you become a Christian, God's Holy Spirit comes to dwell inside of you. God does not have to speak with a loud audible voice, because He is on the inside of you. Jesus said that His sheep would know His voice.

John 10:27 (KJV)
*27 **My sheep hear my voice, and I know them, and they follow me:***

The prophet Isaiah prophesied that people would hear a word behind their ears telling them which way to walk.

Isaiah 30:20-21 (KJV)
*20 And though the Lord give you the bread of adversity, and the water of affliction, yet shall not thy teachers be removed into a corner any more, but thine eyes shall see thy teachers: 21 **And***

thine ears shall hear a word behind thee, saying, This is the way, walk ye in it, when ye turn to the right hand, and when ye turn to the left.

In the New Testament, in the Book of Acts, we can see the Holy Spirit led some people by a vision or a dream.

Acts 16:9 (KJV)
9 And a vision appeared to Paul in the night; There stood a man of Macedonia, and prayed him, saying, Come over into Macedonia, and help us.

The Holy Spirit may lead some people by a dream. We know that dreams played a significant role in leading God's people in the Old Testament.

Acts 2:17 (KJV)
17 And it shall come to pass in the last days, saith God, I will pour out of my Spirit upon all flesh: and your sons and your daughters shall prophesy, and your young men shall see visions, and your old men shall dream dreams:

They were also led by a Word from the Lord as they fasted and ministered to the Lord.

Acts 13:2-3 (KJV)
2 As they ministered to the Lord, and fasted, the Holy Ghost said, Separate me Barnabas and Saul for the work whereunto I have called them. 3 And when they had fasted and prayed, and laid their hands on them, they sent them away.

James, the brother of Jesus, said that it seemed good to them and the Holy Ghost when sending some of the disciples out to confirm how the

Gentiles should live concerning the Law of Moses. This means they had an inward witness of what they were teaching aligned with the Holy Spirit, but it doesn't mean they had a specific word on the matter.

> ### Acts 15:27-28 (KJV)
> *27 We have sent therefore Judas and Silas, who shall also tell you the same things by mouth. 28 **For it seemed good to the Holy Ghost, and to us,** to lay upon you no greater burden than these necessary things;*

As you grow in your walk with God and understand His Word, you will come to experience the Holy Spirit in a more significant way. The Holy Spirit will begin to communicate to you increasingly through the Word of God and His still small voice.

The Holy Spirit will work with your conscience and lead you in the way you should go. Listening to your conscience is one of the most powerful ways to connect with the voice of the Holy Spirit. The Holy Spirit will speak through your conscience when you are not sure what to do or if something is wrong or right.

Being led by the Spirit should be a daily experience of the true sons of God. We are not called to listen to our own understanding, but trust God to lead us.

> ### Proverbs 3:5-6 (KJV)
> *5 Trust in the Lord with all thine heart; and lean not unto thine own understanding. 6 **In all thy ways acknowledge him, and he shall direct thy paths.***

Sons of God acknowledge God in all their ways and only seek to be led by His Spirit. When His Spirit leads you, you will not fulfill the lusts of the flesh, and you will always be in the right place, at the right time, and with the right word. Life becomes easy when you know that God sent the Holy Spirit to guide you in life. If you listen to and obey the Holy Spirit, your life will be blessed.

In conclusion, we can see the importance of being led by the Holy Spirit and being sons of God. God sent His Son to die on the cross and rise again so we can be sons of God. The devil has been fighting and warring against God's people to keep them from entering their Divine destiny as a son of God. When you come into the complete revelation of you being a son of God, you will win the war of words and take your place as a son of God. To do this, you must be led by His Spirit and tell the devil every time he tempts you, *"It is written."* This is how you will win the war of words.

CHAPTER 3

ALL OF YOUR WORDS COME TO PASS

This chapter will reveal that all of your words come to pass. This is true for the wicked and the righteous. In the last chapter, we saw how God created man in His image and gave him dominion over the earth as a son of God. However, many revelations were lost in the fall of Adam. The earth was meant to be governed by the words of humankind. This is a great mystery that has been lost to many generations, but is one of the great truths that Jesus revealed while He ministered on the Earth. This chapter will show that even if people don't realize it, their words are still coming to pass. Incredible things can be accomplished with our words when this truth is understood.

When the Bible speaks of Adam being created in God's image, it refers to him being created in God's resemblance or likeness.

Genesis 1:26 (KJV)
26 And God said, Let us make man in our image, after our likeness: and let them have dominion over the fish of the sea, and over the fowl of the air, and over the cattle, and over all the earth, and over every creeping thing that creepeth upon the earth.

Based on this Scripture, we know that God is a Spirit and doesn't have flesh and blood, so the words image and likeness must be referring to something different. Adam was made with flesh and bone, but he is actually a spirit being. Adam's spirit was meant to live forever on the earth, and never die.

Adam was also made with a soul. The soul is made up of the mind, will, and emotions. So we can say Adam is a spirit who has a soul and lives in a body. Everyone created is a spirit, has a soul, and lives in a body. The real Adam that was meant to live forever was his spirit. Your body may die, but your spirit will live forever. Your spirit will either live with God in Heaven or in hell with the devil. If you believe in your heart that God raised Jesus from the dead and confess with your mouth that Jesus is Lord, you will be saved and live eternally with God in Heaven.

Being created in God's image, Adam was given the ability to speak and cause things to come to pass, just like His Creator did. God is a Creator, and He creates with His Words. Adam was created in God's image and likeness and was given the ability to speak words that had power over the created world. This is an ability that animals do not have. Animals were not made in God's image, and don't have the power of the spoken word.

Being created in God's image is a big subject to study, and this book will not get into the fullness of that teaching. I am only talking about our ability to speak to things and bring things to pass with our words. But, it is important to understand that all of humankind was created in God's image, and therefore, we have power with our words. Evil people use this ability for their own purpose, and good people use this ability for the glory of God. Either way, every created human being has authority with their words, whether they realize it or not.

Before we dive into man and his ability to talk to creation and have it obey him, let's look at what it means for God to be God. We are created in God's image, so it is important to know about the One in whose image we are created. There are certain attributes that make our Creator God. Let's look at some of these attributes together.

We know that God is made up of three persons: the Father, the Son, and the Holy Spirit. We call this unity of the three persons of the Godhead; the Trinity.

Matthew 28:19 (KJV)
19 Go ye therefore, and teach all nations, baptizing them in the name of the Father, and of the Son, and of the Holy Ghost:

There is a seen realm where man and all of creation exist and an unseen realm where angels, demons, and the Heavenly hosts exist. Then there is a realm beyond the unseen realm, where the Trinity first dwelt and created everything. So you can say there is an unseen realm to the unseen realm.

Here is a list of some of the attributes we know about the Trinity from the Bible.

1. There are three persons to the Godhead called the Trinity - The Father, Son, and Holy Spirit.

2. The Trinity is Infinite. The Trinity is Self-Existing, without origin

3. The Trinity is Immutable – The Trinity never changes

4. The Trinity is Self-Sufficient – The Trinity has no needs

5. The Trinity is the Creator of Everything by their Words – Everything comes from the Trinity

35

6. The Trinity has Authority over Everything

7. The Trinity owns Everything

8. The Trinity has the Power to do Anything

9. The Trinity is Omnipresent = God's presence is everywhere at the same time

10. The Trinity is Omniscient = The Trinity knows everything, including the future

11. The Trinity is Omnipotent = The Trinity is all powerful and unlimited in power

12. The Trinity has the right to sit as Judge over anything and everything

13. The Trinity has the right to rule over anything and everything

14. The Trinity is the First and the Last, the Beginning and the End

15. The Trinity is not bound by time or space

16. The Trinity is eternal

In some ways, humankind can operate in some of the attributes of God on the earth. We can have delegated authority and speak to things. We can think and make decisions for ourselves. We are compatible enough with our Maker to be married to Christ one day. We are called sons of God and follow in the example of the Son of God, Jesus the Christ. When we see Him, we will be just like Him according to the Book of 1 John Chapter 3.

1 John 3:1-2 (KJV)

*1 Behold, what manner of love the Father hath bestowed upon us, that we should be called **the sons of God:** therefore the world knoweth us not, because it knew him not. 2 **Beloved, now are we***

the sons of God, and it doth not yet appear what we shall be:
but we know that, when he shall appear, we shall be like him;
for we shall see him as he is.

When Jesus came to the earth, He did not come in the form of any animal or angelic being. He came as the Son of Man and had to take on the form of a man. Jesus came in the form of a man because mankind was already made in His image. While He was on the earth, He revealed that man was supposed to take dominion over the earth, and that is exactly what Jesus did.

The authority given to mankind was only over the earth they were placed in. Humankind was not given dominion over the Heavens but only over the earth. Let's look at an important verse that proves this point.

Psalm 115:15-16 (KJV)

15 Ye are blessed of the Lord which made Heaven and earth. 16 ***The Heaven, even the Heavens, are the Lord's: but the earth hath he given to the children of men.***

Ultimately, God is the owner of all that He has created, but He has given dominion to mankind to rule on the earth. The devil knowing this, went through Eve to get to Adam to steal his authority. He succeeded by getting Adam to disobey the very Words of the God who created him. When Adam disobeyed God, he handed the dominion of the earth to the devil on a silver platter, and the devil became the god of this world.

2 Corinthians 4:3-4 (KJV)

3 But if our gospel be hid, it is hid to them that are lost: 4 ***In whom the god of this world hath blinded the minds of them*** *which believe not, lest the light of the glorious gospel of Christ, who is the image of God, should shine unto them.*

The devil maintained his authority until Jesus came and defeated him at the cross and resurrection. Jesus took the position of being ruler over the earth from the devil because He obeyed the voice of God to the point of death. The devil illegally killed an innocent man and hung Him on a cross to die. Because Jesus suffered the death of the cross and rose again from the dead, He was legally entitled to take back all authority that was lost to Adam and restore humanity.

Matthew 28:18 (KJV)
*18 And Jesus came and spake unto them, saying, **All power is given unto me in Heaven and in earth.***

The Church is those who accept Jesus as their Lord. Jesus invested His authority in His Church and sent them out into the entire world to teach people to start observing the Commands of God.

Matthew 28:19-20 (KJV)
*19 **Go ye therefore, and teach all nations,** baptizing them in the name of the Father, and of the Son, and of the Holy Ghost: 20 **Teaching them to observe all things whatsoever I have commanded you:** and, lo, I am with you always, even unto the end of the world. Amen.*

Before Jesus, mankind lived on this earth with limited knowledge of the power of their words. In the beginning, they understood this more, but as time passed, they understood it less. All would be lost if we didn't have God's Word and men teaching us throughout history about the power of our words. So, when Jesus came to earth, He taught men the power they had with their tongues and how to use this power to bring things to pass.

It is important to note that just because mankind lost the disconnect of what they were saying and its effect on the outcome of their life doesn't mean their words weren't still coming to pass. Even if you don't see it happening, your words still come to pass. However, people don't connect their words coming to pass because sometimes it takes days, months, or years for their words to come to pass. So, when something bad happens to them, they don't connect what they said days, months, or years before regarding what happened. Either way, people's words created their future reality.

Let's look at some verses together to help us better understand this truth.

> ### Proverbs 16:29-30 (KJV)
> *29 A violent man enticeth his neighbour, and leadeth him into the way that is not good. 30 He shutteth his eyes to devise froward things: **moving his lips he bringeth evil to pass.***

This verse reveals how evil men devise evil things and bring evil to pass by moving their lips. King Solomon wrote this verse, and he was the wisest king ever to live. He understood that people could bring evil to pass with their words.

Now, let's look at what Jesus had to say on this subject.

> ### Matthew 12:34-35 (KJV)
> *34 O generation of vipers, how can ye, being evil, speak good things? **for out of the abundance of the heart the mouth speaketh. 35 A good man out of the good treasure of the heart bringeth forth good things: and an evil man out of the evil treasure bringeth forth evil things.***

Jesus revealed in His teachings that good people bring good things to pass by speaking out of the abundance of their hearts. Evil people also bring evil to pass by speaking out of the abundance of their hearts.

Every word we say causes something to come to pass. This is a great mystery but is true. We are created in the image of God with the ability to speak from the heart and cause things to come to pass. Every idle word we speak, we will give account to God on Judgment Day because of the power our words have on the earth. This is a great responsibility, and we must pray for wisdom to watch what we say.

> **Matthew 12:36-37 (KJV)**
> *36 But I say unto you, **That every idle word that men shall speak, they shall give account thereof in the day of judgment. 37 For by thy words thou shalt be justified, and by thy words thou shalt be condemned.***

Jesus revealed many truths about our hearts and what we say with our mouths. The mouth speaks from the abundance of thoughts in the heart. Jesus was showing this throughout His ministry on the earth. The disciples had a front-row seat to see how God used His Words in the form of a man. This is the way humanity was intended to operate. Jesus was not creating miracles on the earth in His position as God. Instead, Jesus laid down His right to operate as God when He was born as a man. The Book of Philippians reveals this truth.

> **Philippians 2:5-7 (KJV)**
> *5 Let this mind be in you, which was also in Christ Jesus: 6 **Who, being in the form of God, thought it not robbery to be equal with God:** 7 But made himself of no reputation, and took upon him the form of a servant, **and was made in the likeness of men:***

Jesus came and operated as a man to show us how to live as a man. Jesus was operating under an anointing from God as a man, and that is how He did miracles.

Acts 10:38 (KJV)
*38 **How God anointed Jesus of Nazareth with the Holy Ghost
and with power:** who went about doing good, and healing all that
were oppressed of the devil; for God was with him.*

This is a fundamental mystery to understand if you are going to learn
how to operate in your God-given authority. Jesus is your example.
Some Churches teach that we can't be like Jesus, but this is not true.
We are to be exactly like Jesus and follow Him. Follow means to act
and be just like Him. Jesus is our example, and we are to imitate Him.

1 Corinthians 11:1 (KJV)
*1 **Be ye followers of me, even as I also am of Christ.***

One of the most significant areas we can imitate Christ is with our
spoken words. Jesus taught His disciples that if they believed their
words would come to pass, they could speak to a mountain and make it
move. This is how Jesus was operating. Jesus had just spoken to a fig
tree, and it withered from the roots by the next day. Peter saw this
happen and asked Jesus about it. Jesus responded by telling them they
could do the same thing with their words if they believed.

Mark 11:20-24 (KJV)
*20 **And in the morning, as they passed by, they saw the fig tree
dried up from the roots. 21 And Peter calling to remembrance
saith unto him, Master, behold, the fig tree which thou cursedst
is withered away.** 22 And Jesus answering saith unto them, Have
faith in God. 23 **For verily I say unto you, That whosoever shall
say unto this mountain, Be thou removed, and be thou cast into
the sea; and shall not doubt in his heart, but shall believe that
those things which he saith shall come to pass; he shall have
whatsoever he saith.** 24 Therefore I say unto you, What things*

soever ye desire, when ye pray, believe that ye receive them, and ye shall have them.

Jesus knew and operated in the power of the spoken word. In the ministry of Jesus, He spoke to a tree, the wind, the sea, devils, fevers, sickness, diseases, and dead people. Everything Jesus spoke to in the world obeyed His voice. It was amazing the authority Jesus demonstrated with His spoken Words. Jesus not only demonstrated this authority, but He taught His disciples they could have this authority also. When we read the Book of Acts, we see His disciples exercising this same authority that Jesus had as they performed miracles. Before He left this earth, Jesus commanded them to preach the Gospel and that signs would follow the preaching of the Gospel.

Mark 16:15-20 (KJV)

*15 And he said unto them, **Go ye into all the world, and preach the gospel to every creature.** 16 He that believeth and is baptized shall be saved; but he that believeth not shall be damned. 17 And these signs shall follow them that believe; In my name shall they cast out devils; they shall speak with new tongues; 18 They shall take up serpents; and if they drink any deadly thing, it shall not hurt them; they shall lay hands on the sick, and they shall recover. 19 So then after the Lord had spoken unto them, he was received up into Heaven, and sat on the right hand of God. 20 **And they went forth, and preached every where, the Lord working with them, and confirming the word with signs following. Amen.***

Jesus was confirming the Word with signs following the preaching of the Gospel. The Gospel is a revelation of the restoration of man back to God. It is also a revelation of man coming back into the image of the God who created them. This image is someone created in the image of God with the ability to speak to things, and these things will obey what is said. We have the ability to bring things to pass with our words, just like God.

Now that we understand that we have power with our words, let's look at the dark side of this truth with the devil and evil people. There are witches, warlocks, and sorcerers who work with the devil's power to bring evil things to pass with their words. These people use curses and spells to bring evil to pass. What is a curse or spell? Curses and spells are spoken words believed to have magic powers. They use specific words intended to invoke a supernatural demonic power to inflict harm or punishment on someone or something.

Many evil people understand the power of speech and work with dark forces to bring their evil words to pass. These dark forces have taught them to use words to make things happen in the natural world. So the devil uses their words to bring evil to pass. God forbade this practice in the Old Testament.

Deuteronomy 18:9-14 (KJV)

*9 When thou art come into the land which the Lord thy God giveth thee, thou shalt not learn to do after the abominations of those nations. 10 There shall not be found among you any one that maketh his son or his daughter to pass through the fire, **or that useth divination, or an observer of times, or an enchanter, or a witch. 11 Or a charmer, or a consulter with familiar spirits, or a wizard, or a necromancer.** 12 For all that do these things are an abomination unto the Lord: and because of these abominations the Lord thy God doth drive them out from before thee. 13 Thou shalt be perfect with the Lord thy God. 14 **For these nations, which thou shalt possess, hearkened unto observers of times, and unto diviners:** but as for thee, the Lord thy God hath not suffered thee so to do.*

A diviner in the Old Testament named Balaam was known for his words coming to pass. Kings knew if he cursed someone, they would be cursed, and if he blessed someone, they would be blessed.

> **Numbers 22:6 (KJV)**
> *6 Come now therefore, I pray thee, curse me this people; for they are too mighty for me: peradventure I shall prevail, that we may smite them, and that I may drive them out of the land: **for I wot that he whom thou blessest is blessed, and he whom thou cursest is cursed.***

God knew the power this diviner had and stepped in to make sure he did not curse the children of Israel. God knows how powerful words can be in the natural world and would not allow him to curse the children of Israel.

> **Numbers 22:9-12 (KJV)**
> *9 And God came unto Balaam, and said, What men are these with thee? 10 And Balaam said unto God, Balak the son of Zippor, king of Moab, hath sent unto me, saying, 11 Behold, there is a people come out of Egypt, which covereth the face of the earth: come now, curse me them; peradventure I shall be able to overcome them, and drive them out. 12 **And God said unto Balaam, Thou shalt not go with them; thou shalt not curse the people: for they are blessed.***

Balak, the king, was willing to pay Balaam a large amount of money and promote him in his kingdom if he would speak a curse over the children of Israel. Balaam ended up going to Balak, and along the way, an angel was sent from God to kill him. Balaam's donkey saw this angel and stopped going forward, turned aside, and eventually fell to the ground. Balaam was upset with this donkey and started to beat him. The donkey began to talk with Balaam, and Balaam's eyes were opened to see this angel. God put His fear on Balaam and told him only to speak the Word that He spoke to him.

Numbers 22:31-35 (KJV)

31 Then the Lord opened the eyes of Balaam, and he saw the angel of the Lord standing in the way, and his sword drawn in his hand: and he bowed down his head, and fell flat on his face. 32 And the angel of the Lord said unto him, Wherefore hast thou smitten thine ass these three times? **behold, I went out to withstand thee, because thy way is perverse before me:** *33 And the ass saw me, and turned from me these three times: unless she had turned from me, surely now also I had slain thee, and saved her alive. 34 And Balaam said unto the angel of the Lord, I have sinned; for I knew not that thou stoodest in the way against me: now therefore, if it displease thee, I will get me back again. 35 And the angel of the Lord said unto Balaam,* **Go with the men: but only the word that I shall speak unto thee, that thou shalt speak.** *So Balaam went with the princes of Balak.*

This story shows just how important words are. Words can either bring blessings or curses when spoken by someone who understands and has developed themselves to speak these words. This story is about a diviner, but God taught the children of Israel how to recognize a true prophet. When a true prophet spoke, all of his words would come to pass. This was the test to see if they were real prophets of the Lord.

Deuteronomy 18:20-22 (KJV)

20 But the prophet, which shall presume to speak a word in my name, which I have not commanded him to speak, or that shall speak in the name of other gods, even that prophet shall die. 21 And if thou say in thine heart, How shall we know the word which the Lord hath not spoken? 22 **When a prophet speaketh in the name of the Lord, if the thing follow not, nor come to pass, that is the thing which the Lord hath not spoken, but the prophet hath spoken it presumptuously:** *thou shalt not be afraid of him.*

Now let's look into the story of a true prophet of the Lord named Samuel. Samuels's mom had prayed for a child because she was barren. The High Priest Eli granted her request. Hannah, Samuels's mom, made a vow that if God gave her a child, she would give him to the Lord all the days of his life. After Samuel was weaned, Hannah gave Samuel to Eli, the High Priest, to serve God all the days of his life. When Samuel was a little boy, the Word of the Lord came to him. At first, Samuel thought Eli was calling to him. Eli perceived that God was talking to Samuel and told him to answer God by saying, *Speak; for thy servant heareth.*

1 Samuel 3:10 (KJV)

10 And the Lord came, and stood, and called as at other times, Samuel, Samuel. Then Samuel answered, **Speak; for thy servant heareth.**

Samuel was established to be a prophet of the Lord in Israel from this point forward. People knew God was speaking to Samuel and his words had power. Now let's look at an important Scripture that talks about the power of the Prophet Samuel's words.

1 Samuel 3:19-21 (KJV)

19 **And Samuel grew, and the Lord was with him, and did let none of His Words fall to the ground.** *20 And all Israel from Dan even to Beersheba knew that* **Samuel was established to be a prophet of the Lord.** *21 And the Lord appeared again in Shiloh:*

*for **the Lord revealed himself to Samuel in Shiloh by the word of the Lord.***

The statement that *none of his words fall to the ground* meant that all his words had power and came to pass. Samuel was graced with the knowledge and power of God's Word at an early age. Samuel grew to be a mighty prophet of the Lord. He heard God speak to him, and he was used to anoint one of the most powerful kings of Israel. He anointed King David, the giant slayer. During the time of the prophet Samuel, the Philistines were subdued because the hand of the Lord was against them all the days of Samuel. The prayers and words of Samuel the prophet dominated the enemy.

1 Samuel 7:7-13 (KJV)

*7 **And when the Philistines heard that the children of Israel were gathered together to Mizpeh, the lords of the Philistines went up against Israel.** And when the children of Israel heard it, they were afraid of the Philistines. 8 And the children of Israel said to Samuel, **Cease not to cry unto the Lord our God for us, that he will save us out of the hand of the Philistines.** 9 And Samuel took a sucking lamb, and offered it for a burnt offering wholly unto the Lord: **and Samuel cried unto the Lord for Israel; and the Lord heard him.** 10 And as Samuel was offering up the burnt offering, the Philistines drew near to battle against Israel: **but the Lord thundered with a great thunder on that day upon the Philistines, and discomfited them; and they were smitten before Israel.** 11 And the men of Israel went out of Mizpeh, and pursued the Philistines, and smote them, until they came under Bethcar. 12 Then Samuel took a stone, and set it between Mizpeh and Shen, and called the name of it Ebenezer, saying, Hitherto hath the Lord helped us. 13 So the Philistines were subdued, and* *they came no more into the coast of Israel:* **and the hand of the Lord was against the Philistines all the days of Samuel.**

This chapter shows how evil people can bring evil to pass and how good people can bring good to pass with their words. Today, most people do not understand the power of words and say things carelessly. It is essential to come back to the lost knowledge of the power of words. Words have power, and there is a war of words going on all the time. God desires for you to understand the power of your words. We are going to give account for everything we say. Jesus, Himself, wants you to understand this truth and learn how to use your words for good and bring good things to come to pass. He also wants you to know and understand that you can speak to a mountain, make it move, and be cast into the sea if you believe.

In the following few chapters, we will continue to reveal the power, purpose, and the war of words. The battle between God and the devil has been raging since the beginning of time. This book will reveal to the Church where the real war is. The battle is between God's Word and the devil's word. God has always desired humankind to return to Him and start using their words to bring good things to pass. You were not created to be used by the devil to speak evil words. God made you in His image to speak to His creation, and by speaking His Word cause good things to come to pass.

CHAPTER 4

---•◉•---

THE HAND OF THE LORD

T*he Hand of the Lord* is a phrase used many times in the Bible. This phrase, however, has lost its true meaning and impact through time. *The Hand of the Lord* has everything to do with the work of the Lord and how God gets things done. To understand this phrase, you must understand who God is and how He works. This chapter will reveal more about this phrase and bring more profound insight into what God refers to when He uses *The Hand of the Lord* in the Bible.

To start with, let's look at the first day of creation in the Scriptures.

Genesis 1:1-5 (KJV)
*1 In the beginning God created the Heaven and the earth. 2 And the earth was without form, and void; and darkness was upon the face of the deep. **And the Spirit of God moved upon the face of the waters.** 3 And God said, Let there be light: and there was light. 4 And God saw the light, that it was good: and God divided the light from the darkness. 5 And God called the light Day, and the darkness he called Night. And the evening and the morning were the first day.*

We see that the earth was without form and void, and the Spirit of God moved upon the face of the waters. Then, God said, *"Let there be light,"* and there was light. He then divided the light from the darkness. So, what we see here is God creating with His spoken Word, and we also see the mentioning of the Spirit of God. We know about God and Him being three persons in One from the Scriptures and that three entities make up the Godhead. These three entities are the Father, Son, and Holy Spirit, which make up the Trinity. We saw this truth in the last chapter.

In the New Testament, we understand that it was Jesus, the Son of God, who spoke everything into existence. Let's look at some verses in the New Testament that confirm this truth.

John 1:1-3 (KJV)

*1 In the beginning was the Word, and the Word was with God, and the Word was God. 2 The same was in the beginning with God.3 **All things were made by him; and without him was not any thing made that was made.***

John 1:10 (KJV)

*10 **He was in the world, and the world was made by him,** and the world knew him not.*

Hebrews 1:1-3 (KJV)

*1 God, who at sundry times and in divers manners spake in time past unto the fathers by the prophets, 2 Hath in these last days spoken unto us by his Son, whom he hath appointed heir of all things, **by whom also he made the worlds;** 3 Who being the brightness of his glory, and the express image of his person, and upholding all things by the word of his power, when he had by himself purged our sins, sat down on the right hand of the Majesty on high:*

We know that it was Jesus who used His Words to speak into existence all things. Jesus is the Creator found in Genesis Chapter 1. During this time, Jesus did not have a body; He was in Spirit form. Jesus didn't have hands like a human has hands when He spoke and created the universe into existence. It wasn't until He became a man that He had a body with hands like every created man or woman. Jesus only used His Words when creating the universe, but He used His hands as a carpenter to build things as a man.

So, with the understanding that God did not have natural hands when creating and working in the beginning, let's look at some Scriptures that have to do with the Hand of the Lord, and we will start to see what is meant by this term.

The term Hand of the Lord is first mentioned during the time of Moses in the Book of Exodus.

Exodus 9:1-4 (KJV)

*1 Then the Lord said unto Moses, Go in unto Pharaoh, and tell him, Thus saith the Lord God of the Hebrews, Let my people go, that they may serve me. 2 For if thou refuse to let them go, and wilt hold them still, 3 Behold, **the hand of the Lord** is upon thy cattle which is in the field, upon the horses, upon the asses, upon the camels, upon the oxen, and upon the sheep: there shall be a very grievous murrain. 4 And the Lord shall sever between the cattle of Israel and the cattle of Egypt: and there shall nothing die of all that is the children's of Israel.*

The Book of Joshua also mentions the Hand of the Lord.

Joshua 4:23-24 (KJV)

23 For the Lord your God dried up the waters of Jordan from before you, until ye were passed over, as the Lord your God did *to the Red sea, which he dried up from before us, until we were gone over: 24 That all the people of the earth might know **the hand of the Lord**, that it is mighty: that ye might fear the Lord your God for ever.*

The Hand of the Lord was against the Philistines during the days of Samuel the prophet.

1 Samuel 7:13 (KJV)

*13 So the Philistines were subdued, and they came no more into the coast of Israel: **and the hand of the Lord was against the Philistines all the days of Samuel.***

The Hand of the Lord came upon Elijah the prophet and gave him the ability to outrun Ahab.

1 Kings 18:45-46 (KJV)

*45 And it came to pass in the mean while, that the Heaven was black with clouds and wind, and there was a great rain. And Ahab rode, and went to Jezreel. 46 And **the hand of the Lord was on Elijah**; and he girded up his loins, and ran before Ahab to the entrance of Jezreel.*

The Hand of God was upon Ezra, the scribe when he went from Babylon to Jerusalem.

Ezra 7:6 (KJV)

*6 This Ezra went up from Babylon; and he was a ready scribe in the law of Moses, which the Lord God of Israel had given: and the king granted him all his request, **according to the hand of the Lord his God upon him.***

Elisha the prophet called for a minstrel to play so he could prophesy. When the minstrel played, the Hand of the Lord came upon him.

2 Kings 3:15 (KJV)
*15 But now bring me a minstrel. And it came to pass, when the minstrel played, **that the hand of the Lord came upon him.***

The Psalmist said the right hand of the Lord does valiantly.

Psalm 118:15-16 (KJV)
*15 The voice of rejoicing and salvation is in the tabernacles of the righteous: **the right hand of the Lord doeth valiantly.** 16 The right hand of the Lord is exalted: **the right hand of the Lord doeth valiantly.***

The Book of Proverbs says the king's heart is in the Hand of the Lord.

Proverbs 21:1 (KJV)
*1 **The king's heart is in the hand of the Lord,** as the rivers of water: he turneth it whithersoever he will.*

Isaiah the prophet prophesied that the Hand of the Lord would be known toward His servants.

Isaiah 66:14 (KJV)
*14 And when ye see this, your heart shall rejoice, and your bones shall flourish like an herb: and **the hand of the Lord** shall be known toward his servants, and his indignation toward his enemies.*

Ezekiel said that the Hand of the Lord was strong upon him.

Ezekiel 3:14 (KJV)
14 So the spirit lifted me up, and took me away, and I went in bitterness, in the heat of my spirit; **but the hand of the Lord was strong upon me.**

During the time of Daniel, Belshazzar, the king of Babylon, saw the fingers of a man's hand appear out of nowhere and write on the wall. Belshazzar, the king of Babylon, sinned against the Lord by drinking from the golden vessels of the Lord that were stolen from the Temple of God when Babylon invaded Jerusalem. So God sent His Hand and wrote a message of judgment against this wicked king that only Daniel could interpret.

Daniel 5:5-6 (KJV)
*5 **In the same hour came forth fingers of a man's hand**, and wrote over against the candlestick upon the plaister of the wall of the king's palace: **and the king saw the part of the hand that wrote.** 6 Then the king's countenance was changed, and his thoughts troubled him, so that the joints of his loins were loosed, and his knees smote one against another.*

The Hand of the Lord was with John the Baptist.

Luke 1:66 (KJV)
*66 And all they that heard them laid them up in their hearts, saying, What manner of child shall this be! And **the hand of the Lord was with him.***

The Hand of the Lord was with the early Christians in the Book of Acts.

Acts 11:21 (KJV)
*21 **And the hand of the Lord was with them**: and a great number believed, and turned unto the Lord.*

Saul, the apostle, cursed Elymas, the sorcerer, for trying to turn the deputy away from the faith, and the Hand of God came upon him and made him blind.

> ### Acts 13:8-11 (KJV)
> *8 But Elymas the sorcerer (for so is his name by interpretation) withstood them, seeking to turn away the deputy from the faith. 9 Then Saul, (who also is called Paul,) **filled with the Holy Ghost,** set his eyes on him. 10 And said, O full of all subtilty and all mischief, thou child of the devil, thou enemy of all righteousness, wilt thou not cease to pervert the right ways of the Lord? 11 And now, behold, **the hand of the Lord is upon thee, and thou shalt be blind, not seeing the sun for a season.** And immediately there fell on him a mist and a darkness; and he went about seeking some to lead him by the hand.*

All these Scriptures point to the Hand of the Lord, but we are not sure what the Hand of the Lord is until we get to the ministry of Jesus. Jesus was casting a devil out of someone, and some people said He was casting out devils by Beelzebub, the chief of devils. Jesus went on to tell them that He cast out devils by the finger of God and made reference to the Kingdom of God coming upon them. The Kingdom of God refers to the rule and reign of God by His Holy Spirit.

> ### Luke 11:14-20 (KJV)
> *14 And he was casting out a devil, and it was dumb. And it came to pass, when the devil was gone out, the dumb spake; and the people wondered. 15 But some of them said, He casteth out devils through Beelzebub the chief of the devils. 16 And others, tempting him, sought of him a sign from Heaven. 17 But he, knowing their thoughts, said unto them, Every kingdom divided against itself is brought to desolation; and a house divided against a house*

falleth. 18 If Satan also be divided against himself, how shall his kingdom stand? because ye say that I cast out devils through Beelzebub. 19 And if I by Beelzebub cast out devils, by whom do your sons cast them out? therefore shall they be your judges. 20 **But if I with the finger of God cast out devils, no doubt the kingdom of God is come upon you.**

Jesus went on to say that He cast out devils by the Spirit of God, and the Kingdom of God was coming to them.

Matthew 12:22-28 (KJV)

22 Then was brought unto him one possessed with a devil, blind, and dumb: and he healed him, insomuch that the blind and dumb both spake and saw. 23 And all the people were amazed, and said, Is not this the son of David? 24 But when the Pharisees heard it, they said, This fellow doth not cast out devils, but by Beelzebub the prince of the devils. 25 And Jesus knew their thoughts, and said unto them, Every kingdom divided against itself is brought to desolation; and every city or house divided against itself shall not stand: 26 And if Satan cast out Satan, he is divided against himself; how shall then his kingdom stand? 27 And if I by Beelzebub cast out devils, by whom do your children cast them out? therefore they shall be your judges. 28 **But if I cast out devils by the Spirit of God, then the kingdom of God is come unto you.**

From the first passage, we see Jesus referring to the finger of God, which is another way of saying Hand of the Lord. Hands are your palm, fingers, and thumb. When you put the two passages together, you see the finger of God and the Spirit of God are the same. Jesus said when He was casting devils out of people; the Kingdom of God was coming to them and upon them. The statement *Kingdom of God* refers to the rule and reign of the Holy Spirit. The Book of Romans says that God's Kingdom is not meat and drink but righteousness, peace, and joy in the Holy Ghost.

> **Romans 14:17 (KJV)**
> *17 **For the kingdom of God is not meat and drink; but righteousness, and peace, and joy in the Holy Ghost.***

We also know from Scriptures that Jesus did not start His ministry until He was baptized by John the Baptist and the Holy Spirit came upon Him like a dove. He then went into the wilderness to be tempted by the devil. However, once Jesus successfully defeated the devil's three temptations, He returned in the power of the Spirit.

> **Luke 4:13-14 (KJV)**
> *13 And when the devil had ended all the temptation, he departed from him for a season. 14 **And Jesus returned in the power of the Spirit into Galilee:** and there went out a fame of him through all the region round about.*

From all of these Scriptures, we can see that the Holy Spirit is the Hand of the Lord referred to in the Scriptures. The Holy Spirit has always worked with Jesus. He worked with Jesus at the beginning of creation, and He also worked with Him while He ministered to people during His earthly ministry. The Holy Spirit is also the one mentioned in the Old Testament as the Hand of the Lord when working with men of God.

Now, let's get into why God refers to the Holy Spirit as the Hand of the Lord. God refers to the Holy Spirit as the Hand of the Lord because He wants us to know that it is His Spirit that does the work of what God Commands with His Mouth. We, as humans, use our hands to work and get things done. We use them in almost every area of our life. God, however, doesn't have hands like us to get things done because God is a Spirit and does not have a body.

When God speaks, it is the Holy Spirit who goes out and does whatever God says. When Jesus spoke during creation, the Holy Spirit did the work of what He was saying. While Jesus ministered as a man during His ministry on earth, the Holy Spirit carried out His Words. The Holy Spirit is referred to as the Hand of the Lord because it is the Holy Spirit that carries out and works God's spoken Word. Our hands are how we get things done, and the Holy Spirit is the one doing the actual work of God's Words.

Before the first Adam fell, he was also working by speaking, and it was the Holy Spirit who carried out his words. This is one of the things that Adam lost in the curse. He had to work by the sweat of his brow and lost the anointing of the Holy Spirit when he sinned against God. When Jesus died and rose again from the dead, the Holy Spirit came back on the earth and gave believers the ability to speak, and the Hand of the Lord would carry out their words. The Holy Spirit is the Hand of the Lord who carries out the spoken Word of God. The Holy Spirit works in the unseen realm, behind the scene, and makes things happen in the natural world.

In conclusion, this truth is fundamental to understand if you are going to start speaking, working, and warring with your words. The very *Hand of God*, which is the Holy Spirit, will carry out and perform your words. You no longer are called to just work with your natural hands. You can now work with your spoken words, and the Holy Spirit will be there as the Hand of the Lord to carry out what you say. This is an honor beyond all comprehension that we can work with the Holy Spirit in this way. You cannot see the Holy Spirit, but He is always there, working to bring your words to pass. Now you can work and fight with the words of your mouth, and the Hand of the Lord will be there helping you to win the war of words.

CHAPTER 5

DOUBLE PORTION OF HIS SPIRIT

A double portion of His Spirit is a term many Christians use when seeking to be anointed by God. This term came from the story of Elisha and Elijah when Elijah was taken to Heaven by God in a whirlwind. Elisha asked Elijah for a double portion of his spirit before he left. God chose Elisha to be the prophet who would take the place of Elijah. Elisha knew he needed the anointing of the spirit on Elijah to accomplish his call as a prophet. In this chapter, I will reveal what Elisha was really asking of Elijah when he asked for a double portion of his spirit.

Earlier on in the ministry of Elijah, Jezebel made a death threat to Elijah. This threat was very real because she had already killed the prophets of the Lord. Elijah was sent to her husband, Ahab, the King of Israel, and through a powerful standoff, Elijah demonstrated the power of God. He killed all the prophets of baal in front of Ahab after the fire of God fell on Elijah's sacrifice. Jezebel made a death threat to Elijah because he had her prophets of baal killed. Because of this death threat, Elijah left that area and went to Mount Sinai, the very mountain where God spoke the Ten Commandments directly to the children of Israel and established the Law of Moses.

While Elijah was on this mountain, God spoke to him and told Elijah to anoint Elisha, the son of Shaphat, in his place as a prophet of the Lord. Elijah then left Mount Sinai and found Elisha plowing with twelve yokes of oxen. Let's look at this encounter found in 1 Kings 19.

1 Kings 19:19-21 (KJV)

19 So he departed thence, and found Elisha the son of Shaphat, who was plowing with twelve yoke of oxen before him, and he with the twelfth: **and Elijah passed by him, and cast his mantle upon him.** *20 And he left the oxen, and ran after Elijah, and said, Let me, I pray thee, kiss my father and my mother, and then I will follow thee. And he said unto him, Go back again: for what have I done to thee? 21 And he returned back from him, and took a yoke of oxen, and slew them, and boiled their flesh with the instruments of the oxen, and gave unto the people, and they did eat.* **Then he arose, and went after Elijah, and ministered unto him.**

The mantle of Elijah represented the authority he was clothed in to be a prophet of the Lord. When God calls someone to a ministry, He wraps them in a mantle of authority to do the job He called them to do. This authority comes from the Spirit of God. The Holy Spirit clothes the man or woman to do the work of the ministry. The mantle is just a symbol of the anointing of the Spirit.

In the case of a prophet, they are called to be a spokesperson for God. We know from Scriptures that all the words of a true prophet had to come to pass.

Deuteronomy 18:21-22 (KJV)
*21 And if thou say in thine heart, How shall we know the word which the Lord hath not spoken? 22 **When a prophet speaketh in the name of the Lord, if the thing follow not, nor come to pass, that is the thing which the Lord hath not spoken,** but the prophet hath spoken it presumptuously: thou shalt not be afraid of him.*

It was a great responsibility to be a true prophet of the Lord. The responsibility and commitment to be a true prophet of the Lord were going to come on Elisha, and he spent several years ministering to the needs of Elijah to learn from him. One day this mighty mantle from Elijah the prophet would be passed down to Elisha.

The time finally came for Elijah to leave the earth; God was going to take him away in a whirlwind. Elisha stayed right by his side. Elisha would not leave Elijah no matter what. This is important to note because when Elijah was running for his life when Jezebel threatened his life, Elijah asked his servant (Elijah's first unnamed servant) to stay behind in a location, and he did. When it came to Elisha, he was asked three times by Elijah to stay in a place, and he refused to. His refusal was one of the key factors in obtaining Elijah's mantle. Too many Christians give up when they need to press in. Just because you are asked to stop doesn't mean you stop. It is just a test to see if you have the never-give-up spirit.

Elijah and Elisha traveled first from Gilgal, and then to Bethel. From Bethel, they went to Jericho, and from Jericho, they crossed the Jordan River. Elijah used his mantle to strike the Jordan River, the waters parted, and they crossed over on dry ground. When they got to the other side, Elisha asked Elijah for a double portion of his spirit. Elijah said he asked a hard thing, but it would be so if he saw him when he was taken from him.

Then, suddenly, a chariot of fire appeared, which separated them, and Elijah was taken. As he was going up, Elijah's mantle fell to the earth.

Elisha took up Elijah's mantle and started walking in the authority and power of Elijah. This was when Elisha started doing mighty signs and wonders by the Word of the Lord.

2 Kings 2:8-14 (KJV)

*8 **And Elijah took his mantle, and wrapped it together, and smote the waters,** and they were divided hither and thither, so that they two went over on dry ground. 9 **And it came to pass, when they were gone over, that Elijah said unto Elisha, Ask what I shall do for thee, before I be taken away from thee. And Elisha said, I pray thee, let a double portion of thy spirit be upon me.** 10 **And he said, Thou hast asked a hard thing:** nevertheless, if thou see me when I am taken from thee, it shall be so unto thee; but if not, it shall not be so. 11 And it came to pass, as they still went on, and talked, that, behold, there appeared a chariot of fire, and horses of fire, and parted them both asunder; and Elijah went up by a whirlwind into Heaven. 12 And Elisha saw it, and he cried, My father, my father, the chariot of Israel, and the horsemen thereof. **And he saw him no more: and he took hold of his own clothes, and rent them in two pieces. 13 He took up also the mantle of Elijah that fell from him, and went back, and stood by the bank of Jordan; 14 And he took the mantle of Elijah that fell from him, and smote the waters, and said, Where is the Lord God of Elijah? and when he also had smitten the waters, they parted hither and thither: and Elisha went over.***

I want to dig in deeper at Elisha's statement to Elijah about a *double portion of his spirit* on the day that Elijah was taken up in the whirlwind. This statement is many times used in the wrong way. You must go back to the Hebrew text to understand what was being asked by Elisha to Elijah when he asked him, "*let a double portion of thy spirit be upon me*." You have to understand the word *portion* to understand what he was actually asking for. Let's look at the definition of the word *portion* in the Hebrew language.

The word **Portion** comes from the Hebrew word **peh** and means mouth, literally or figuratively, particularly speech. It also means command, sentence, sound, speech, spoken, and talk.

So, another way of understanding what he was asking would be, *"Let the Spirit of God speak through me twice as much as He spoke through you."* I know this may change people's understanding of what had happened here. I will reveal this truth in more Scriptures, but this aligns with what a prophet was called to do. They were called to be a mouthpiece for God. God's Holy Spirit would come on them, and they would speak. Whenever they spoke by the Spirit of God, miracles would occur. Everything spoken by the Spirit of God came to pass.

Let's now turn our eyes to Jesus the Christ Himself. Jesus was **The Prophet** that was to come. Let's look at the prophecy made by Moses in the Book of Deuteronomy together about this **Prophet** to come.

> ### Deuteronomy 18:15-19 (KJV)
> *15 **The Lord thy God will raise up unto thee a Prophet from the midst of thee**, of thy brethren, like unto me; unto him ye shall hearken; 16 According to all that thou desiredst of the Lord thy God in Horeb in the day of the assembly, saying, Let me not hear again the voice of the Lord my God, neither let me see this great fire any more, that I die not. 17 And the Lord said unto me, They have well spoken that which they have spoken. 18 **I will raise them up a Prophet from among their brethren**, like unto thee, **and will put my words in his mouth; and he shall speak unto them all that I shall command him. 19 And it shall come to pass, that whosoever will not hearken unto my words which he shall speak in my name, I will require it of him.***

God said He would raise up a *Prophet* from their midst, and He would put His Words in His mouth, and He would speak all that God commanded Him to speak. Being a true prophet of the Lord had everything to do with God putting His Words in your mouth. We see this with many other prophets God raised up, like Isaiah, Jeremiah, and Ezekiel. But, this *Prophet* to come would be unique from all other prophets. This *Prophet* would speak Words in God's name, and every Word He spoke would be required of people. Jesus is that *Prophet* to come.

Acts 3:22-26 (KJV)

*22 For Moses truly said unto the fathers, **A prophet shall the Lord your God raise up unto you of your brethren,** like unto me; **him shall ye hear in all things whatsoever he shall say unto you.** 23 And it shall come to pass, that every soul, **which will not hear that prophet,** shall be destroyed from among the people. 24 Yea, and all the prophets from Samuel and those that follow after, as many as have spoken, have likewise foretold of these days. 25 Ye are the children of the prophets, and of the covenant which God made with our fathers, saying unto Abraham, And in thy seed shall all the kindreds of the earth be blessed. 26 **Unto you first God, having raised up his Son Jesus, sent him to bless you,** in turning away every one of you from his iniquities.*

Now, let's get back to a double portion of his spirit and its meaning. God speaking twice as much through Elisha was how he would perform more miracles than Elijah. Elisha was asking for a double portion of God speaking through him. This means how much God speaks through someone by His Spirit can be measured. We find in the Scriptures that Elijah performed eight recorded miracles, and Elisha performed sixteen recorded miracles.

Let's look at the verse spoken about Jesus, **The Prophet** by John the Baptist. John reveals how God's Spirit can be measured by what is spoken, but Jesus has no limit of how much the Spirit of God would speak through Him.

John 3:34 (KJV)
*34 **For he whom God hath sent speaketh the Words of God : for God giveth not the Spirit by measure unto him.***

Jesus had an unlimited measure of God speaking through Him by the Holy Spirit. This powerful verse shows that God speaking through someone can be measured. There was no measure when it came to Jesus, but with Elijah and Elisha, it could be measured. Many verses talk about *the measure*. Let's look at some of them together.

2 Corinthians 10:13-14 (KJV)
*13 But we will not boast of things without our **measure**, but according to the **measure** of the rule which God hath distributed to us, a **measure** to reach even unto you. 14 For we stretch not ourselves beyond our **measure**, as though we reached not unto you: for we are come as far as to you also in preaching the gospel of Christ:*

Ephesians 4:7 (KJV)
*7 But unto every one of us is given grace according to **the measure of the gift of Christ.***

Ephesians 4:13 (KJV)
*13 Till we all come in the unity of the faith, and of the knowledge of the Son of God, unto a perfect man, **unto the measure of the stature of the fulness of Christ:***

Ephesians 4:16 (KJV)

*16 From whom the whole body fitly joined together and compacted by that which every joint supplieth, according to the effectual working in the **measure** of every part, maketh increase of the body unto the edifying of itself in love.*

God works with people where they are spiritually and wants to increase the measure of Him working through them by His Spirit. This working through you will depend on how much of God's Word will get into you, and you speak by His Spirit. The Apostle Paul had gone up into paradise and heard Words that could not even be uttered.

2 Corinthians 12:2-4 (KJV)

*2 I knew a man in Christ above fourteen years ago, (whether in the body, I cannot tell; or whether out of the body, I cannot tell: God knoweth;) such an one caught up to the third Heaven. 3 And I knew such a man, (whether in the body, or out of the body, I cannot tell: God knoweth;) 4 How that he was caught up into paradise, **and heard unspeakable words, which it is not lawful for a man to utter.***

God has an exceedingly high speech, and He speaks at such a level that man cannot say these Words now. But, we are given a measure on this earth, and that measure of God speaking through us can grow. We are called to speak by faith, and there is a measure of faith given to every man.

Romans 12:1-3 (KJV)

1 I beseech you therefore, brethren, by the mercies of God, that ye present your bodies a living sacrifice, holy, acceptable unto God, which is your reasonable service. 2 And be not conformed to this world: but be ye transformed by the renewing of your mind, that ye may prove what is that good, and acceptable, and *perfect, will of God. 3 For I say, through the grace given unto me, to every man that is among you, not to think of himself more highly than he ought to think; but to think soberly, **according as God hath dealt to every man the measure of faith.***

From this Scripture, we can see that God dealt to every man the measure of faith. Faith can be measured, and faith can grow.

2 Thessalonians 1:3 (KJV)

*3 We are bound to thank God always for you, brethren, as it is meet, because that your **faith groweth exceedingly,** and the charity of every one of you all toward each other aboundeth;*

Your faith has everything to do with what you believe in your heart and speak out of your mouth.

2 Corinthians 4:13 (KJV)

*13 **We having the same spirit of faith**, according as it is written, **I believed, and therefore have I spoken; we also believe, and therefore speak;***

This means what you believe and speak out of your mouth can grow in measures. As you stay faithful to God and grow in His Word, your faith can grow. This also means the impact of your faith-filled words can grow. In essence, your ability to speak to things can grow as your faith grows.

This concept is fundamental to understand when it comes to the war of words. Not everyone's level of faith to speak to things is at the same place. We are all given a measure of faith, but we are responsible for how it grows as we obey God. Jesus is also called the *Author* and *Finisher* of our faith.

Hebrews 12:2 (KJV)
2 Looking unto Jesus the author and finisher of our faith; who
for the joy that was set before him endured the cross, despising
the shame, and is set down at the right hand of the throne of God.

A big part of the ministry of Jesus is to not only be the *Author* of the faith in our hearts but to be the *Finisher* of the faith that He started in us. The word finish in Greek means to complete. So Jesus will complete what He started in regards to our faith. Now, getting back to the point I was making, faith can be measured, which has everything to do with the authority of our words. God has destined for you to mature where He can speak through you by His Spirit and enable you to move mountains with your words.

You will only move mountains in accordance with where your faith has grown. You will also need the Holy Spirit to speak God's Word to win the war of words. The Holy Spirit desires to find people of God that He can use to speak through. As you learn and grow in your walk with God, God will begin to speak through you more. If you remain faithful, His Word can increase on the inside of you as you release greater levels of the voice of God on the earth.

In conclusion, to win the war of words, the Spirit of God must speak through you. One of the main reasons Jesus came to the earth was to get people walking in the anointing once again. Those who walk in the anointing will have the authority to speak to mountains and make them move. Mountains represent anything standing in the way of God and His will. God has destined you to walk in a measure of the Holy Spirit so He can speak through you. This is one of the greatest mysteries of your destiny.

CHAPTER 6

LAW OF FAITH

To win the war of words, you have to understand the Laws of God. God operates by laws and governs the whole universe by His Laws. The devil knows this and tries to use God's laws against Him. God, however, always outsmarts the devil and knows all of the loopholes found in His Laws. Learning about the *Law of Faith* will help you defeat the devil and stay in right standing with God. Then, when you are in right standing with God, you can pray, move mountains with your faith, and win the war of words.

Many people do not know that faith is a law. Faith is a law that governs how a Christian lives, speaks, and acts. The *Law of Faith* is made up of many laws, and we will be going over these laws in the following chapters. When you learn the *Laws of Faith*, you will no longer be ignorant of why your prayers are not answered. Hosea, the prophet, said that God's people were destroyed for lack of knowledge. If you don't understand the *Law of Faith*, you could also perish. What I mean by perishing is that you may need a healing, a financial miracle, or protection from a demonic spirit, but don't get your answer due to the ignorance of the *Law of Faith*. If you don't understand the *Law of Faith*, you may not get the breakthrough you seek.

> **Hosea 4:6 (KJV)**
> *6 My people are destroyed for lack of knowledge: because thou hast rejected knowledge, I will also reject thee, that thou shalt be no priest to me: seeing thou hast forgotten the Law of thy God, I will also forget thy children.*

God's answer to helping people is to bring them to an understanding of how things work in His Kingdom. So, you will not perish when you understand God, His ways, and His Laws. Let's look deeper into the *Law of Faith* and see how we are to live and not perish. The Book of Romans is where we see that God calls faith a law. Let's look at this verse together.

> **Romans 3:27 (KJV)**
> *27 Where is boasting then? It is excluded. By what law? of works? Nay:* ***but by the law of faith.***

A law is a rule made by someone who has the authority over people, places, and things and has the ability to enforce with punishments or rewards depending on if the law is broken or kept. The word law can also be defined by outcomes when the same factors and conditions are put into motion. These laws are governing rules, structural factors, principles, parameters, universal programming codes, and influences that never change. God's governing rules maintain the order, integrity, and outcome of all that happens in His created universe. God has bound Himself to the laws He made. These laws keep things running smoothly, and when violated, things don't work right.

However, when the Laws of God are understood and worked with, anyone can have the desired outcome they seek 100% of the time. The Laws of God govern the spiritual world just as they do the physical world. Spiritual laws, however, supersede natural laws. Most people think that God only wrote the Law of Moses, but in the Scriptures, we see God has many Laws.

Here is a list of laws found in the Bible:

1. Law of Moses (Joshua 8:31)

2. Law of the Burnt Offering (Leviticus 6:9)

3. Law of the Meat Offering (Leviticus 6:14)

4. Law of the Sin Offering (Leviticus 6:25)

5. Law of the Trespass Offering (Leviticus 7:1)

6. Law of the Sacrifice of Peace Offerings (Leviticus 7:11)

7. Law of the beasts, the fowl, and every living creature that moves in the waters and of every creature that creeps upon the earth. (Leviticus 11:46)

8. Law of the Plague of Leprosy in a Garment (Leviticus13:59)

9. Law of the Leper (Leviticus 14:2)

10. Law of him that hath an Issue (Leviticus15:32)

11. Law of Jealousies (Numbers 5:29)

12. Law of the Nazarite (Numbers 6:13)

13. Law of the House (Ezekiel 43:12)

14. Law of thy Mouth (Psalm 119:72)

15. Law of thy Mother (Proverbs 1:8)

16. Law of the Wise (Proverbs 13:14)

17. Law of Kindness (Proverbs 31:26)

18. Law of Truth (Malachi 2:6)

19. Law of Faith (Romans 3:27)

20. Law of her husband (Romans 7:2)

21. Law of My Mind (Romans 7:23)

22. Law of Sin and Death (Romans 8:2)

23. Law of the Spirit of Life in Christ Jesus (Romans 8:2)

24. Law of Righteousness (Romans 9:31)

25. Law of Christ (Galatians 6:2)

26. Law of Liberty (James 1:25)

One of the most powerful laws that God created was the *Law of Faith*. The *Law of Faith* supersedes all of His Laws, just as the Law of Lift supersedes the Law of Gravity. The *Law of Faith*, however, is misunderstood many times. When the *Law of Faith* is not understood, religion will start to make up false doctrines and statements that are not true. Some of these statements are that you can't figure God out, or maybe God put sickness on someone, or God answers some people's prayers and not others.

Jesus had to die and rise again to fulfill God's Laws for us to be saved. Satan knows that God is a God of Laws, and therefore, he tries to use His Laws against Him. God, however, knows how to maneuver through all His Laws because He is wise beyond all comprehension. Satan killed Jesus, an innocent man; therefore, the righteousness of Jesus the Christ could be imputed to guilty people if they believe and have faith in Him.

This faith is expressed by believing in your heart that God raised Jesus from the dead and confessing with your mouth that Jesus is Lord. This is how we are saved by faith.

Romans 10:8-10 (KJV)

*8 But what saith it? The Word is nigh thee, even in thy mouth, and in thy heart: that is, the Word of faith, which we preach; 9 **That if thou shalt confess with thy mouth the Lord Jesus, and shalt believe in thine heart that God hath raised him from the dead, thou shalt be saved. 10 For with the heart man believeth unto righteousness; and with the mouth confession is made unto salvation.***

God has encoded the secret *Law of Faith* into the framework of all creation and supersedes all laws by faith in Him. When you understand how the *Law of Faith* operates, you can get healed or have God answer any prayer you need from Him 100% of the time. I have listed what I have found from the Word of God to be some of the different laws that make up the *Law of Faith*. The *Law of Faith* is made up of many laws, just as Moses' Law consists of many individual laws, but we still call it the Law of Moses.

I want to note that Jesus said you could sum up the whole Law of Moses into two laws. The first law was to love the Lord your God with all of your heart, soul, mind, and strength. The second law was to love your neighbor as yourself.

Mark 12:28-31 (KJV)

28 And one of the scribes came, and having heard them reasoning together, and perceiving that he had answered them well, asked him, Which is the first commandment of all? 29 And Jesus answered him, The first of all the Commandments is, Hear, O

Israel; The Lord our God is one Lord: 30 **And thou shalt love the Lord thy God with all thy heart, and with all thy soul, and with all thy mind, and with all thy strength: this is the first commandment.** *31 And the second is like, namely this,* **Thou shalt love thy neighbour as thyself.** *There is none other commandment greater than these.*

For faith to work, it has to work by love. The *Law of Faith* is one of God's most powerful laws, but faith only works by love. We will get into this truth more later in the chapter *Faith Works by Love.*

Another truth I want to bring out is about all created matter. In the Book of Hebrews, the Word of God says that faith is the substance of things hoped for, so there is real substance to faith.

Hebrews 11:1 (KJV)
11 **Now faith is the substance** *of things hoped for, the evidence of things not seen.*

Through faith, we understand that the Word of God framed the worlds, and the Word of His power upholds everything.

Hebrews 11:3 (KJV)
3 **Through faith we understand that the worlds were framed by the Word of God**, *so that things which are seen were not made of things which do appear.*

Hebrews 1:1-3 (KJV)
1 God, who at sundry times and in divers manners spake in time past unto the fathers by the prophets, 2 Hath in these last days spoken unto us by his Son, whom he hath appointed heir of all things, by whom also he made the worlds; 3 Who being the brightness of his glory, and the express image of his person, **and**

upholding all things by the Word of his power, when he had by himself purged our sins, sat down on the right hand of the Majesty on high:

Let's talk about creation and the foundation of creation being atoms. When God created the earth, we know from science that He used atoms as the building blocks. These atoms can hear, understand, and speak (Think – Hear – Communicate). I know this concept may seem strange to some, but it will make more sense as you read this book. In the next chapter, we will see how Jesus and many other people in the Bible spoke to trees, mountains, wind, waves, demons, altars, the sun, fevers, rocks, and more. When they talked to them, they heard and obeyed what was said.

To understand the war of words we are in, you must realize that everything can hear, understand, and communicate. However, the creation of God is neutral, and is only responding to what is being communicated to it by human beings. The war comes in when an evil person is talking to God's creation or if a good person is speaking to His creation. The devil is in the background, and so is God, speaking to people. The devil wants to create evil things and bring evil things to pass, so he puts thoughts in people's hearts and minds so they will speak it and bring evil to pass. On the other hand, God is putting His thoughts into people's hearts and minds so they will speak His thoughts and bring good to pass.

Many people do not understand this war and think many of their thoughts are their own. So, let's look at a powerful verse in the Bible that shows this warfare of thoughts in the mind.

2 Corinthians 10:3-6 (KJV)
*3 For though we walk in the flesh, **we do not war after the flesh:** 4 (**For the weapons of our warfare** are not carnal, but mighty through God to the pulling down of strong holds;) 5 **Casting down imaginations, and every high thing that exalteth itself***

against the knowledge of God, and bringing into captivity every thought to the obedience of Christ; 6 And having in a readiness to revenge all disobedience, when your obedience is fulfilled.

We, as Christians, must cast down any and every thought that does not line up with the Word or will of God. The devil is trying to get people to speak his thoughts to bring evil to pass. The war starts in the mind. But, God is trying to get people to say His thoughts so He can bring good to pass. This war has been raging since the beginning of time. Let's look at what Paul wrote about this war in the Book of Ephesians, Chapter 6.

Ephesians 6:10-20 (KJV)

*10 Finally, my brethren, be strong in the Lord, and in the power of his might. 11 Put on the whole armour of God, that ye may be able to stand against **the wiles of the devil.** 12 **For we wrestle not against flesh and blood, but against principalities, against powers, against the rulers of the darkness of this world, against spiritual wickedness in high places.** 13 **Wherefore take unto you the whole armour of God**, that ye may be able to withstand in the evil day, and having done all, to stand. 14 Stand therefore, having your loins girt about with truth, and having on the breastplate of righteousness; 15 And your feet shod with the preparation of the gospel of peace; 16 **Above all, taking the shield of faith, wherewith ye shall be able to quench all the fiery darts of the wicked.** 17 And take the helmet of salvation, **and the sword of the Spirit, which is the Word of God:** 18 Praying always with all prayer and supplication in the Spirit, and watching thereunto with all perseverance and supplication for all saints; 19 **And for me, that utterance may be given unto me, that I may open my mouth boldly, to make known the mystery of the gospel, 20 For*** *which I am an ambassador in bonds: that therein I may speak boldly, as I ought to speak.*

Apostle Paul is talking about the war of the New Testament Christian. The darts of the devil are the thoughts that come through the principalities, powers, rulers of darkness, and spiritual wickedness in high places. These evil darts of thoughts have to be stopped by the shield of faith that God gave you. Then you have to take the Word of God, which is the Sword of the Spirit and attack the enemy's words. It is an attack or assault of demonic words that try to get you to speak or have been spoken by other people. You have to defeat these thoughts and spoken words of the devil with the Word of God and by taking every thought captive to the obedience of Christ.

Very few people have ever seen the devil or a demon. So, when the Bible talks of them, they have difficulty recognizing where their attack is coming from. Demons and fallen angels are spirits that do not appear in the natural world. They can affect the natural world and rarely appear in it. They attack the mind and pressure people to speak their thoughts because they know it takes a human living in the natural world to speak words into the air that will cause things to come to pass.

Once you learn where your battle is coming from, you are better equipped to fight this battle. The battle starts in your mind and is finished by what you say out of your mouth. The devil has been blinding the minds of people to this war for centuries.

2 Corinthians 4:3-4 (KJV)
*3 But if our gospel be hid, it is hid to them that are lost: 4 **In whom the god of this world hath blinded the minds of them which believe not,** lest the light of the glorious gospel of Christ, who is the image of God, should shine unto them.*

People have been speaking thoughts from the devil since the beginning of time. We can see this truth in the story of Job from the Bible. When the devil attacked Job, he tried to get him to curse God with his mouth. However, Job refused to speak against God and charge God foolishly.

Job 1:9-11 (KJV)

*9 Then Satan answered the Lord, and said, Doth Job fear God for nought? 10 Hast not thou made an hedge about him, and about his house, and about all that he hath on every side? thou hast blessed the work of his hands, and his substance is increased in the land. 11 **But put forth thine hand now, and touch all that he hath, and he will curse thee to thy face.***

The devil was trying to get Job to curse God to His face. Job, however, loved God and refused to do so. As a result of this attack, Job had almost his whole life wiped out by the enemy, but let's look at what Job said.

Job 1:20-22 (KJV)

*20 Then Job arose, and rent his mantle, and shaved his head, and fell down upon the ground, and worshipped, 21 **And said, Naked came I out of my mother's womb, and naked shall I return thither: the Lord gave, and the Lord hath taken away; blessed be the name of the Lord. 22 In all this Job sinned not, nor charged God foolishly.***

Job watched his tongue during the worst attack of his life. He was also attacked again by the devil in his body. The devil said Job would curse God to His face if he faced an infirmity in his body. Job, however, kept his integrity and didn't sin with his lips. It is interesting to note that Job's wife unknowingly picked up on the words spoken in the spirit world and said what the devil said.

Job 2:9-10 (KJV)
*9 Then said his wife unto him, Dost thou still retain thine integrity? curse God, and die. 10 But he said unto her, **Thou speakest as one of the foolish women speaketh**. What? shall we receive good at the hand of God, and shall we not receive evil? In all this did not Job sin with his lips.*

Job declared that while he had breath in him, and the Spirit of God in his nostrils, his lips would not speak wickedness and that his tongue would not utter deceit. Job was not going to lose his integrity no matter what happened.

Job 27:3-5 (KJV)
*3 All the while my breath is in me, and the spirit of God is in my nostrils; 4 **My lips shall not speak wickedness, nor my tongue utter deceit**. 5 God forbid that I should justify you: **till I die I will not remove mine integrity from me**.*

There is a war raging, and it's over what is in your heart and what comes out of your mouth. The devil is warring to control what people believe in their hearts and speak out of their mouths so he can curse them and the world around them. On the other hand, God is warring to get people to repent of their evil thoughts and words, bring His Law into their hearts, and speak His Words out of their mouths.

Isaiah 55:6-9 (KJV)
*6 Seek ye the Lord while he may be found, call ye upon him while he is near: 7 **Let the wicked forsake his way, and the unrighteous man his thoughts**: and let him return unto the Lord, and he will have mercy upon him; and to our God, for he will abundantly pardon. 8 **For my thoughts are not your thoughts**, neither are your ways my ways, saith the Lord. 9 **For as the***

Heavens are higher than the earth, so are my ways higher than your ways, and my thoughts than your thoughts.

God sent Jesus, His Word, and prophets to teach people His ways and how to speak. God has desired from the beginning that His people know what to believe, think, and speak. Whatever you believe in your heart and speak out of your mouth is where the battlefield begins and ends. The devil knows if God's people learn and understand this truth, he is doomed. God's Word never returns void and always prospers where it is sent.

Isaiah 55:10-11 (KJV)

*10 For as the rain cometh down, and the snow from Heaven, and returneth not thither, but watereth the earth, and maketh it bring forth and bud, that it may give seed to the sower, and bread to the eater: 11 **So shall my Word be that goeth forth out of my mouth: it shall not return unto me void, but it shall accomplish that which I please, and it shall prosper in the thing whereto I sent it.***

I mentioned before that God's people perish for lack of knowledge of His Laws and ways. To win the war of words, you have to understand you have two battles you have to win. The first battle is a legal battle before the Throne of God. To win this war, you must be in right standing with God and pray according to His will. You cannot be living in sin or be operating outside of the *Law of Faith* to get your prayers answered. The person you are praying for also must repent if they are in sin before God.

James 5:15-16 (KJV)

*15 **And the** Prayer of Faith **shall save the sick,** and the Lord shall raise him up; and if he have committed sins, they shall be* *forgiven him. 16 **Confess your faults one to another, and pray one for another, that ye may be healed. The effectual fervent prayer of a righteous man availeth much.***

Once the issue of sin is cleared up, you have a right to pray to God to get an answer. When God sees that everything you ask aligns with the *Law of Faith*, you have His blessing upon whatever you request. The devil knows this is a legal battle in Heaven and will try to put up a fight, but the *blood* of Jesus will always prevail. Jesus' *blood* always prevails because you are applying what He did for you on the cross. All legal battles are won in Heaven when someone repents and applies the *blood* of Jesus. Once the legal battle is won in Heaven, and you are in the will of God, you have a right to speak to whatever mountain you are facing, and it will move.

Speaking and enforcing the will of God with your faith and words is the second battle. Just because you won the legal battle in Heaven doesn't mean the mountain has moved. Moving mountains is enforced by the words of faith coming out of your mouth. The *Prayer of Faith* is the enforcement of God's will on earth.

We will learn more about the laws that govern your faith in the following few chapters. I will be revealing 16 laws or principles that govern your faith. God said the just shall live by his faith. The following chapters will reveal truths that will help you in your walk with God. Learning the *Laws of Faith* will help you understand how to live in right standing with God. You will also learn laws on how to speak to mountains. Jesus revealed many spiritual truths that govern His Kingdom, and when you abide by His New Covenant Laws, you too can have what you say and win the war of words.

God has called you to bring good things to pass by speaking good things out of your mouth. He also wants you to learn that you can rebuke evil things and demons and cause them to stop operating. Speaking to things by the Word of God is how you bring the will of God to pass on the earth. This is how you bring Heaven to earth and live in all the blessings and promises of God.

——●◆●——

CHAPTER 7

LAW #1

SPEAK DIRECTLY TO THE MOUNTAIN

To operate in the *Law of Faith*, you have to believe you can speak to the mountain and that it will obey you. This also includes rebuking anything that does not line up with the Word and will of God. Jesus taught His disciples the spiritual truth of speaking to mountains. A mountain represents anything standing in your way. God has revealed His will that His people speak directly to mountains to cause His will to come to pass in the earth. This is how you inherit promises from God.

> *Mark 11:23 (KJV)*
> *23 For verily I say unto you, **That whosoever shall say unto this mountain,** Be thou removed, and be thou cast into the sea; and shall not doubt in his heart, but shall believe that those things which he saith shall come to pass; he shall have whatsoever he saith.*

To understand that we can speak to a mountain, you must know how God created the world and all of creation; He created everything to have intelligence. This means everything God created in the known universe has the ability to hear, think and speak. This is important to understand if you are going to believe you will speak to something, and it will listen to you and obey you.

One thing to note is God has a universal language; He doesn't just speak in the English language. So, a better way to say hear, speak, and think is to say communicate. Everything has the ability to communicate with God and humankind. This concept may sound new and strange to some people, but you will see this truth more as we study the Scriptures in this chapter.

I also want to add that most of humanity sees the created world as something solid, but it is virtual to God. What I mean is that man sees things in a solid form that must be moved by their hands, whereas God knows the world is virtual and is moved or manipulated by words. Let me show you this truth from the story of Moses meeting God for the first time.

During the first exchange between God and Moses, God asks Moses to do something. Let's read this story and see what God asks Moses to do.

> ### Exodus 4:6-7 (KJV)
> *6 And the Lord said furthermore unto him,* **Put now thine hand into thy bosom. And he put his hand into his bosom: and when he took it out, behold, his hand was leprous as snow.** *7 And he said, Put thine hand into thy bosom again.* **And he put his hand into his bosom again; and plucked it out of his bosom, and, behold, it was turned again as his other flesh.**

God was able at will to turn Moses' hand leprous and then back to normal again within seconds. God can do this because He created the world through His Words and has complete control over it with His Words. God can change anything in the created world into anything He wants to by speaking to it. The devil knows this and tested Jesus to turn the stones into bread when He was hungry. Jesus defeated the devil in this test by saying that man not only lives by bread but by every Word that proceeds out of the mouth of God.

Matthew 4:3-4 (KJV)

*3 And when the tempter came to him, he said, If thou be the Son of God, **command that these stones be made bread.** 4 But he answered and said, It is written, **Man shall not live by bread alone, but by every word that proceedeth out of the mouth of God.***

The created world is more virtual than most people understand it to be. That is why what you say matters. You were created in the image of God, and you have the ability to speak to things, and they will listen to you. This is because they were designed to listen to you. This is why the Bible says nothing is impossible with God, and nothing is impossible to him who believes. Anything and everything is possible to God because He can speak to all of His creation, and it obeys His Words.

Mark 10:27 (KJV)

*27 And Jesus looking upon them saith, With men it is impossible, but not with God: **for with God all things are possible.***

Luke 1:37 (KJV)

*37 **For with God nothing shall be impossible.***

If you have faith in God, nothing will be impossible for you either.

Matthew 17:20 (KJV)

*20 And Jesus said unto them, Because of your unbelief: for verily I say unto you, If ye have faith as a grain of mustard seed, ye shall say unto this mountain, Remove hence to yonder place; and it shall remove; **and nothing shall be impossible unto you.***

The power of His Word upholds all things.

Hebrews 1:1-3 (KJV)

*1 God, who at sundry times and in divers manners spake in time past unto the fathers by the prophets, 2 Hath in these last days spoken unto us by his Son, whom he hath appointed heir of all things, by whom also he made the worlds; 3 Who being the brightness of his glory, and the express image of his person, **and upholding all things by the word of his power**, when he had by himself purged our sins, sat down on the right hand of the Majesty on high:*

Many people in the Bible understood the truth of speaking to things and operated in this truth, not just Jesus. Let's look into these stories in the Bible and see how Jesus and other men of God spoke to things, and they obeyed them.

JESUS CURSING THE FIG TREE

Mark 11:12-14 (KJV)

*12 And on the morrow, when they were come from Bethany, he was hungry: 13 And seeing a fig tree afar off having leaves, he came, if haply he might find any thing thereon: and when he came to it, he found nothing but leaves; for the time of figs was not yet. 14 And **Jesus answered and said unto it**, No man eat fruit of thee hereafter for ever. And his disciples heard it.*

In verse 14, you see that Jesus answered and spoke to the fig tree. You only answer something that is talking to you. Jesus explains to the disciples the next day; that when they see the fig tree dried up by the roots, if you have faith in God, you must speak to the mountain, and it will obey you. If you believe what you say comes to pass, you will have what you say. Jesus told them to talk to the mountain. Mountains represent problems or anything you need as an answer from God. If a mountain or problem is in your way, you must speak to it for it to move.

SPEAK TO THE MOUNTAIN

Mark 11:20-24 (KJV)

*20 And in the morning, as they passed by, they saw the fig tree dried up from the roots. 21 And Peter calling to remembrance saith unto him, Master, behold, the fig tree which thou cursedst is withered away. 22 And Jesus answering saith unto them, **Have faith in God.** 23 For verily I say unto you, **That whosoever shall say unto this mountain**, Be thou removed, and be thou cast into the sea; and shall not doubt in his heart, but shall believe that those things which he saith shall come to pass; he shall have whatsoever he saith. 24 Therefore I say unto you, What things soever ye desire, when ye pray, believe that ye receive them, and ye shall have them.*

Jesus taught His disciples they had to speak to the mountain for it to be moved. The mountain represents any problem you are facing. Jesus used the word mountain as a figure of speech to what was standing in the way of God. The mountain has to be spoken to from a believing heart for it to move. Tell the mountain what you want it to do, and if you believe, it will move.

The spiritual truth of moving mountains originated in the Old Testament. God wanted His people to know the mountain would move by His Spirit and not by the might or power of man.

Zechariah 4:6-7 (KJV)

*6 Then he answered and spake unto me, saying, This is the word of the Lord unto Zerubbabel, saying, **Not by might, nor by power,***

89

*but by my spirit, saith the Lord of hosts. 7 **Who art thou, O great mountain?** before Zerubbabel thou shalt become a plain: and he shall bring forth the headstone thereof with shoutings, crying, Grace, grace unto it.*

JESUS SPEAKING TO THE WIND AND THE SEA

Mark 4:35-41 (KJV)

*35 And the same day, when the even was come, he saith unto them, Let us pass over unto the other side. 36 And when they had sent away the multitude, they took him even as he was in the ship. And there were also with him other little ships. 37 And there arose a great storm of wind, and the waves beat into the ship, so that it was now full. 38 And he was in the hinder part of the ship, asleep on a pillow: and they awake him, and say unto him, Master, carest thou not that we perish? 39 **And he arose, and rebuked the wind, and said unto the sea, Peace, be still.** And the wind ceased, and there was a great calm. 40 And he said unto them, Why are ye so fearful? how is it that ye have no faith? 41 And they feared exceedingly, and said one to another, **What manner of man is this, that even the wind and the sea obey him?***

Jesus rebuked the wind. To rebuke means giving a verbal reprimand or scolding something or someone. Jesus verbally reprimanded the wind. He also said to the sea, *Peace, be still.* The word peace here has to do with muzzling the mouth. He told the sea to be quiet or stop speaking.

MOSES SPEAKING TO THE ROCK

Numbers 20:2-13 (KJV)

2 And there was no water for the congregation: and they gathered themselves together against Moses and against Aaron. 3 And the people chode with Moses, and spake, saying, Would God that we *had died when our brethren died before the Lord! 4 And why have ye brought up the congregation of the Lord into this wilderness, that we and our cattle should die there? 5 And wherefore have ye made us to come up out of Egypt, to bring us in unto this evil place? it is no place of seed, or of figs, or of vines, or of pomegranates; neither is there any water to drink. 6 And Moses and Aaron went from the presence of the assembly unto the door of the tabernacle of the congregation, and they fell upon their faces: and the glory of the Lord appeared unto them. 7 And the Lord spake unto Moses, saying, 8 Take the rod, and gather thou the assembly together, thou, and Aaron thy brother, **and speak ye unto the rock before their eyes; and it shall give forth his water, and thou shalt bring forth to them water out of the rock:** so thou shalt give the congregation and their beasts drink. 9 And Moses took the rod from before the Lord, as he commanded him. 10 And Moses and Aaron gathered the congregation together before the rock, and he said unto them, Hear now, ye rebels; must we fetch you water out of this rock? 11 And Moses lifted up his hand, and with his rod he smote the rock twice: and the water came out abundantly, and the congregation drank, and their beasts also. 12 And the Lord spake unto Moses and Aaron, Because ye believed me not, to sanctify me in the eyes of the children of Israel, therefore ye shall not bring this congregation into the land which I have given them. 13 This is the water of Meribah; because the children of Israel strove with the Lord, and he was sanctified in them.*

In this famous story, God told Moses to speak to the rock, and it would bring forth water. However, in his anger, Moses hit the rock with his rod. The rock still brought forth water, but he was kept from going into the Promised Land because he disobeyed the Lord. The speaking to the rock was supposed to be a prophetic example of us speaking to things, and they will listen. God wanted to reveal to the children of Israel that they could speak to things, and they would obey them. Just as Moses was kept from the Promised Land for not speaking to the rock, many of God's children will be kept from their Promised Land if they do not start talking to things.

JOSHUA SPEAKING TO THE SUN AND MOON

Joshua 10:12-14 (KJV)

12 Then spake Joshua to the Lord in the day when the Lord delivered up the Amorites before the children of Israel, and he said in the sight of Israel, **Sun, stand thou still upon Gibeon; and thou, Moon, in the valley of Ajalon. 13 And the sun stood still, and the moon stayed, until the people had avenged themselves upon their enemies.** *Is not this written in the Book of Jasher?* **So the sun stood still in the midst of Heaven, and hasted not to go down about a whole day.** *14 And there was no day like that before it or after it, that the Lord hearkened unto the voice of a man: for the Lord fought for Israel.*

Joshua spoke directly to the sun and the moon. He spoke to the sun and moon to stand still to have more time to fight and destroy their enemies. This story is amazing because it's one thing to speak to something on the earth and another thing to speak to the sun and the moon, and they obey you.

GOD REBUKES THE RED SEA

Psalm 106:9 (KJV)

9 He rebuked the Red sea also, and it was dried up: so he led them through the depths, as through the wilderness.

God spoke angrily with the Red Sea when the children of Israel were leaving Egypt. The Red Sea was in the way of the children of Israel and their deliverance from the Egyptians and Pharaoh. God also used the Red Sea to destroy the Egyptians when they followed the Israelites as they passed through the Red Sea. Anything that stands in the way of God's plan or purpose, God will rebuke for His children.

THE PROPHET SPEAKING TO THE ALTAR

1 Kings 13:1-6 (KJV)

*1 And, behold, there came a man of God out of Judah by the word of the Lord unto Bethel: and Jeroboam stood by the altar to burn incense. 2 **And he cried against the altar in the word of the Lord, and said, O altar, altar, thus saith the Lord;** Behold, a child shall be born unto the house of David, Josiah by name; and upon thee shall he offer the priests of the high places that burn incense upon thee, and men's bones shall be burnt upon thee. 3 And he gave a sign the same day, saying, This is the sign which the Lord hath spoken; **Behold, the altar shall be rent, and the ashes that are upon it shall be poured out.** 4 And it came to pass, when king Jeroboam heard the saying of the man of God, which had cried against the altar in Bethel, that he put forth his hand from the altar, saying, Lay hold on him. And his hand, which he put forth against him, dried up, so that he could not pull it in again to him. 5 **The altar also was rent, and the ashes poured out from the altar, according to the sign which the man of God had given by the word of the Lord.** 6 And the king answered and said unto the man of God, Intreat now the face of the Lord thy God, and pray for me, that my hand may be restored me again. And the man of God besought the Lord, and the king's hand was restored him again, and became as it was before.*

The prophet, in this story, spoke directly to the altar, and the altar did exactly what he said.

THE STONES WILL CRY OUT

Luke 19:37-40 (KJV)

*37 And when he was come nigh, even now at the descent of the mount of Olives, the whole multitude of the disciples began to rejoice and praise God with a loud voice for all the mighty works that they had seen; 38 Saying, Blessed be the King that cometh in the name of the Lord: peace in Heaven, and glory in the highest. 39 And some of the Pharisees from among the multitude said unto him, Master, rebuke thy disciples. 40 And he answered and said unto them, I tell you that, **if these should hold their peace, the stones would immediately cry out.***

When Jesus entered Jerusalem shortly before He was crucified, the whole multitude rejoiced and praised God with a loud voice for all of the mighty works they had seen. The Pharisees wanted Jesus to rebuke the multitude; however, Jesus said if they didn't cry out, the stones would immediately cry out. Once you understand that the creation of God can hear, understand, and speak, this verse makes sense. All of creation can and will declare the glory of God.

SPEAKING TO A SYCAMINE TREE

Luke 17:5-6 (KJV)

*5 And the apostles said unto the Lord, Increase our faith. 6 And the Lord said, If ye had faith as a grain of mustard seed, **ye might say unto this sycamine tree,** Be thou plucked up by the root, and be thou planted in the sea; **and it should obey you.***

Jesus told His disciples to speak directly to the sycamine tree, and it would obey them. To obey someone, it must hear and comprehend what it is told to do.

TESTIMONY

There was a faith healer, and one day after he was speaking, a woman came up to him and said, "I don't believe in what you are teaching." This faith healer had an experience with God where he went up to Heaven, and Jesus told him that if he would believe and not doubt, He would heal his daughter of all the growths that were on her. So, he came back from that Heavenly experience, started believing God, and speaking to his daughter's growths on her body. His daughter was completely healed in about 40 days of speaking to the growths. Those growths had been on his daughter for years. This faith healer taught people how to believe God and how to be healed from Matthew 21.

> ### Matthew 21:21-22 (KJV)
> *21 Jesus answered and said unto them, Verily I say unto you, If ye have faith, and doubt not, ye shall not only do this which is done to the fig tree, **but also if ye shall say unto this mountain, Be thou removed, and be thou cast into the sea; it shall be done.** 22 And all things, whatsoever ye shall ask in prayer, believing, ye shall receive.*

The woman who came up to this minister had a husband who died from cancer at an early age. The woman said her husband was a Christian, they prayed, and people from all over the world had prayed for him to be healed. When he died, they were all devastated. This woman was mad at this faith healer for teaching that people could get healed if they believed God because her husband had died when they tried to believe

God for healing. Remember that the Bible says that God's people perish for lack of knowledge.

> ### Hosea 4:6a (KJV)
> **6 My people are destroyed for lack of knowledge: because thou hast rejected knowledge,...**

At that moment, God revealed to the man of God that yes, they had prayed for him to be healed, but he and no one else ever spoke directly to the cancer. He could have been healed if he or someone of faith had spoken directly to the cancer. So many people die and go without for lack of understanding of using their faith to speak to things.

You must speak to things after you pray to God when you believe for a miracle. You have to speak to the mountain for it to move. The mountain will not move until you talk to it. God wants you to know that you have the authority to speak to mountains, and they will move if you believe they will move, using your faith-filled words.

I want to show you a very powerful story in the Bible that illustrates this truth where someone was raised from the dead. When Jesus came to the tomb of Lazarus, he had been dead four days, and his body had the smell of death on it. Jesus came up to the tomb and made a fascinating statement before He raised Lazarus from the dead that many people overlook.

> ### John 11:41-42 (KJV)
> *41 Then they took away the stone from the place where the dead was laid. And Jesus lifted up his eyes, and said, **Father, I thank thee that thou hast heard me. 42 And I knew that thou hearest me always:** but because of the people which stand by I said it, that they may believe that thou hast sent me.*

Jesus had already prayed to the Father about raising Lazarus from the dead and received an answer. However, Lazarus was still dead. How can Jesus have prayed, the Father heard Him, and Lazarus still is dead? The answer is simple. Jesus needed to come to the tomb and speak directly to Lazarus for him to be raised from the dead. Jesus had to speak to Lazarus and not just pray to the Father. The Father heard Jesus' prayer, but Jesus revealed the truth of having to speak to things for the answer from God to come to pass. If you just pray to God and never speak to your problem, your problem will stay dead.

John 11:43-44 (KJV)

43 And when he thus had spoken, he cried with a loud voice, Lazarus, come forth. 44 And he that was dead came forth, bound hand and foot with graveclothes: and his face was bound about with a napkin. Jesus saith unto them, Loose him, and let him go.

In conclusion, many people pray to God, and God answers them, but they fail to realize if they do not speak to their mountain after they get an answer from God, the mountain will never move. Mountains only move when they are spoken to. To win the war of words, you have to understand that someone has to speak directly to the mountain. When you put God's Word in your mouth and speak to the mountain, you will win the war of words every time.

CHAPTER 8

LAW #2
BELIEVE WHAT YOU SAY
WILL COME TO PASS

B elieving in what you say will come to pass and that you can have what you say is a very vital *Law of Faith*. This is one of the most important *Laws of Faith* because if you don't believe you can speak to something and it will obey you, you can't use your voice to command anything to come to pass. Jesus said you should not doubt in your heart if you want what you say to come to pass. He also said you have to believe what you say will come to pass for your faith to work.

Let's look at the verse in Mark Chapter 11 where Jesus spoke this truth to understand better what He was teaching.

> ### *Mark 11:23 (KJV)*
> *23 For verily I say unto you, That whosoever shall say unto this mountain, Be thou removed, and be thou cast into the sea; **and shall not doubt in his heart, but shall believe that those things which he saith shall come to pass;** he shall have whatsoever he saith.*

For your faith to work, you have to believe in your *Believer*. What I mean by this is the first place to apply your faith is in your own faith. You must have faith in your faith. You have to believe you can speak to things, and they will obey you for your faith to work. Everything in God's Kingdom works by faith, and therefore you have to have faith to make things work. Faith works by believing in your heart and speaking with your mouth what you believe. Doing this is how God and everyone created in His image makes things come to pass.

Most people, however, do not understand this truth and don't believe their words have any power. If you do not understand and operate in this truth, your unbelief could work against your faith. If your own faith says you don't have the power to speak to things, you won't have the power to speak to things. For your faith to work, you must believe in your heart it can work, and when you speak to a mountain, it will move. The more you believe this, the more it will work for you.

When someone doesn't believe their words have power, they don't realize their faith just worked. If you believe your words have no power, your words will have no power. But they actually had power in that your words will now have no power because that is what you believe and spoke. You can short circuit your faith by not believing that you can speak by faith and have your words come to pass. This is called doubt in the heart.

Whatever you believe will be true for you. Doubt is a form of belief in the wrong direction. We are creative beings, so if you do not believe in your ability to speak to things, you just shut down your ability to speak to things, but your words still came to pass. I know this sounds tricky, but you can come into genuine faith when you understand the truth about your ability to believe or not believe. You can start believing in your ability to believe because when you get right down to it, believing is a choice. Humankind was created with free will, and this free will includes believing in whatever you want to believe. All humankind was made to believe in something.

Now let's turn our attention back to Mark 11:23. In Mark 11:23, it doesn't say that you are to believe God can do it? Why is this? We already know God can do all things, but God wants you to come to the place where you believe in your God-given ability to speak by faith and cause things to come to pass. Doing this is extremely hard for some Christians to come to terms with. They want God to do everything for them. They have no problem believing Jesus can do miracles, but they shrink at the fact that God has called them to speak to mountains and make them move. Some Christians want God to speak to the mountain for them.

Jesus said that those who believe in Him would do greater works than Him.

> ### John 14:12-13 (KJV)
> *12 Verily, verily, I say unto you, He that believeth on me, the works that I do shall he do also; and greater works than these shall he do; because I go unto my Father. 13 And whatsoever ye shall ask in my name, that will I do,* that the Father may be glorified in the Son.

This truth that Jesus taught is astounding! Jesus was doing miracles regularly. When you understand you were created in God's image, you will start speaking to mountains and regularly see miracles in your life. For this to happen, the image of God has to be built on the inside of you. For your faith to work, you have to come to the revelation that you were created in God's image, and just like God spoke everything into existence, you can also speak to things, and they will obey your words.

If you want your words to have power, however, you have to be changed into the image of God's dear Son. You have to see yourself as someone who was created in God's image with the ability to have the power to speak to things. We come into God's image by looking at Jesus. Jesus is the *Author* and *Finisher* of our faith.

Hebrews 12:2 (KJV)

*2 **Looking unto Jesus the author and finisher of our faith**; who for the joy that was set before him endured the cross, despising the shame, and is set down at the right hand of the throne of God.*

Colossians 1:14-15 (KJV)

*14 In whom we have redemption through his blood, even the forgiveness of sins: 15 **Who is the image of the invisible God**, the firstborn of every creature:*

As we look at Jesus through prophetic insight in the Word of God, by the Holy Spirit, we are changed from glory to glory.

2 Corinthians 3:18 (KJV)

*18 **But we all, with open face beholding as in a glass the glory of the Lord, are changed into the same image from glory to glory, even as by the Spirit of the Lord.***

As we look at the glorious image of Jesus from the Word of God, we are to put on this new image and put off our old image. The new image is called the new man in the New Testament, and the old image is called the old man.

Colossians 3:8-14 (KJV)

*8 **But now ye also put off all these;** anger, wrath, malice, blasphemy, **filthy communication out of your mouth.** 9 Lie not* *one to another, **seeing that ye have put off the old man with his deeds; 10 And have put on the new man, which is renewed in knowledge after the image of him that created him:** 11 Where there is neither Greek nor Jew, circumcision nor uncircumcision, Barbarian, Scythian, bond nor free: but Christ is all, and in all. 12 **Put on therefore, as the elect of God,** holy and beloved, bowels of mercies, kindness, humbleness of mind, meekness, longsuffering; 13 Forbearing one another, and forgiving one another, if any man have a quarrel against any: even as Christ forgave you, so also do ye. 14 **And above all these things put on charity,** which is the bond of perfectness.*

Putting on the new man is something we must do. As you put on this new man, you will go from glory to glory and from faith to faith. God speaks His identity and image to people by His Word. As you draw closer to God, He will speak more of His image into you. Sometimes God will also find someone not looking for Him and speak His image into them. In the Old Testament, there is a man named Gideon who God came to and spoke into his image. Let's look at this fascinating story and see how God spoke into his image.

The Israelites had sinned against the Lord, and the Lord delivered them into the hand of the Midianites. As a result, the Midianites were keeping the children of Israel in poverty.

Judges 6:1-6 (KJV)

*1 **And the children of Israel did evil in the sight of the Lord: and the Lord delivered them into the hand of Midian seven years.** 2 And the hand of Midian prevailed against Israel: and because of the Midianites the children of Israel made them the dens which are in the mountains, and caves, and strong holds. 3 And so it was, when Israel had sown, that the Midianites came* *up, and the Amalekites, and the children of the east, even they came up against them; 4 **And they encamped against them, and destroyed the increase of the earth, till thou come unto Gaza, and left no sustenance for Israel, neither sheep, nor ox, nor ass.** 5 For they came up with their cattle and their tents, and they came as grasshoppers for multitude; for both they and their camels were without number: and they entered into the land to destroy it. 6 **And Israel was greatly impoverished because of the Midianites; and the children of Israel cried unto the Lord.***

God was allowing the children of Israel to be stolen from by their enemies because they sinned against Him. Their sins had caused the protection of God to be pulled back, and the Midianites came in and were stealing their food. The Midianite army was so big that the Israelites couldn't do anything about it. One thing worth noting about God is that if you cry to Him and repent of your sins, He will always come and deliver you. Let's now see how God chose to deliver the children of Israel through Gideon and how this applies to the image of God.

Gideon was in hiding from the Midianites when God first appeared to him.

Judges 6:11-13 (KJV)

*11 And there came an angel of the Lord, and sat under an oak which was in Ophrah, that pertained unto Joash the Abiezrite: **and his son Gideon threshed wheat by the winepress, to hide it from the Midianites.** 12 And the angel of the Lord appeared unto him, and said unto him, **The Lord is with thee, thou mighty man of valour.** 13 And Gideon said unto him, **Oh my Lord, if the Lord be with us, why then is all this befallen us? and where be all his miracles which our fathers told us of,** saying, Did not the Lord bring us up from Egypt? but now the Lord hath forsaken us, and delivered us into the hands of the Midianites.*

God's answer to their problem with the Midianites was to send an angel to Gideon. The angel told Gideon that the Lord was with him and that he was a mighty man of valor. God spoke into Gideon's image. Gideon was hiding from the Midianites as he threshed the wheat. Only God can come in and see something in someone and talk into their identity when no one else can. God was putting His faith into Gideon so Gideon could put his faith in God. Gideon, however, at first, challenged the angel about God being with them. He tried to blame God for their problems when it was their sin that caused evil to come upon the children of Israel.

This is an excellent story in revealing how God works. Everyone wants God to come in and do everything. God, however, always rose up a deliverer. He always uses people, but that person has to believe God is with them and that they are a mighty person of valor. So, when you become a Christian, you are enlisted into the army of God, and God wants you to believe that you too are a mighty person of valor.

2 Timothy 2:3-4 (KJV)
*3 Thou therefore endure hardness, **as a good soldier of Jesus Christ.** 4 No man that warreth entangleth himself with the affairs of this life; **that he may please him who hath chosen him to be a soldier.***

This is why we put on the armor of God and fight the good fight of faith. For the children of Israel to be delivered, Gideon had to believe he was a mighty man of valor. He could only come into this image by believing God was with him and that God was sending him.

Judges 6:14 (KJV)
*14 And the Lord looked upon him, and said, **Go in this thy might, and thou shalt save Israel from the hand of the Midianites: have not I sent thee?***

The rest of Chapter 6 is filled with Gideon not believing, and God had to convince Gideon that He was with him. It took some time and tests before Gideon came into the image of being that mighty man of valor that God said he was. God's Word always prevails and creates what He speaks. God created the image of a mighty man of valor in Gideon by speaking it into him.

In the following verse, we can see where Gideon's image was before God came to him. Gideon saw himself as the least in his father's house.

Judges 6:15 (KJV)

*15 And he said unto him, Oh my Lord, wherewith shall I save Israel? behold, my family is poor in Manasseh, **and I am the least in my father's house.***

After God revealed Himself to Gideon, he still asked God for a sign. God gives Gideon the sign so he will believe what He is saying to him is true.

Judges 6:17-21 (KJV)

*17 And he said unto him, If now I have found grace in thy sight, **then shew me a sign that thou talkest with me.** 18 Depart not hence, I pray thee, until I come unto thee, and bring forth my present, and set it before thee. And he said, I will tarry until thou come again. 19 And Gideon went in, and made ready a kid, and unleavened cakes of an ephah of flour: the flesh he put in a basket, and he put the broth in a pot, and brought it out unto him under the oak, and presented it. 20 And the angel of God said unto him, Take the flesh and the unleavened cakes, and lay them upon this rock, and pour out the broth. And he did so. 21 Then the angel of the Lord put forth the end of the staff that was in his hand, and touched the flesh and the unleavened cakes; **and there*** *rose up fire out of the rock, and consumed the flesh and the unleavened cakes. Then the angel of the Lord departed out of his sight.*

After this sign, Gideon goes on to ask God for more signs. Gideon asked God to put a sign on a fleece of wool. First, Gideon asked God to put dew on the fleece of wool only and not on anything else by morning. Then Gideon asks God to put the dew on everything else but the fleece of wool the next day. This is the story that many people use to ask God for a fleece or a sign when they are praying and want to know that God heard their prayer. The fleece is symbolic of a sign for them to believe that God heard them or what they are doing is in God's will.

Judges 6:36-40 (KJV)

*36 And Gideon said unto God, If thou wilt save Israel by mine hand, as thou hast said, 37 **Behold, I will put a fleece of wool in the floor; and if the dew be on the fleece only, and it be dry upon all the earth beside, then shall I know that thou wilt save Israel by mine hand, as thou hast said.** 38 And it was so: for he rose up early on the morrow, **and thrust the fleece together, and wringed the dew out of the fleece, a bowl full of water.** 39 And Gideon said unto God, Let not thine anger be hot against me, and I will speak but this once: **let me prove, I pray thee, but this once with the fleece;** let it now be dry only upon the fleece, and upon all the ground let there be dew. 40 **And God did so that night:** for it was dry upon the fleece only, and there was dew on all the ground.*

After this, God gives Gideon one more sign by going near the enemy's camp to hear what they have to say. While Gideon is near the enemy's camp, he overhears two men telling about a dream where God delivers the Midianites into his hand. This is the final sign that tips Gideon to fully believe that God was with him and that he had the victory.

> *Judges 7:15 (KJV)*
> *15 And it was so, when Gideon heard the telling of the dream, and the interpretation thereof, that he worshipped, and returned into the host of Israel, and said, Arise; for the Lord hath delivered into your hand the host of Midian.*

God had also reduced Gideon's army to only 300 men, and these 300 men went on to defeat the whole army of the Midianites. This story is so powerful because it reveals how God works. First, God had to get Gideon to believe He was with him. Second, God spoke to the image of Gideon when He told him he was a mighty man of valor. Third, God called those things that be not as though they were in Gideon's identity. Once Gideon believed in who God said he was, he became that mighty man of valor and went on to defeat the Midianites.

Now, getting back to how this story applies to you and believing that what you say will come to pass. First, you have to believe God is with you and that you are a mighty person of valor. The inner image of God has to be built on the inside of you before you can speak to things and they obey you. You have to see yourself as a son or daughter of God who has power with their words. You have to believe in what God has done on the inside of you.

Once the inner image of Christ is built on the inside of you, you will do the works that Jesus did.

> *John 14:12 (KJV)*
> *12 Verily, verily, I say unto you, He that believeth on me, the works that I do shall he do also; and greater works than these shall he do; because I go unto my Father.*

Jesus taught His disciples that they could do greater works than He did. Jesus left Heaven and was born of a woman and did what He did as a man to be an example to us. The Book of Philippians tells us what mindset we should have because of this.

> **Philippians 2:5-8 (KJV)**
> **5 Let this mind be in you, which was also in Christ Jesus: 6 Who, being in the form of God, thought it not robbery to be equal with God: 7 But made himself of no reputation, and took** upon him the form of a servant, **and was made in the likeness of men:** 8 And being found in fashion as a man, he humbled himself, and became obedient unto death, even the death of the cross.

God is calling His people to come into their destined image. Anyone who tells you otherwise is a thief and a liar. It is time for you to come into the image of who you were created to be. It is important to note that Jesus was not the only person who did miracles in the Bible. The Old and New Testament is filled with stories of God's people doing extraordinary miracles. The same God that used people to do miracles in the Bible is the same God using people of faith to do miracles in our time. And it is the same God that will use you to speak to mountains and make them move by your faith.

One thing I do to help build the inner image of God in me is speak confessions about who God says I am. I confess that I can do all things through Christ who strengthens me. I am the righteousness of God in Christ Jesus, and I am strong in the Lord and the power of His might. We have to say to ourselves what God's Word says we are. *I am* statements are one of the most powerful ways to do this. Jesus made many *I Am* confessions about who He was. Let's look at some of the *I Am* statements Jesus made about Himself.

John 6:35 (KJV)
*35 And Jesus said unto them, **I am the bread of life:** he that cometh to me shall never hunger; and he that believeth on me shall never thirst.*

John 8:12 (KJV)
*12 Then spake Jesus again unto them, saying, **I am the light of the world:** he that followeth me shall not walk in darkness, but shall have the light of life.*

John 10:9 (KJV)
*9 **I am the door:** by me if any man enter in, he shall be saved, and shall go in and out, and find pasture.*

John 10:11 (KJV)
*11 **I am the good shepherd:** the good shepherd giveth his life for the sheep.*

John 10:36 (KJV)
*36 Say ye of him, whom the Father hath sanctified, and sent into the world, Thou blasphemest; because I said, **I am the Son of God?***

John 11:25 (KJV)
*25 Jesus said unto her, **I am the resurrection, and the life:** he that believeth in me, though he were dead, yet shall he live:*

Jesus knew who He was, and He wants us to know who we are. We declare who we are by *I am* statements. When you say *I am* statements, you declare who God says you are out of your mouth. Now, to tie this all together, let's go back to you believing what you say will come to pass and not doubt in your heart. For you to do this, you have to be a believer. All Christians are called to be believers. The word *believer* has been watered down or thrown out there as one who believes in Jesus as the Christ.

Yes, a *believer* is a Christian in the fundamental understanding. However, being a *believer* has a much deeper meaning. Being a *true believer* in Christ means you believe many things. First, you believe Jesus is the Christ. You also believe that God raised Jesus from the dead. You believe you are a son or daughter of God. You believe the Bible is God's Word. You believe God exists. You believe in Heaven and hell. You believe you are going to Heaven. You believe in Judgment Day. As a believer, you believe many things.

A *believer* also believes their words come to pass. A *believer* believes they can speak to a mountain and make it move with faith-filled words coming out of their mouth. A *believer* has the spirit of faith and speaks what they believe and what they believe and speak comes to pass.

> *2 Corinthians 4:13 (KJV)*
> *13 We having the same spirit of faith, according as it is written, I believed, and therefore have I spoken; we also believe, and therefore speak;*

The point to all of this is true. *Believers* believe in many things about God and themselves. Now I want to turn your attention to an amusing Scripture about believers not believing, and being reprimanded by the Lord. The story is found in Mark 16 after Jesus died and rose again. Jesus was always working on His believers believing.

> *Mark 16:9-11 (KJV)*
> *9 Now when Jesus was risen early the first day of the week, he appeared first to Mary Magdalene, out of whom he had cast seven devils. 10 And she went and told them that had been with*

*him, as they mourned and wept. 11 **And they, when they had
heard that he was alive, and had been seen of her, believed not.***

When Jesus appeared to Mary Magdalene after His resurrection, she
went and told the other believers that Jesus rose from the dead, but they
didn't believe her. So now, let's see what happens next.

Mark 16:12-13 (KJV)

*12 After that he appeared in another form unto two of them, as
they walked, and went into the country. 13 And they went and told
it unto the residue: **neither believed they them.***

Next, Jesus appeared to two people while they were walking, and when
they went and told the believers, they didn't believe them. In the next
verse, Jesus appears to them. Let's see what He says to them.

Mark 16:14 (KJV)

*14 Afterward he appeared unto the eleven as they sat at meat,
**and upbraided them with their unbelief and hardness of heart,
because they believed not them which had seen him after he was
risen.***

When Jesus appeared to His believing apostles, He upbraided them for
their unbelief. I am pointing out this story of them not believing because
I am revealing that you could be an unbelieving believer. Faith is
something that must be built inside of us, and God requires us to believe
Him if we say we are a believer. We cannot please God without faith.

Hebrews 11:6 (KJV)

*6 **But without faith it is impossible to please him:** for he that
cometh to God must believe that he is, and that he is a rewarder
of them that diligently seek him.*

Our faith in God is vital to God, and it is one of the highest ways we can please God. God desires His children to come into the image of a complete believing *believer*. After Jesus reprimanded His followers for not believing, He told them to go and preach the Gospel, and whoever believed would be saved. These unbelieving believers needed to be converted to believe God in all things to preach to others to believe. Jesus also said that whoever didn't believe would be damned.

> ### Mark 16:15-18 (KJV)
> *15 And he said unto them, Go ye into all the world, and preach the Gospel to every creature. 16 **He that believeth and is baptized shall be saved; but he that believeth not shall be damned.** 17 **And these signs shall follow them that believe;** In my name shall they cast out devils; they shall speak with new tongues; 18 They shall take up serpents; and if they drink any deadly thing, it shall not hurt them; they shall lay hands on the sick, and they shall recover.*

I know this story is humorous in these believers not believing, but our faith in God is serious. God requires us to believe if we are true believers. Therefore, as a Christian, it is crucial to come into the image of being a true *believer*. True believers will speak to mountains and not doubt in their hearts. A true believer is someone who has come into the image of God and is strong in faith.

As true believers, we can never let words of doubt or unbelief come out of our mouths. We also cannot self-defecate on ourselves by speaking of any negative image about ourselves that does not align with who God says we are. We also have to watch what others say about ourselves. Never let anyone speak into your image or identity if they are not speaking God's Word and image into you. The devil loves to use other people to speak into our identities. Sometimes kids can be the worst violators of speaking negative image words to other kids. I am sure most people reading this book had this happen to them by someone in their life.

In conclusion, for you to believe that what you say will come to pass, you have to believe in the image of God on the inside of you. You have to believe you are a person made in God's image who has what they say, and your words come to pass. You have to be a *believing* believer.

If you are going to win the war of words, you have to believe you are a mighty warrior with God's Word in your mouth. You are not a weak Christian; you are strong in the Lord and the power of His might. The stronger you come into the image of God and confess what God says over your life, the more outstanding victory you will have over the enemy.

You are a child of the Most High God, and you have power with your words to bring things to pass. Today is the day for you to come into the full image of God as a *believer*.

CHAPTER 9

LAW #3

BELIEVE YOU HAVE RECEIVED

B elieve you have received is one of the most powerful *Laws of Faith*. To understand this law, you must understand time. This chapter will teach you what time is and how this applies to the *Law of Faith*. I will also reveal how everything was already done before you were born according to the Word of God.

To start with, let's talk about time. What is time? We measure time by the moon going around the earth, which makes up 31 days or a month. Then it is measured by the world rotating around the sun in a 12-month circuit. This 12-month circuit around the sun makes up a year for those living on the earth. Time is also measured by how long it takes to get from one place to another. Time has a beginning and ending based upon where you start and finish. Time is also measured in terms of events that succeed from the past, through the present to the future.

Now that I have defined time, the question that has to be asked is, "How is God measured by time?" The answer is, "God is not measured by time as we know it," because God is not just on the earth but is everywhere at the same time. God created time and is eternal, so how could you measure time with an infinite God that is everywhere? God is everywhere at the same time. God is not bound by time or space. God is not bound to the earth and our time because God is not just on the earth.

So, let's take this train of thought about time with God and dig deep into believing you have received. Take someone who has a sickness and goes to God in prayer for healing. The Bible says in 1 Peter, *By whose stripes, ye were healed.* According to this verse, healing took place long ago when Jesus took stripes on His back before He went to the cross. According to God's Word, healing already happened before you were born. Your healing is not *going to happen* because, according to God's Word, you were *already* healed.

1 Peter 2:24 (KJV)
24 Who his own self bare our sins in his own body on the tree that we, being dead to sins, should live unto righteousness: **by whose stripes ye were healed.**

Did you notice how this is a past tense statement? This is past tense because when Jesus took those stripes on His back, healing was being paid for everyone. So, if you need healing and you ask *to be healed*, you do not believe that Jesus already paid the price for your healing. You should rather say, "Thank you, God, that I am healed." Then speak to the sickness, rebuke it, and call forth your healing now. If you come to God and ask to be healed, then you are proclaiming that Jesus did not pay the price for your healing in the past when He went to the cross.

From God's perspective, everything is happening now because He is not only on the earth or bound by time. So, He sees you healed now and not in the future. You don't even have to ask God to be healed because to Him, you are already healed. All you have to do is believe this Gospel truth and apply your healing by speaking to the mountain and commanding your illness to leave you. Speak to the mountain of pain, sickness, and disease and tell it to leave you, and by faith, it will leave you. You are not going to be healed because it is already done. Healing is not something in your future; it is something in your past that can be applied in your now.

If you speak or think about timing on the earth, most people think the answer to their prayer is in the future. Therefore, if your belief is in the future, the answer to your prayer will remain in the future and not in the now. Because your faith is in the future, you will never receive what was already freely given. You have to believe it is already done, and you already have it. You have to appropriate the answer from God with your mouth. You do this by decreeing and declaring you are healed.

With this understanding, you can see why Jesus said when you pray, you have to believe you received it.

Mark 11:24 (KJV)
*24 Therefore I say unto you, What things soever ye desire, when ye pray, **believe that ye receive them**, and ye shall have them.*

Believe that you received is a past tense statement. Jesus taught that when you pray, believe you already have it because it is already done as far as God is concerned. God does not live in just the past, present, or future. God is eternal and simultaneously lives in the past, present, and future. We as humans can only live in the present. We can't go into the past, and we can't go into the future as mere humans. We live in the now. God, however, is everywhere at the same time, and everything is happening *Now* for Him.

With this understanding, you can better understand Hebrews 11 v. 1.

Hebrews 11:1 (KJV)
1 Now faith is the substance of things hoped for, the evidence of things not seen.

Faith is now. God speaks in the now because God does not live in our timeframe. According to God, you either have it or don't have it when it comes to God and His timing based upon your faith. You say you have it now and agree with God by faith. When you start to think, believe, and speak this way, your manifestation of what you believe God for will appear faster.

So, when you come to God, you have to speak His language and in His timing. Don't ask to be healed; believe that the Eternal God already knows what you need and made provision for your prayer before you even ask. Your prayer should be more about thanking Him for what He has done and believing you have received. This may be a new train of thought for some, but God wants you to understand this truth, so your prayers will be answered.

If you constantly talk as things are in the future, they will remain in the future. They will stay in your future because that is where your faith is. Everything works for you according to your faith and what you believe. Believe you have received it now, and it will appear now. All things work according to the *Law of Faith*. What do you believe? Jesus said continually to people, ***"According to your faith be it unto you."***

Matthew 9:29 (KJV)
*29 Then touched he their eyes, saying, **According to your faith be it unto you**.*

Jesus said when you ask God for something in prayer; you are to believe you received it. This is a past tense prayer. You don't go to God and ask

Him for something He has already done or given. Instead, you thank Him for what was freely given, and you speak to your mountain and make it move.

Mark 11:22-24 (KJV)

*22 And Jesus answering saith unto them, **Have faith in God.** 23 For verily I say unto you, That whosoever shall say unto this mountain, Be thou removed, and be thou cast into the sea; and shall not doubt in his heart, but shall believe that those things which he saith shall come to pass; he shall have whatsoever he saith. 24 Therefore I say unto you, What things soever ye desire, when ye pray, **believe that ye receive them, and ye shall have them.***

This is a good place for us to talk about the ***Blessing of Abraham*** and how it applies to you receiving from God. Many Christians do not understand that everything works off the covenant God made with Abraham over 4,000 years ago. Before you were born, God made a covenant with Abraham that has every provision you will ever need in your lifetime. Your healing, wealth, peace, blessing, prosperity, and every answer to your prayers are all found in the covenant God made with Abraham.

When you don't understand God's covenant with Abraham, you could go without when you don't need to go without. Let's look at the Scriptures to better understand God's covenant with Abraham and how this covenant applies to you. One of the best places to understand the covenant and blessing of Abraham is in Galatians 3. I will walk you through this whole chapter to help you better understand the *Blessing and Covenant of Abraham*.

Galatians 3:1-5 (KJV)

*1 O foolish Galatians, who hath bewitched you, that ye should not obey the truth, before whose eyes Jesus Christ hath been evidently set forth, crucified among you? 2 This only would I learn of you, **Received ye the Spirit by the works of the law, or by the hearing of faith?** 3 Are ye so foolish? having begun in the Spirit, are ye now made perfect by the flesh? 4 Have ye suffered so many things in vain? if it be yet in vain. 5 **He therefore that ministereth to you the Spirit, and worketh miracles among you, doeth he it by the works of the law, or by the hearing of faith?***

This portion of the chapter talks about Jesus Christ being crucified, and because of His crucifixion, you can receive the Holy Spirit and miracles by faith. You can receive the Spirit and miracles by faith because He was crucified in your place. You do not get healed or receive miracles by the works of the law. This means you cannot work to be healed or get an answer to your prayers by keeping the Law of Moses. You can do nothing as far as works of the flesh are concerned to receive anything from God; you have to receive all of God's blessings by faith.

Galatians 3:6-9 (KJV)

*6 Even as Abraham believed God, and it was accounted to him for righteousness. 7 **Know ye therefore that they which are of faith, the same are the children of Abraham.** 8 And the Scripture, foreseeing that God would justify the heathen through faith, **preached before the Gospel unto Abraham, saying, In thee shall all nations be blessed. 9 So then they which be of faith are blessed with faithful Abraham.***

He is now using Abraham, believing God to receive righteousness, as an example. He says that if you have faith, you can be blessed like faithful Abraham. Then Paul, the writer of Galatians, says when God said to Abraham, *In thee shall all nations be blessed*, this is the preaching of the Gospel. We know the Gospel was the Good News Jesus preached and healed people by.

Matthew 4:23 (KJV)

*23 And Jesus went about all Galilee, teaching in their synagogues, **and preaching the Gospel of the kingdom**, and healing all manner of sickness and all manner of disease among the people.*

Matthew 9:35 (KJV)

*35 And Jesus went about all the cities and villages, teaching in their synagogues, **and preaching the Gospel of the kingdom, and healing every sickness and every disease among the people.***

Jesus was healing the Jewish people and showing them it was their right to be healed if they believed because they were children of Abraham. The Jewish people were entering into the blessing of Abraham through the preaching of the Gospel through Christ. The blessing of Abraham or the Good News of the Gospel entitled them to be healed, prosper, and be blessed in every area of their life. God made provisions for the Jewish people before they were born through the covenant He made with Abraham. Abraham was the father of faith, and through his example, we know how to have faith in God. Abraham revealed his faith in God when he believed God saying he could have a child in his old age with Sarah, his wife. Sarah's womb at that time had stopped working because of her age, and it would have to be a miracle for her to have a child.

Romans 4:17-20 (KJV)

*17 (As it is written, I have made thee a father of many nations,) **before him whom he believed, even God**, who quickeneth the*

dead, and calleth those things which be not as though they were.
*18 **Who against hope believed in hope, that he might become***
***the father of many nations,** according to that which was spoken,*
*So shall thy seed be. 19 **And being not weak in faith, he***
considered not his own body now dead, when he was about an
hundred years old, neither yet the deadness of Sarah's womb:
20 He staggered not at the promise of God through unbelief; but
was strong in faith, giving glory to God;

If you are going to receive any miracle from God, you have to believe as Abraham believed. When Abraham believed God, he entered into a covenant with God, and anyone who was of his lineage could enter into this covenant. The Old Testament is story after story of God's blessing and answering the Jewish people's prayers. The Jewish people were the offspring of Abraham. God did all those miracles in the Old Testament that we read about based upon the promise He made with Abraham and not by the works of the law.

Galatians 3:10-14 (KJV)

10 For as many as are of the works of the law are under the curse:
for it is written, Cursed is every one that continueth not in all
things which are written in the Book of the law to do them. 11 But
that no man is justified by the law in the sight of God, it is evident:
*for, The just shall live by faith. 12 **And the law is not of faith:***
*but, The man that doeth them shall live in them. 13 **Christ hath***
redeemed us from the curse of the law, being made a curse for
us: for it is written, Cursed is every one that hangeth on a tree:
*14 **That the blessing of Abraham might come on the Gentiles***
through Jesus Christ; that we might receive the promise of the
Spirit through faith.

Because of the death of Christ on the cross, you have been redeemed from the curse of the law. The curse of the law can be found in Deuteronomy 28:15-68 and Leviticus 26:14-39. Everything you read in both of those passages of Scriptures; you have been redeemed from. The word *Redeemed* means that someone paid the price so you could be released as an enslaved person and be restored. This redemption happened before you were born. As a Christian, you are first entering into the covenant that God made with Abraham to bless the whole world, and second, you are entering into the covenant of God in the death, burial, and resurrection of Jesus the Christ. This is why we call it the New Covenant. Jesus was the official *Seed* of Abraham and died in your place, so you not only can go to Heaven but be redeemed from every curse found in the law. Jesus paid the price for your redemption on the cross.

Galatians 3:15-18 (KJV)

15 Brethren, I speak after the manner of men; Though it be but a man's covenant, yet if it be confirmed, no man disannulleth, or addeth thereto. 16 Now to Abraham and his seed were the promises made. **He saith not, And to seeds, as of many; but as of one, And to thy seed, which is Christ.** *17 And this I say, that the covenant, that was confirmed before of God in Christ,* **the law, which was four hundred and thirty years after, cannot disannul, that it should make the promise of none effect.** *18 For if the inheritance be of the law, it is no more of promise:* **but God gave it to Abraham by promise.**

God's actual covenant was with Abraham and his *Seed*. The *Seed* represents Christ. Christ was the *Seed* of Abraham. God's covenant to bless the whole world through faith was made with Jesus Christ through Abraham. All of this happened many years ago before you were born.

The promise was made to Abraham after the flood of Noah. Jesus came to fulfill this promise. The law was in place until this revelation of faith would come. Jesus revealed to people how to receive the blessing of Abraham by faith. This is why faith was so important to Jesus. Jesus taught faith and always pointed to people's faith when they were healed.

> **Galatians 3:19-23 (KJV)**
> *19 **Wherefore then serveth the law? It was added because of transgressions, till the seed should come to whom the promise was made;** and it was ordained by angels in the hand of a mediator. 20 Now a mediator is not a mediator of one, but God is one. 21 **Is the law then against the promises of God? God forbid:** for if there had been a law given which could have given life, verily righteousness should have been by the law. 22 **But the Scripture hath concluded all under sin, that the promise by Faith of Jesus Christ might be given to them that believe. 23 But before faith came, we were kept under the law, shut up unto the faith which should afterwards be revealed.***

Jesus brought the understanding of faith. Jesus is the *Author* and *Finisher* of our Faith. This is why I am teaching the *Law of Faith*. Only through faith can you be healed, saved, and delivered. Jesus died so that you can be blessed *Now* through the covenant He made with Abraham. Yes, Jesus died so you can go to Heaven, but He also died to redeem you from the curse of the law. Speaking to mountains is how you enforce this blessing of Abraham upon your life and the life of others. The Law of Moses was only a schoolmaster to bring us to Christ. The law came in later only to confirm the promise made to Abraham. Once Christ came, we were called to live by faith. When you get baptized in water, you put on Christ by faith. You are found in Christ by faith when you become a Christian.

Galatians 3:24-27 (KJV)
*24 Wherefore the law was our schoolmaster to bring us unto Christ, **that we might be justified by faith. 25 But after that faith is come, we are no longer under a schoolmaster. 26 For ye are all the children of God by faith in Christ Jesus. 27 For as many of you as have been baptized into Christ have put on Christ.***

You must be found in Christ to inherit the blessing of Abraham. Believing in your heart that God raised Jesus from the dead, confessing with your mouth, and being baptized in water is what places you in Christ. This is how you put on Christ. You also must put off the old man and put on the new man. Then, you are entitled to inherit all the promises of Abraham and are redeemed from the curse of the law.

Colossians 3:8-14 (KJV)
*8 **But now ye also put off all these;** anger, wrath, malice, blasphemy, filthy communication out of your mouth. 9 Lie not one to another, **seeing that ye have put off the old man with his deeds; 10 And have put on the new man, which is renewed in knowledge after the image of him that created him:** 11 Where there is neither Greek nor Jew, circumcision nor uncircumcision, Barbarian, Scythian, bond nor free: but Christ is all, and in all. 12 **Put on therefore,** as the elect of God, holy and beloved, bowels of mercies, kindness, humbleness of mind, meekness, longsuffering; 13 Forbearing one another, and forgiving one another, if any man have a quarrel against any: even as Christ forgave you, so also do ye. 14 And above all these things **put on charity,** which is the bond of perfectness.*

Jesus was healing the Jewish people through the Abrahamic Covenant before He died. When Christ took those stripes on His back, died on the cross, and rose again from the dead, He opened up salvation to the whole world. You may not be a Jew by birth, but you can access the Abrahamic Covenant made with Christ the *Seed* if you accept Jesus Christ as your Lord and Savior and put on the new man. The covenant was made with Christ, so once we are in Christ, put off the old man, and put on the new man, we can access all the blessings found in the covenant that God made with Abraham and Christ his *Seed*.

Galatians 3:28-29 (KJV)

*28 There is neither Jew nor Greek, there is neither bond nor free, there is neither male nor female: for ye are all one in Christ Jesus. 29 **And if ye be Christ's, then are ye Abraham's seed, and heirs according to the promise.***

If you are *In Christ*, you are Abraham's seed and an heir to the promises of God. When Jesus was on the earth, He was healing people based upon the covenant God made with Abraham to bless the whole world. All they had to do was believe what He was saying about the Gospel, and they could receive their healing. They had to believe they received. What did they believe they received? They believed they received all God promised to Abraham and that He would bless them. The word blessing means healing, saving, delivering, and empowering them to prosper.

During the time of Jesus, most people did not know that He was the Son of God. This truth that He was the Son of God wasn't revealed to the masses until later after His death, burial, and resurrection. People did not believe they were being healed during the ministry of Jesus while He was on the earth because they thought He was the Son of God. Most people thought Jesus was just a prophet while He was on the earth. Jesus even asked His disciples, *"Who do men say that I am?"* Most of the answers were not that He was the Christ. Let's read how His disciples answered this question.

Matthew 16:13-14 (KJV)

*13 When Jesus came into the coasts of Caesarea Philippi, he asked his disciples, saying, **Whom do men say that I the Son of man am?** 14 And they said, **Some say that thou art John the Baptist: some, Elias; and others, Jeremias, or one of the prophets.***

The Jewish people of Jesus' day thought He was a prophet and were getting healed because He was anointed and brought the blessing of Abraham to them. Now, after all of these years, we know that Jesus is the Christ and died for our redemption. Jesus was revealing people could get healed based upon the promise God made to Abraham. This was the good news of the Gospel. They were promised healing many years before they were born through the covenant of Abraham.

Everything you pray about has already been promised as an answer from God before you were born. This is why you have to believe you received it and then act on your faith. You act on your faith by speaking to the mountain. You are not trying to get God to do anything. God has already done everything He is going to do. He is waiting for you to wake up to the revelation that it is already done.

You have to enforce the blessing of Abraham upon your situation by speaking to it by faith. This is why Jesus said you have to believe you received it. This is a past tense statement because God already answered your prayer a long time ago during the time of Abraham. Believing you received is an essential *Law of Faith*. When you understand this aspect of the law, you are better equipped to face your problems. It is easier to believe something will come to pass if it was already promised and paid for. What you are believing God for has already been purchased. Believe and receive it!

This concept is complex for some people to grasp, but it is easy to receive answers from God once you learn this truth. When you know it is already done, it is easy to believe God for the manifestation. You have the title deed to what you are praying for. All you have to do is believe you receive, and you shall have what you are praying for. You are no longer praying and asking God if it is His will, you know it is His will, and all you have to do is speak His will out by faith.

This chapter has been fun to write because I know how this truth has changed my life. It is easy to believe God when you come into a complete revelation that everything is already done. God worked six days and then rested on the seventh day. As Christians, we are to believe to enter into this rest. The rest of God has to do with everything being completed. God has already done everything He set out to do. You just have to enter into His rest and receive what He has freely done for us all.

> *Hebrews 4:1-5 (KJV)*
> *1 Let us therefore fear, lest, a promise being left us of entering into his rest, any of you should seem to come short of it. 2 For unto us was the Gospel preached, as well as unto them: but the word preached did not profit them, not being mixed with faith in them that heard it. 3 For we which have believed do enter into rest, as he said, As I have sworn in my wrath, if they shall enter into my rest: although the works were finished from the foundation of the world. 4 For he spake in a certain place of the seventh day on this wise, And God did rest the seventh day from*

*all his works. 5 And in this place again, **If they shall enter into my rest.***

The Gospel rest He is talking about is God finishing all His works in the first six days of creation. God is not working anymore. All His work has been done. It is now up to humankind to believe and receive all He has done for us in creation, the covenant of Abraham, and the work of Jesus on the cross. This revelation, when fully understood, will change how you think, act, pray and believe. It will help you receive answers to your prayers and overcome the devil.

To win the war of words, you have to know that the war is already won. We are speaking from a place of victory. We are not trying to win the war; we are only applying the victory already won for us. Jesus won the victory when He said it was finished on the cross. Jesus defeated the devil, death, hell, and the grave when He died and rose again. You already won the war of words if you believe what God has already done. You are victorious because God is victorious. All you have to do is believe in your heart and speak what you believe out of your mouth to receive miracles from God. It really is that simple. When you tie all the *Laws of Faith* together, you will walk in the victory that God has already paid for you and you will win the war of words.

CHAPTER 10

LAW #4
No Doubt in Your Heart

The opposite of believing is doubting. Doubt is what kept the children of Israel out of the *Promised Land*. If you don't overcome doubts in your heart, you will not move mountains by faith or be able to believe God for any miracle. Doubting will also prevent you from winning the war of words. In this chapter, I will help you see where doubt comes from and how to overcome it.

To start, let's look at what doubt is. Doubt is not believing in what God says in His Word to be true. Doubt is to be uncertain and unsure about the truth of what God says. A person in doubt is wavering, has questions, reservations and is uncertain when it comes to all the wonderful miraculous promises of God. A person who doubts may want to believe God, but their heart has too much uncertainty. Doubts cause a person to waver in what they believe to be true, resulting in a lack of conviction about what God says.

Some people doubt because God is challenging everything they have ever known about this natural world to be true. Most people born into this world only see how the natural world operates. As they grow up and live in this world, they see people go through life with no supernatural miracles. They see people live, get sick, face problems, die, and the cycle of natural life continues from generation to generation.

Natural life has been going on for thousands of years. Then one day, a man named Jesus Christ of Nazareth shows up and starts doing miracles. What is a miracle? A miracle is when God disrupts the natural order of life and does something that is not normal. For instance, when someone dies, we all know they stay dead, and we bury them. When Jesus started raising people from the dead, He disrupted the regular order of life and death.

Another example is when someone would get sick, they would either die of the sickness or, in time, the person would get better. Jesus came along and started healing people of sicknesses. He disrupted the ordinary course of sickness and miraculously healed people. When Jesus healed them, they didn't die or wait for the natural healing process to take place. Miracles from God bypass natural laws and create outcomes that humankind cannot produce by themselves.

Without God, humankind is limited to the natural laws of life and death. God works in the realm of miracles and the supernatural. Humanity has limitations, but God is limitless. God has no limits because He is God and is not like a natural man. God is a Spirit, and He is so much more powerful than we could ever imagine.

We understand from the Bible that God is a *Being* of far greater intelligence and power than our natural minds can comprehend. He is from everlasting to everlasting and created all things. We know God made everything with His Words. His Words have the power to create planets and entire universes. When God speaks, things come into being. God's power, however, is not fully known or understood by humankind.

Humankind only knows how to work with their hands. Until Jesus came along, few people understood the power of speech. A few men throughout history tapped into the miraculous power of God. These men were people like Moses, Samuel, Elijah, Elisha, and other men of God. But, they were very far and few in between.

When Jesus came on the scene, He started opening people up to far greater possibilities in God than they had ever known. Yet, some still doubted because Jesus was teaching a whole new way of living by the *Law of Faith*. Jesus taught people that they could believe God for miracles. The teachings of Jesus are a game-changer for the natural man. However, when the truth of the Gospel is preached, you choose to either believe or disbelieve. As far as God sees it, all things are possible if you believe. It is only when a man decides to stay connected to the old natural way of doing things that he misses out on the miraculous promises of God. It is their loss if they don't believe God's amazingly Good News of the Gospel that all can be saved, healed, and delivered of whatever is troubling them.

Let's look at some of the stories of Jesus and how people responded. We will start with Jesus walking on water and showing Peter that he also could walk on water.

Matthew 14:22-31 (KJV)
22 And straightway Jesus constrained his disciples to get into a ship, and to go before him unto the other side, while he sent the multitudes away. 23 And when he had sent the multitudes away, he went up into a mountain apart to pray: and when the evening

was come, he was there alone. 24 But the ship was now in the midst of the sea, tossed with waves: for the wind was contrary. 25 And in the fourth watch of the night Jesus went unto them, walking on the sea. 26 And when the disciples saw him walking on the sea, they were troubled, saying, It is a spirit; and they cried out for fear. 27 But straightway Jesus spake unto them, saying, **Be of good cheer; it is I; be not afraid. 28 And Peter answered him and said, Lord, if it be thou, bid me come unto thee on the water.** *29 And he said, Come. And when Peter was come down out of the ship, he walked on the water, to go to Jesus. 30 But when he saw the wind boisterous, he was afraid; and beginning to sink, he cried, saying, Lord, save me. 31 And immediately Jesus stretched forth his hand, and caught him, and said unto him,* **O thou of little faith, wherefore didst thou doubt?**

Up to this point in history, no one had ever walked on water that we know of. Jesus is now walking on water and showing Peter that he could also walk on water. The great thing about this story is Peter walked on water for a while. He could have continued to walk on water with Jesus if he would not have doubted. Jesus expanded a new possibility to Peter and all of humanity. Walking on water is now a possibility if you believe.

Let's look at another story where someone was healed and received a miracle that had never been done before in the history of the world.

John 9:1-7 (KJV)
1 And as Jesus passed by, he saw a man which was blind from his birth. 2 And his disciples asked him, saying, Master, who did sin, this man, or his parents, that he was born blind? 3 Jesus answered, Neither hath this man sinned, nor his parents: but that the works of God should be made manifest in him. 4 I must work

the works of him that sent me, while it is day: the night cometh, when no man can work. 5 As long as I am in the world, I am the light of the world. 6 When he had thus spoken, he spat on the ground, and made clay of the spittle, and he anointed the eyes of the blind man with the clay, 7 And said unto him, Go, wash in the pool of Siloam, (which is by interpretation, Sent.) **He went his way therefore, and washed, and came seeing.**

No one had ever been born blind and made to see until Jesus came and performed this miracle. Jesus was showing how God can do anything. Nothing is impossible with God. But unfortunately, the Jews and religious leaders did not believe this miracle was real.

John 9:18-21 (KJV)

*18 **But the Jews did not believe concerning him, that he had been blind, and received his sight, until they called the parents of him that had received his sight.** 19 And they asked them, saying, Is this your son, who ye say was born blind? how then doth he now see? 20 His parents answered them and said, We know that this is our son, and that he was born blind: 21 But by what means he now seeth, we know not; or who hath opened his eyes, we know not: he is of age; ask him: he shall speak for himself.*

Jesus was shocking the world with miracles that had never been done before. The power of the Gospel was causing people to either believe or not believe. In many cases, it seemed just too good to be true. Jesus was disrupting the natural order of known life and bringing new possibilities to those who would believe. Up to this point in the history of the world, no one had ever received sight after being born blind. Only God can do these types of miracles. Let's see what the blind man had to say.

John 9:30-33 (KJV)

*30 The man answered and said unto them, Why herein is a marvellous thing, that ye know not from whence he is, and yet he hath opened mine eyes. 31 Now we know that God heareth not sinners: but if any man be a worshipper of God, and doeth his will, him he heareth. 32 **Since the world began was it not heard that any man opened the eyes of one that was born blind.** 33 If this man were not of God, he could do nothing.*

Jesus changed the world with miracles from God. Jesus expanded what people believed was possible. He was teaching people to believe God for the miraculous, and God was performing miracles. Once someone witnesses a miracle from God, they are never the same. Miracles open us up to all of the possibilities of God.

God wants to free your mind from the limitations of this world. You were born in the limited capacity of walking and living as a human. You were bound to all of the laws of nature and gravity. But, then, here comes Jesus walking on water, raising the dead, casting out devils, and healing the sick. Jesus defied things known to the everyday natural man. He expanded the levels of possibility. God always raises the bar of what is possible when He comes on the scene.

God not only raises the bar of the possibility of what He can do, but He raises the possibility of what humankind can do if they believe Him. This is why Jesus taught us to speak to mountains, and they will move if we don't doubt in our hearts. We all know that God and Jesus can move mountains, but religion has a hard time believing that man can speak to a mountain, and it will move through faith in God. This is where doubt comes in.

Doubt is a byproduct of living in this natural world without knowing the All-Powerful God. Jesus taught that if we would not doubt in our heart but believe what we say would come to pass, we would have what we say. This is one of the powerful *Laws of Faith*. You can have what you say; if you don't doubt, the words coming out of your mouth will come to pass.

> **Mark 11:23 (KJV)**
> *23 For verily I say unto you, That whosoever shall say unto this mountain, Be thou removed, and be thou cast into the sea;* ***and shall not doubt in his heart, but shall believe that those things which he saith shall come to pass;*** *he shall have whatsoever he saith.*

Jesus taught that out of the abundance of the heart, the mouth speaks. We also know that faith works by speaking what you believe. So, what you speak is necessary, but what you believe about what you are speaking is crucial. You have to believe and be 100% persuaded that what you say will come to pass for faith to work. According to the Bible, you are called a double-minded person if you have faith and doubt simultaneously.

> **James 1:5-8 (KJV)**
> *5 If any of you lack wisdom, let him ask of God, that giveth to all men liberally, and upbraideth not; and it shall be given him. 6* ***But let him ask in faith, nothing wavering.*** *For he that wavereth is like a wave of the sea driven with the wind and tossed. 7* ***For let not that man think that he shall receive any thing of the Lord. 8 A double minded man is unstable in all his ways.***

When people compete in the Olympics, they are trained not to think or speak of losing. They are trained to only think and speak about winning the Gold Medal. They have to control every thought in their mind and every word that comes out of their mouth. They must think and talk about their victory before getting to the Olympics to win.

There are mental management systems that teach you how to control your thoughts. Unfortunately, some Christians have not mastered their thoughts and let doubt rule them. The Bible says we are to battle any thought that does not line up with the knowledge of God and bring it into captivity. Mentally strong people take captive every disobedient thought. This is what we have to do to win the war of words.

> *2 Corinthians 10:3-6 (KJV)*
> *3 For though we walk in the flesh, we do not war after the flesh:*
> *4 (For the weapons of our warfare are not carnal, but mighty through God to the pulling down of strong holds;) 5 Casting down imaginations, and every high thing that exalteth itself against the knowledge of God, and bringing into captivity every thought to the obedience of Christ; 6 And having in a readiness to revenge all disobedience, when your obedience is fulfilled.*

Most people are not mentally strong and speak just about any thought the devil throws at them. This is why we must take the shield of faith, quench these thoughts, and battle every thought with the Word of God, which is the sword of the Spirit (Ephesians 6:16-17). You have to build up and strengthen your mind in the Word of God daily. Then, as you meditate on the Word, you will be able to conquer any thoughts the enemy shoots at you.

To get to the place where there is no doubt in your heart takes training, correction, and confession of the Word of God. Thoughts in the heart must be battled against by the Word of God. Sometimes this battle can get very heated. Spiritual warfare is not for the weak of heart. When someone is going to believe God for anything, they must be full of faith. If you have faith and doubt simultaneously, this double-mindedness hinders God from answering your prayer. There is, however, a place of cross-over where you battle the thought of unbelief with intercessory prayer and confession until you get the victory.

I call it the cross-over place because that is exactly what it feels like. You must be in the *Law of Faith* for a prayer to be answered. Until you cross over in full faith, your prayer will undoubtedly be hindered. When you cross over in full faith, you will know that you know you have the answer. This is where God lives. Unfortunately, many Christians never press in deep enough to reach this elevated place of faith. If you will stay in prayer and keep confessing the Word of God for your answer over and over, you will get to the place where you believe you have what you say. You won't even care if the opposite occurs. You will believe God despite what you see or hear.

This kind of faith is where Jesus lived, and as the *Author* and *Finisher* of our faith, He is working to get us to live in this same realm of faith. When you understand faith at this level, it is easy to understand the stories of Jesus. When Jesus was faced with impossible situations, He handled them with the boldness of faith. He believed until He manifested the power of God. You can see this in the case of Jairus, a leader of the Synagogue in Capernaum. Jesus was on his way to heal his daughter when someone came to Jairus and said not to bother the Master because his daughter had died. Right at that moment, Jesus told Jairus to *Be not afraid, only believe.* Jesus then went and raised his daughter from the dead. Let's look at this miraculous story of faith together.

Mark 5:35-43 (KJV)

*35 While he yet spake, there came from the ruler of the synagogue's house certain which said, Thy daughter is dead: why troublest thou the Master any further? 36 As soon as Jesus heard the word that was spoken, he saith unto the ruler of the synagogue, **Be not afraid, only believe.** 37 And he suffered no man to follow him, save Peter, and James, and John the brother of James. 38 And he cometh to the house of the ruler of the synagogue, and seeth the tumult, and them that wept and wailed greatly. 39 And when he was come in, he saith unto them, Why make ye this ado, and weep? the damsel is not dead, but sleepeth. 40 And they laughed him to scorn. But when he had put them all out, he taketh the father and the mother of the damsel, and them that were with him, and entereth in where the damsel was lying. 41 **And he took the damsel by the hand, and said unto her, Talitha cumi; which is, being interpreted, Damsel, I say unto thee, arise. 42 And straightway the damsel arose, and walked;** for she was of the age of twelve years. And they were astonished with a great astonishment. 43 And he charged them straitly that no man should know it; and commanded that something should be given her to eat.*

Jesus was living in a place where He was never moved. Sometimes, when you believe God for a miracle, it can get worse. But, if you keep believing God and not doubt or move in fear, you will get your answer. Your faith can get so strong that you don't flinch at an evil report because you know God answered you. You are just in a battle for manifestation. If you stay strong in faith, the answer will come 100% of the time because it is a law. Faith works by a law, and you can count on laws to work 100% of the time.

This is where the war of words comes in. The Word of God coming out of your mouth has to be stronger than any other word. If you speak to a mountain and keep speaking to it in faith, it will move. The *Law of Faith* will force it to move if you don't doubt. Once doubt is removed, the miracle will manifest every time. Your faith in God forces the miracle to occur.

Abraham is called the father of our faith for a good reason. God had promised him a son when he was about 75 years old. The Bible says he believed God, and it was counted unto him for righteousness, but his promised son Isaac was not born until he was 99 years old. There is a hidden secret to the birth of Isaac and why it took this long for the promise to take place.

When he was about 99 years old, God came to Abram and changed his name from Abram to Abraham and his wife's name from Sarai to Sarah. Abraham means Father of a Multitude, and Sarah means Mother of Many Nations. Within three months of God changing their name, Isaac was conceived and birthed nine months later. Why was Isaac born so fast after their names were changed? He was born fast after waiting 25 years because they started speaking into existence with faith by saying their new names. They were saying they were a *Father of a Multitude* and a *Mother of Many Nations.* They were using their mouths to create the promise of God. Before this, they were not speaking anything into existence. This is the *Law of Faith* at work. They did not doubt the promise of God and were fully persuaded that what He promised would come to pass. Let's look at how the Book of Romans confirms this truth.

Romans 4:17-21 (KJV)

17 (As it is written, I have made thee a father of many nations,) before him whom he believed, even God, who quickeneth the *dead, and calleth those things which be not as though they were. 18 Who against hope believed in hope, that he might become the father of many nations, according to that which was spoken, So shall thy seed be. 19 And being not weak in faith, he considered not his own body now dead, when he was about an hundred years old, neither yet the deadness of Sarah's womb: 20 **He staggered not at the promise of God through unbelief; but was strong in faith, giving glory to God; 21 And being fully persuaded that, what he had promised, he was able also to perform.***

According to the natural process of life, no one was able to have a child in their old age. The womb in a woman dies at a certain age. Abraham and Sarah believed God could bypass this life's natural law and give them a child in their old age. They believed in God in hope against all hope, and God performed a miracle. Abraham was strong in His faith and did not doubt that God could do this miracle, and this is why he is called the Father of Faith.

If you are in a situation and need a miracle, you can speak to the mountain and make it move. But you have to be fully persuaded in your mind with no doubt in your heart. Getting to this place of faith is possible. Many men and women of God have believed God for miracles and received them. The *Law of Faith* makes all things possible. You can win any war of words and receive miracles from God if you believe and do not doubt in your heart that what you say will come to pass. When you operate in this *Law of Faith*, you will move any mountain facing you with the words of faith coming out of your mouth. Your faith will work for you every time you don't have any doubt in your heart.

CHAPTER 11

---◆●◆---

LAW #5

Call Things that Be Not as Though they Were

God is so powerful that He can speak universes and worlds into existence. He formed planets with just His Words. From the Book of Genesis, we understand that He created by His spoken Word; the universe, the stars, the sun, the moon, the earth, everything in the world, including Adam and Eve, in just six days. The enormity of all of this is beyond what our finite minds could ever comprehend. It will take all of eternity to tap into the vastness of how great and mighty God is.

We as humans have barely tapped into the mystery of the power of God's spoken Word. Since the beginning of creation, man has not fully understood who God is and what He is capable of. We will, however, have all of eternity to get to know God and discover the power of His might. God can call things that be not as though they were. Let's look at the famous verse where this statement is found.

Romans 4:17 (KJV)

*17 (As it is written, I have made thee a father of many nations,) before him whom he believed, even God, who quickeneth the dead, **and calleth those things which be not as though they were.***

In this chapter, I will dig deep into this statement when it comes to us praying to God for answers to our prayers and speaking to mountains. Calling things that be not as though they were is an important statement that has to be explored for faith-believing Christians. Calling things that be not as though they were is also an essential *Law of Faith*.

Many Christians who learn about faith and speaking to mountains sometimes misunderstand this statement. This statement from Romans 4:17 must be accurately understood if we are going to speak to mountains and cause them to move with our words, as Jesus said.

Mark 11:22-23 (KJV)

*22 And Jesus answering saith unto them, Have faith in God. 23 **For verily I say unto you, That whosoever shall say unto this mountain, Be thou removed, and be thou cast into the sea; and shall not doubt in his heart, but shall believe that those things which he saith shall come to pass; he shall have whatsoever he saith.***

We, as Christians, are called to speak to mountains and make them move with our faith. Jesus taught this as a fact in the New Testament. We were made in God's image and have the power to cause things to come to pass with our words, just as God in whose image we were created. But, we can only cause things to come to pass and call things that be not as though they were if we have faith in God. This faith has to be understood for us to operate in it correctly.

Let's go back and look at what the passage in Romans 4:17 *didn't say*.

Romans 4:17 (KJV)

*17 (As it is written, I have made thee a father of many nations,) before him whom he believed, even God, who quickeneth the dead, **and calleth those things which be not as though they were.***

This verse does not say that God calls things that be as though they are not. This small change in how you read this passage makes all the difference in the world. God is not a liar and cannot lie. Therefore, if you call something that is as though it is not, it is a lie. This is an important truth to understand. It is also vital to know how this truth affects how you operate and speak with words of faith.

Let's take the example of someone who has a growth on their face and wants to be healed. If they misunderstand this passage of Scripture, they will say, "I don't have a growth." This is where many faith-believing Christians have been mocked because everyone can see they have a growth. To say it is not there is a lie. What they should say is, "I am healed, and I call forth healing to come and heal me of this growth. By the stripes of Jesus, I am healed. I speak directly to you growth and command you to leave my body! I curse you growth at your roots and command you to leave me!" If a minister is praying for them, they should say, "Be healed according to your faith." This growth should be rebuked at its roots. No one should say it is not there because that would be a lie.

Faith calls healing into the seen realm from the unseen realm. Faith is not a denial of the truth but rather an overcoming of natural facts. God has not called us to lie about facts but to overcome any fact that does not align with His Word and will. Some people of faith have misunderstood the ways of God and try to deny they don't have a problem when they do have a problem. It is okay to admit you have a problem if you do. Problems are considered mountains in the New Testament. Jesus faced many difficulties and overcame them by faith. Jesus never conquered a problem by denying it existed.

Let's look at the story of Jesus healing blind Bartimaeus to understand this truth better.

Mark 10:46-52 (KJV)

*46 And they came to Jericho: and as he went out of Jericho with his disciples and a great number of people, **blind Bartimaeus**, the son of Timaeus, sat by the highway side begging. 47 And when he heard that it was Jesus of Nazareth, he began to cry out, and say, Jesus, thou son of David, have mercy on me. 48 And many charged him that he should hold his peace: but he cried the more a great deal, Thou son of David, have mercy on me. 49 And Jesus stood still, and commanded him to be called. And they call the blind man, saying unto him, Be of good comfort, rise; he calleth thee. 50 And he, casting away his garment, rose, and came to Jesus. 51 And Jesus answered and said unto him, **What wilt thou that I should do unto thee?** The blind man said unto him, **Lord, that I might receive my sight.** 52 And Jesus said unto him, Go thy way; thy faith hath made thee whole. **And immediately he received his sight,** and followed Jesus in the way.*

Jesus, Bartimaeus, and everyone else knew that he was blind. Jesus, however, asked blind Bartimaeus what He should do for him. Jesus did not deny the fact that Bartimaeus was blind. Jesus wanted blind Bartimaeus to speak what he wanted. Blind Bartimaeus did not say he wasn't blind. Jesus wanted him to be specific, and then Jesus would call those things that be not as though they were. Blind Bartimaeus asked that he might receive his eyesight, and then he received his eyesight from Jesus. Denial of a problem will never make it go away; in fact, a problem can get worse. The woman with the issue of blood had that problem for 12 years, and when she went to the doctors, it just got worse. She also spent all her money on the issue.

> ### Mark 5:25-26 (KJV)
> 25 And a certain woman, which had an issue of blood twelve years, 26 **And had suffered many things of many physicians, and had spent all that she had,** and was nothing bettered, **but rather grew worse,**

The woman with the issue of blood was healed by Jesus when no one else could heal her. She didn't deny she had a problem. Jesus will heal you, and you can get answers from God if you are honest and genuine with your faith in God. True faith does not deny problems exists, but instead calls for an answer from God to overcome the problems.

> ### Mark 5:27-29 (KJV)
> 27 When she had heard of Jesus, came in the press behind, and touched his garment. 28 For she said, If I may touch but his clothes, I shall be whole. 29 **And straightway the fountain of her blood was dried up; and she felt in her body that she was healed of that plague.**

Now let's turn our attention to how God talks when He speaks things into creation or performs miracles. From the Scriptures, we see that God has a specific word He often uses when He is calling things that be not as though they were. This word has often been overlooked and understudied. We will see from the Scriptures that this small two-letter word was used many times by God in the first six days of creation, and it was also used many times in the ministry of Jesus Christ.

The two-letter word I am referring to is **BE.** God used the word **Be** many times to speak things into creation and perform miracles. It is a small word with a significant impact. **Be** means to exist, become, occur, happen, come to pass, or be done. It means something has just come into existence or occurred just as God said it would. The word for **Be** in the Hebrew language is *hâyâh* (*haw-yaw'*).

Now, let's look at how God used the word **BE** in the first six days of creation.

Genesis 1:1-3 (KJV)
*1 In the beginning God created the Heaven and the earth. 2 And the earth was without form, and void; and darkness was upon the face of the deep. And the Spirit of God moved upon the face of the waters. 3 **And God said, Let there be light:** and there was light.*

Genesis 1:6 (KJV)
*6 **And God said, Let there be** a firmament in the midst of the waters, and let it divide the waters from the waters.*

Genesis 1:9 (KJV)
*9 **And God said, Let the waters under the Heaven be** gathered together unto one place, and let the dry land appear: and it was so.*

Genesis 1:14-15 (KJV)
*14 **And God said, Let there be lights** in the firmament of the Heaven to divide the day from the night; and let them be for signs, and for seasons, and for days, and years: 15 **And let them be for lights** in the firmament of the Heaven to give light upon the earth: and it was so.*

Genesis 1:21-22 (KJV)
21 And God created great whales, and every living creature that moveth, which the waters brought forth abundantly, after their kind, and every winged fowl after his kind: and God saw that it

*was good. 22 **And God blessed them, saying, Be fruitful, and multiply,** and fill the waters in the seas, and let fowl multiply in the earth.*

Genesis 1:27-28 (KJV)

*27 So God created man in his own image, in the image of God created he him; male and female created he them. 28 And God blessed them, **and God said unto them, Be fruitful, and multiply,** and replenish the earth, and subdue it: and have dominion over the fish of the sea, and over the fowl of the air, and over every living thing that moveth upon the earth.*

As you can see from the above Scriptures, the word **Be** played an important role when God created everything. The word **Be** is a commanding word. The word **Be** is a command from God for something to come into existence, come to pass, or fulfill a purpose. Light, the firmament, the sun, the moon, and all living creatures were commanded to **Be**. All animals were commanded to **Be** fruitful and multiply. Adam and Eve were also commanded to **Be** fruitful, multiply, replenish the earth and subdue it.

Be is one of God's most powerful words for creation. It is a short word with a significant impact. When God speaks the word **Be**, it has to **Be**. God is full of authority and power, and when He speaks, nothing can resist His will. When God speaks, His Word will not return to Him void but will accomplish whatever He pleases it to do.

Isaiah 55:9-11 (KJV)

9 For as the Heavens are higher than the earth, so are my ways higher than your ways, and my thoughts than your thoughts. 10 For as the rain cometh down, and the snow from Heaven, and returneth not thither, but watereth the earth, and maketh it bring *forth and bud, that it may give seed to the sower, and bread to the eater: 11 **So shall my word be that goeth forth out of my mouth: it shall not return unto me void, but it shall accomplish that which I please, and it shall prosper in the thing whereto I sent it.***

Now let's turn our attention to how Jesus used the word *Be* in His ministry while on the earth. God is made of three entities; The Father, The Son, and The Holy Spirit. In an earlier chapter, we talked about the Holy Spirit and His role in creation as the Hand of God. From the Books of John and Hebrews, we know it was Jesus who was the God who spoke the Words of creation. Jesus is God the Creator in Genesis Chapter 1, who spoke everything into existence.

John 1:1-3 (KJV)

*1 In the beginning was the Word, and the Word was with God, and the Word was God. 2 The same was in the beginning with God. 3 **All things were made by him; and without him was not any thing made that was made.***

Hebrews 1:1-2 (KJV)

*1 God, who at sundry times and in divers manners spake in time past unto the fathers by the prophets, 2 **Hath in these last days spoken unto us by his Son,** whom he hath appointed heir of all things, **by whom also he made the worlds;***

From the beginning, Jesus was with the Father and the Holy Spirit and created all things. Jesus used the word *Be* many times when He created everything in Genesis Chapter 1. We will see in the following Scriptures Jesus used the same word *Be* to perform many miracles during His ministry on the earth. The word for *Be* in the Greek language is *ginomai* (*ghin'-om-ahee*). The word in Greek means to cause to be, come into being, be performed, or be fulfilled.

Let's look at some of the miracles Jesus performed where He used the word ***Be***. One of the first times we see Jesus use the word ***Be*** in His ministry on earth is in the story of the healing of the leper.

Matthew 8:1-3 (KJV)
1 When he was come down from the mountain, great multitudes followed him. 2 And, behold, there came a leper and worshipped him, saying, Lord, if thou wilt, thou canst make me clean. 3 And Jesus put forth his hand, and touched him, saying, I will; ***be thou clean.*** *And immediately his leprosy was cleansed.*

He then used this same word, ***Be***, to heal the Centurions servant, who was grievously tormented and sick of palsy.

Matthew 8:13 (KJV)
13 And Jesus said unto the centurion, Go thy way; and as thou hast believed, so ***be it done unto thee***. *And his servant was healed in the selfsame hour.*

Jesus used the word ***Be*** to heal the two blind men that came to Him.

Matthew 9:27-30 (KJV)
27 And when Jesus departed thence, two blind men followed him, crying, and saying, Thou son of David, have mercy on us. 28 And when he was come into the house, the blind men came to him: and Jesus saith unto them, Believe ye that I am able to do this? They said unto him, Yea, Lord. 29 Then touched he their eyes, saying, According to your faith ***be it unto you.*** *30 And their eyes were opened; and Jesus straitly charged them, saying, See that no man know it.*

The word **Be** was also used with the woman's healing of the issue of blood. This woman was plagued with the issue of blood for over twelve years before Jesus healed her.

Mark 5:34 (KJV)
*34 And he said unto her, Daughter, thy faith hath made thee whole; go in peace, and **be whole of thy plague.***

We also find a story where Jesus healed a Gentile woman's daughter of a demon vexing her and used the word **Be**.

Matthew 15:28 (KJV)
*28 Then Jesus answered and said unto her, O woman, great is thy faith: **be it unto thee even as thou wilt.** And her daughter was made whole from that very hour.*

Finally, we see Jesus speaking to a storm with the word **Be**. This storm tried to kill Jesus and His disciples on the Sea of Galilee.

Mark 4:36-39 (KJV)
*36 And when they had sent away the multitude, they took him even as he was in the ship. And there were also with him other little ships. 37 And there arose a great storm of wind, and the waves beat into the ship, so that it was now full. 38 And he was in the hinder part of the ship, asleep on a pillow: and they awake him, and say unto him, Master, carest thou not that we perish? 39 And he arose, and rebuked the wind, and said unto the sea, Peace, **be still.** And the wind ceased, and there was a great calm.*

As we can see from these Scriptures, the word **Be** played a significant role in the ministry of Jesus. Jesus used this powerful word when speaking at the beginning of creation and into His earthly ministry.

Jesus used the word *Be* to create worlds and perform miracles. We cannot underestimate the power of the creative word *Be*.

Now I want to turn your attention to how this powerful two-letter word *Be* applies to the *Law of Faith* and us. We know that faith has everything to do with believing in our hearts and speaking what we believe out of our mouths. Jesus taught this truth in Mark 11:22-24. Unfortunately, today, many Christians have lost some of the powerful truths that Jesus taught concerning prayer. Jesus had much to say about prayer and how a New Testament believer was to pray.

Jesus taught His early disciples to use the word *Be* when speaking to a mountain. We were created in God's image, and it has always been the plan of God for His children to be like Him. So, if God uses the word *Be* to get things done, we should also use the word *Be* to get things done. Now, we are not creating anything new, but when it comes to God's creation, He wants us to use the word *Be* just like Jesus did when performing miracles and praying for mountains to be moved. Let's read Mark Chapter 11, verse 23, and see what Jesus says about us using the word *Be*.

> ### *Mark 11:22-23 (KJV)*
> *22 And Jesus answering saith unto them, Have faith in God. 23 For verily I say unto you, That whosoever shall say unto this mountain, **Be thou removed**, and **be thou cast into the sea;** and shall not doubt in his heart, but shall believe that those things which he saith shall come to pass; he shall have whatsoever he saith.*

Jesus taught us to have faith in God and speak to mountains. He said that whosoever, not just Him or His apostles, but *whosoever* would dare to speak to a mountain, it would move if they believed. Jesus said we could move a mountain with our words by telling it to *Be* removed and *Be* cast into the sea. Jesus taught us to use the same word *Be* that He was using. I know this may be a new concept to some people, but it is right here in the Scriptures for all to see. This same statement can also be found in Matthew Chapter 21, verse 21.

> *Matthew 21:21 (KJV)*
> *21 Jesus answered and said unto them, Verily I say unto you, If ye have faith, and doubt not, ye shall not only do this which is done to the fig tree, but also if ye shall say unto this mountain, **Be thou removed**, and **be thou cast into the sea**; it shall be done.*

Some of the most significant truths of God are hidden in plain sight. People have read the Bible for years and overlooked many powerful truths. However, the truths of God have to be revealed for us to see and apply them to our lives. When God reveals these truths to us, He wants us to live in them. You are called to move mountains by faith, and He is teaching you how to do it. He wants you to move mountains in the same way Jesus did. God calls things that be not as though they were and performs miracles with His Words. You can speak to a mountain with the word *Be*, just like Jesus did.

Jesus has called His Church to call things that be not as though they were. The Scripture from where I am quoting refers to Abraham and Sarah having a child in their old age.

> *Romans 4:17-18 (KJV)*
> *17 (As it is written, I have made thee a father of many nations,) before him whom he believed, even God, who quickeneth the dead, **and calleth those things which be not as though they were.** 18 Who against hope believed in hope, that he might become the*

father of many nations, according to that which was spoken, So shall thy seed be.

God spoke a child into existence when Abraham and Sarah were past the age of having children. He quickened Sarah's womb, and she became pregnant with Isaac. God creates worlds and works miracles, and He does it all by faith. When we believe Him, we too can see miracles. You have the right to call things that be not as though they were. Jesus called blind eyes to *Be* healed, and this same God is in our midst, ready to work miracles.

If you are going to win the war of words, you have to learn the power of God's creative Word, how He speaks, and the Words He uses. This powerful two-letter word *Be* is a word you can use to move mountains. So many people perish for lack of knowledge, but this won't be you. God is revealing tremendous and powerful truths in these last days for us to be overcoming faith-filled believers. You are called to help accomplish the will of God on the earth by speaking His Word and moving mountains. Calling things that be not as though they were is a powerful *Law of Faith* that can produce many miracles. Dare to believe God for the miraculous and win the war of words.

CHAPTER 12

LAW #6
The Will of God

God has a destiny and a plan for every person born on this planet. He also has a will and direction for the whole world. Finding and doing God's will is the most important thing you can do in your lifetime. Jesus Christ never did anything outside of the will of God. For you to please God, you must find, do, and become the will of God. In this chapter, we will discover the importance of the will of God in the life of a believer.

To fulfill your purpose on the earth, you must do the will of God. God destined your life for a purpose before you were born. God planned, designed, mapped out, and orchestrated all He was going to do and create before He spoke light into existence in the Book of Genesis. The concept of how great and mighty God is can overwhelm your mind. We were created by a Creator who is All-Knowing, All-Powerful, and Everywhere at the same time and eternal. He is the Almighty God, and yet He is loving, thoughtful, and caring.

God lovingly created the world and everyone that was born into it. God, in His love, also created everyone with a free will. God gave everyone a choice to serve and obey Him or serve and obey themselves. Serving and obeying yourself is serving and obeying the devil. When He placed Adam and Eve in the Garden of Eden, He gave them a commandment not to eat from the Tree of the Knowledge of Good and Evil. Adam and Eve disobeyed God's commandment and ate of that tree. They then entered into the devil's will and were kicked out of the Garden of Eden.

God created and destined Adam to obey Him, tend to the garden, multiply and fill the earth. Adam and Eve were given delegated authority over the whole world in the beginning.

Genesis 1:26-28 (KJV)

*26 And God said, Let us make man in our image, after our likeness: **and let them have dominion** over the fish of the sea, and over the fowl of the air, and over the cattle, and over all the earth, and over every creeping thing that creepeth upon the earth. 27 So God created man in his own image, in the image of God created he him; male and female created he them. 28 **And God blessed them, and God said unto them, Be fruitful, and multiply, and replenish the earth, and subdue it: and have dominion over the fish of the sea, and over the fowl of the air, and over every living thing that moveth upon the earth.***

After the fall of Adam and Eve, they started having children and multiplying on the earth. God began to allow people to be born, and every person born was given an opportunity to do God's will or not. God wanted to see if they would obey Him and do good or disobey Him and do evil.

Many people think they have control over their whole life, but they don't. We live in a simulated world where we believe we have control. We, however, have limited control over our lives, and what control we do have in this life is only to see if we are going to obey God or not.

Let me explain this to you in a more profound way. You have no control of being born or given life itself. You have no control over the time in history you were born in. You have no control over who your parents are going to be. You have no control if you would be a boy or a girl. You have no control over what ethnicity you would be. You also have no control over world events such as wars, conflict, and natural disasters during the time you were born and live on the earth.

I know these thoughts are intense, but they are true. In reality, you have very little control over your life. Most people live to be about 60 to 100 years before they die. The whole time people live on the earth, God writes what people choose to speak and do in books. Everything you say and do is recorded in the books of Heaven. At the end of the world, we will all stand before the Judgement Seat of God and be judged for what we did while alive on the earth. God will open these books on Judgment Day and judge us based upon what is written in them. There is also a Book of Life, and people who choose to accept Jesus Christ as their Savior are found written in that Book.

Revelation 20:11-13 (KJV)

*11 And I saw a great white throne, and him that sat on it, from whose face the earth and the Heaven fled away; and there was found no place for them. 12 **And I saw the dead, small and great, stand before God; and the books were opened: and another book was opened, which is the Book of life: and the dead were judged out of those things which were written in the books, according to their works.** 13 And the sea gave up the dead which were in it; and death and hell delivered up the dead which were in them: **and they were judged every man according to their works.***

The Bible says, *It is appointed unto man once to die, and then you are judged.* There is no coming back to this earth for a second chance of life once you die.

> ### Hebrews 9:27 (KJV)
> **27 *And as it is appointed unto men once to die, but after this the judgment:***

You are given one life to glorify and choose Jesus as your Lord. Jesus taught and preached a lot about the will of God. He taught His disciples that the only people going to Heaven were the ones who did the will of His Father. Doing the will of God has everything to do with knowing Jesus and not doing iniquity.

> ### Matthew 7:21-23 (KJV)
> *21 Not every one that saith unto me, Lord, Lord, shall enter into the kingdom of Heaven;* **but he that doeth the will of my Father which is in Heaven.** *22 Many will say to me in that day, Lord, Lord, have we not prophesied in thy name? and in thy name have cast out devils? and in thy name done many wonderful works? 23* ***And then will I profess unto them, I never knew you: depart from me, ye that work iniquity.***

Jesus also taught His disciples to pray that God's will be done on earth as it is in Heaven. We have to pray for God's will to be done on the earth; it doesn't just happen.

> ### Matthew 6:9-13 (KJV)
> *9 After this manner therefore pray ye: Our Father which art in Heaven, Hallowed be thy name. 10* ***Thy kingdom come, Thy will be done in earth, as it is in Heaven.*** *11 Give us this day our daily bread. 12 And forgive us our debts, as we forgive our debtors. 13*

And lead us not into temptation, but deliver us from evil: For thine is the kingdom, and the power, and the glory, for ever. Amen.

One of the primary purposes for Jesus to be born was to die for our sins. Jesus came to earth and lived as a man so He could die as a man and redeem us back to God. Jesus dying on the cross was the only way to defeat the devil and take dominion back from him that Adam and Eve had lost. However, when it came close to the time for Jesus to die on the cross, He struggled in Himself and asked the Father if there was any other way than for Him to have to die a horrific crucifixion.

This is understandable because Jesus dying on the cross meant being humiliated, beaten, and killed in one of the most horrific ways possible; the cross. The cross was a slow and torturous way the Romans killed people they considered criminals in their society. First, they would hang them on the cross with their feet and hands nailed to the wood that supported them. Then, the person crucified would lift themselves in agonizing pain for air because their feet were nailed to the cross. This would go on for hours until they couldn't raise themselves to breathe anymore or until the Roman soldiers broke their legs. We can see what great sacrifice and trial Jesus went through to save us by knowing all of this.

Because the cross was so horrific, Jesus prayed to the Father if there was another way to save us. However, there was no other way, and Jesus being the powerful person that He is, chose to obey the will of the Father over His own will and die the death on the cross. In the Scriptures, we can see the prayer Jesus prayed about the will of God before He went to the cross. Let's look at this important passage of Scripture.

Matthew 26:36-44 (KJV)

*36 Then cometh Jesus with them unto a place called Gethsemane, and saith unto the disciples, Sit ye here, while I go and pray yonder. 37 And he took with him Peter and the two sons of Zebedee, **and began to be sorrowful and very heavy.** 38 Then saith he unto them, My soul is exceeding sorrowful, even unto death: tarry ye here, and watch with me. 39 And he went a little farther, and fell on his face, and prayed, saying, **O my Father, if it be possible, let this cup pass from me: nevertheless not as I will, but as thou wilt.** 40 And he cometh unto the disciples, and findeth them asleep, and saith unto Peter, What, could ye not watch with me one hour? 41 Watch and pray, that ye enter not into temptation: the spirit indeed is willing, but the flesh is weak. 42 He went away again the second time, and prayed, saying, **O my Father, if this cup may not pass away from me, except I drink it, thy will be done.** 43 And he came and found them asleep again: for their eyes were heavy. 44 **And he left them, and went away again, and prayed the third time, saying the same words.***

We know from history that Jesus chose to do the will of the Father and died on the cross for our sins. He decided to do the will of the Father. Thank God that He did, or we wouldn't have the opportunity to be saved, go to Heaven, and live forever with God. God sent Jesus to do His will. It is also important to note that Jesus did die on the cross, but before this event, Jesus was continually doing God's will during His life. Let's look at some truths Jesus taught concerning the will of God while He was on the earth.

John 4:34 (KJV)

*34 Jesus saith unto them, **My meat is to do the will of him that sent me,** and to finish his work.*

John 5:30 (KJV)

*30 I can of mine own self do nothing: as I hear, I judge: and my judgment is just; because **I seek not mine own will, but the will of the Father which hath sent me.***

John 6:38 (KJV)

*38 **For I came down from Heaven, not to do mine own will, but the will of him that sent me.***

Doing the will of God was very important to Jesus. Therefore, doing the will of God must be very important to us as well. Some people say they struggle with finding and knowing what the will of God is for their life. For something to be in the will of God, two elements must be in place. The first thing is it must line up with the known will of God from the Scriptures. The next thing is the Holy Spirit must lead you. Being led by the Spirit proves you are a child of God, and this is how we stay in the will of God during our lives. The Holy Spirit will only lead you to God's perfect will every time.

Romans 8:14 (KJV)

*14 For as many as are **led by the Spirit of God, they are the sons of God.***

Jesus was always led by the Spirit and operated within the will of God according to the Scriptures. This is why His Words always came to pass. It is also important to see that when the devil was tempting Jesus in the wilderness, the devil tried to get Him to speak to the rocks to become bread. Jesus refused to be led by the devil and told him that *man should not live by bread alone but by every Word that proceeds from the mouth of God.*

Matthew 4:2-4 (KJV)

2 And when he had fasted forty days and forty nights, he was afterward an hungred. 3 And when the tempter came to him, he *said, If thou be the Son of God, command that these stones be made bread. 4 But he answered and said, It is written, **Man shall not live by bread alone, but by every word that proceedeth out of the mouth of God.***

God's will always lines up with His spoken and written Word. As you grow in your walk with God, you must study the Word of God to find out the will of God and how you should live. As you are growing, the Holy Spirit will begin to talk to you on the inside of your heart and lead you into His Divine will for your life. The voice of the Holy Spirit works with your conscience. Sometimes you have choices you have to make, but always make sure you choose what the Holy Spirit wants, even if it is challenging. To hear and do God's will, your mind must be renewed.

Romans 12:2 (KJV)

*2 And be not conformed to this world: **but be ye transformed by the renewing of your mind, that ye may prove what is that good, and acceptable, and perfect, will of God.***

We see there is a choice between God's good, acceptable, and perfect will from this Scripture. Always choose the perfect will of God. God will never lead you astray, and if you always choose His perfect will, you will be blessed. You will always be in the right place, at the right time, and with the right word. God will use you to do mighty things. When you are in God's will, you have a right to pray for things to come to pass that is in His will.

1 John 5:14-15 (KJV)

*14 And this is the confidence that we have in him, that, if we ask **any thing according to his will**, he heareth us: 15 And if we know that he hear us, **whatsoever we ask, we know that we have the petitions that we desired of him.***

When you pray the will of God, God will hear you and answer your prayers. You have a right to speak to situations, and they will change and conform to the will of God. It is important to understand that God's will doesn't just happen on the earth. Someone on this earth has to choose to obey God and speak His will into existence. You will go down into eternal Heavenly history as one that obeyed God if you choose to speak and do God's will. Your works will be written in His Book, and you will be rewarded on Judgment Day.

The will of God is also not something you just do, but it is something you become. Many people want to know what God's will is for their life, such as what career path they should take, who they should marry, and many more life decisions such as these. People are looking for God's will and what they should do, which is important, but let me pose another thought for you to consider about the will of God.

God not only wants you to seek Him for what you should do in life, but who you are while you are doing what you are called to do. God chose King Saul to be the King of Israel, but when he became king, he disobeyed God twice and killed some of the priests of the Lord. His character was not in alignment with the will of God. He was doing God's will by being the King of Israel but missed the will of God in his character and actions. It is just as important to God that your character aligns with His will as you do the assignment you are called to do in this life.

The devil wants to take people captive to do his will. Therefore, the devil continues to tempt people and try to get them to disobey God and do his will.

2 Timothy 2:24-26 (KJV)

24 And the servant of the Lord must not strive; but be gentle unto all men, apt to teach, patient, 25 In meekness instructing those that oppose themselves; if God peradventure will give them repentance to the acknowledging of the truth; 26 And that they may recover themselves out of the snare of the devil, **who are taken captive by him at his will.**

Doing the will of God is imperative to winning the war of words. You can only win the war of words if you obey God and do His will. We are not here to live and do our own will. God has a plan for you, which entails victory over the devil, but you can only defeat the devil by doing God's will.

I wrote the will of God as one of the *Laws of Faith* because God's will is the law. God rules over all, and His will is the law. If you disobey God and His will, you are a lawbreaker. We are not here to obey a set of rules, but we are here to come into fellowship with and obey the living God. He wants us to be in fellowship with Him as we do His will for our lives. His will is for us to love and obey Him. It is also His will that we love others. When you get right down to it, the only thing that matters in life is accepting Jesus as your Lord, loving God with all of your heart, and doing the will of God. Nothing else matters.

In conclusion, obeying God is paramount to winning the war of words. When you speak to a mountain and command it to move, you must be praying in the will of God. If you live doing the will of God and pray according to the will of God, you will always be heard by God. When God hears you, you have the answer you were praying for, and you have a right to speak to any mountain and command it to move. By the *Law of Faith*, it will move. God's will for you is to be blessed, healed, healthy and prosperous as your soul prospers.

3 John 1:2 (KJV)
2 Beloved, I wish above all things that thou mayest prosper and be in health, even as thy soul prospereth.

CHAPTER 13

LAW #7

Forgive Everyone from the Heart

Forgiveness plays a crucial part in the working of your faith, and for your faith to work, you have to be in right standing with God. We will explore this thought and see why you have to have a forgiving heart if you want to speak to mountains and have them listen to you. Forgiving people from the heart plays a vital role in the *Laws of Faith.*

In the Lord's Prayer found in the Book of Matthew, it says, *"Forgive us our debts as we forgive our debtors."*

Matthew 6:12 (KJV)
12 And forgive us our debts, as we forgive our debtors.

God is a very fair and just God and treats us how we treat others. God went to great lengths in the death, burial, and resurrection of Jesus for you to have your sins forgiven. The blood of Jesus is of the highest value in the Kingdom of God. It is only through His shed blood that your sins are forgiven. The only way to enter Heaven is by God forgiving us of our sins when we repent and ask Him to forgive us.

There is a parable found in the Book of Matthew where a man was forgiven an enormous amount of debt from a king and then turned around and wouldn't forgive another man a small debt. When the king heard of this, he brought the man back before him, threw him into jail, and required the entire debt to be repaid that he owed him. Jesus spoke this parable as an example of how God will treat those in whom He forgives their sins, but they don't forgive others their sins committed against them. Let's read this parable together.

> *Matthew 18:23-35 (KJV)*
> *23 Therefore is the kingdom of Heaven likened unto a certain king, which would take account of his servants. 24 And when he had begun to reckon, one was brought unto him, which owed him ten thousand talents. 25 But forasmuch as he had not to pay, his Lord commanded him to be sold, and his wife, and children, and all that he had, and payment to be made. 26 The servant therefore fell down, and worshipped him, saying, Lord, have patience with me, and I will pay thee all. 27 **Then the Lord of that servant was moved with compassion, and loosed him, and forgave him the debt.** 28 But the same servant went out, and found one of his fellowservants, which owed him an hundred pence: and he laid hands on him, and took him by the throat, saying, **Pay me that thou owest.** 29 And his fellowservant fell down at his feet, and besought him, saying, **Have patience with me, and I will pay thee all.** 30 **And he would not: but went and cast him into prison, till he should pay the debt.** 31 So when his fellowservants saw what was done, they were very sorry, and came and told unto their Lord all that was done. 32 Then his Lord, after that he had called him, said unto him, O thou wicked servant, I forgave thee all that debt, because thou desiredst me: 33 **Shouldest not thou also have had compassion on thy fellowservant, even as I had pity on**

thee? 34 And his Lord was wroth, and delivered him to the tormentors, till he should pay all that was due unto him. 35 So likewise shall my Heavenly Father do also unto you, if ye from your hearts forgive not every one his brother their trespasses.

This passage of Scripture gives us great insight into the mind and thoughts of God concerning forgiveness. God treats you the way you treat others. If you don't forgive others, He won't forgive you. If you forgive others, He will forgive you. The forgiveness of God is not to be taken lightly; neither is forgiving others to be taken lightly. Your whole salvation rests upon God forgiving you. For God to not hold your sins against you, you have to forgive others. God expects you to forgive everyone from your heart, just as He forgave you.

Now let's turn out attention to the Book of James and see what it has to say about forgiveness and people getting healed. In this book, James talks about those who want to be prayed for by the Church elders for healing.

James 5:14-18 (KJV)
14 Is any sick among you? let him call for the elders of the Church; and let them pray over him, anointing him with oil in the name of the Lord: 15 And the Prayer of Faith shall save the sick, and the Lord shall raise him up; and if he have committed sins, they shall be forgiven him. 16 Confess your faults one to another, and pray one for another, that ye may be healed. The effectual fervent prayer of a righteous man availeth much. 17 Elias was a man subject to like passions as we are, and he prayed earnestly that it might not rain: and it rained not on the earth by the space of three years and six months. 18 And he prayed again, and the Heaven gave rain, and the earth brought forth her fruit.

A person who needs healing also must repent and confess their sins to be healed. When they confess their sins, the *Prayer of Faith* can be offered on their behalf for them to be healed. The *Prayer of Faith* is the speaking to the mountain. The *Prayer of Faith* has to be offered by a righteous man. Another way to say a righteous man is to say a man in right standing with God.

For a man of God to be in right standing with God and considered righteous, their sins have to be forgiven. For their sins to be forgiven, they must have repented and been walking in obedience to the Holy Spirit. To be forgiven, they must also not be holding any unforgiveness toward anyone because God will not forgive you if you have not forgiven others. Therefore, for the *Prayer of Faith* to be offered by a righteous man, they must forgive everyone from their heart. If the person offering the *Prayer of Faith* has any unforgiveness in their heart, they are not considered in right standing with God because their sins are not forgiven.

To be forgiven, you have to have repented of all your sins, walking in a clean conscience, and have forgiven from your heart anyone who has sinned against you. If you do not forgive others, you are regarding iniquity in your heart, and the Lord will not hear those who are not forgiven of their sins. Let's look at this truth from the Scripture found in the Book of Psalms.

> ### *Psalm 66:17-19 (KJV)*
> *17 I cried unto him with my mouth, and he was extolled with my tongue. 18 **If I regard iniquity in my heart, the Lord will not hear me:** 19 But verily God hath heard me; he hath attended to the voice of my prayer.*

The man born blind from birth that Jesus healed in John 9 also understood this truth. He had greater insight into the ways of God than many of the religious leaders of his day.

John 9:31-33 (KJV)
*31 **Now we know that God heareth not sinners:** but if any man be a worshipper of God, and doeth his will, him he heareth. 32 Since the world began was it not heard that any man opened the eyes of one that was born blind. 33 If this man were not of God, he could do nothing.*

Isaiah, the prophet, also revealed this truth in the 59th chapter of the Book of Isaiah. Let's read what he had to say concerning this subject.

Isaiah 59:1-2 (KJV)
*1 Behold, the Lord's hand is not shortened, that it cannot save; neither his ear heavy, that it cannot hear: 2 But your iniquities have separated between you and your God, **and your sins have hid his face from you, that he will not hear.***

Now you can see why forgiveness is so essential when offering the *Prayer of Faith*, because God doesn't hear sinners. You have to be in right standing with God to offer the *Prayer of Faith*. Being forgiven and forgiving others is crucial for your prayers being heard by God. If God does not hear your prayers, the mountain will not move when you speak to it.

Let's look at the Scripture found in Mark 11 to see deeper into this truth.

Mark 11:22-26 (KJV)
22 And Jesus answering saith unto them, Have faith in God. 23 For verily I say unto you, That whosoever shall say unto this mountain, Be thou removed, and be thou cast into the sea; and

*shall not doubt in his heart, but shall believe that those things which he saith shall come to pass; he shall have whatsoever he saith. 24 Therefore I say unto you, What things soever ye desire, when ye pray, believe that ye receive them, and ye shall have them. 25 **And when ye stand praying, forgive, if ye have ought against any: that your Father also which is in Heaven may forgive you your trespasses. 26 But if ye do not forgive, neither will your Father which is in Heaven forgive your trespasses.***

After Jesus taught His disciples to have faith in God and speak to mountains, He taught about forgiveness. Nothing can stop your prayers faster from being answered than an unforgiving heart. Forgiveness and being in right standing with God are vital for your faith to work. Many ministers teach the importance of forgiveness, but not all of them tie it into your prayers being answered or not. Forgiveness is vital in the walk of every believer.

On a side note, I want to add in a secret that I learned from the Lord when it comes to forgiveness. I used to be of the mindset that when someone did something wrong to me, I would take my time in forgiving them. This mode of operation, however, kept me weak. Sometimes I would hold my forgiveness back for weeks and then finally forgive someone. Unfortunately, I was kept back from fellowshipping with the Lord during this time.

The Lord graciously taught me a secret when it comes to forgiveness. The Lord led me to forgive people even before they did anything wrong. When a wrong is done to someone, most people go through a process of thought before they forgive others or not. They have to think about what was done and work through the pain in their heart as they consider forgiving someone or not. The Lord watches all of this take place. Jesus also taught that offenses would come and being hurt or wronged by others is a part of this life.

Matthew 18:7 (KJV)

7 Woe unto the world because of offences! ***for it must needs be that offences come;*** *but woe to that man by whom the offence cometh!*

Because offenses are going to come in life, we must be prepared when it happens. I will reveal the secret that God taught me regarding forgiving others and keeping my heart free. God told me to think of every evil thing that could be done to me. He wanted me to think of everything, and I mean everything. It took me some time, but I thought this through.

The next thing He told me to do was forgive anyone and everything that could be done to me in advance. This was a new way of living for me. I was used to being hurt and then working through the process of forgiving someone. Forgiving someone in advance was a paradigm shift in my thinking and living. I never even thought of forgiving people in advance. This was a game-changer for me.

This new way of thinking and living regarding forgiveness changed my whole life. I could see how something terrible would happen to people (myself included), and it would knock them off course for weeks or months by them not forgiving in advance. When someone offends you, you can be knocked off your spiritual foothold with God if you are not walking in forgiveness. But, if you are walking in forgiveness, you can always stay in right standing with God by forgiving in advance.

Unforgiveness did not stick in my heart by forgiving in advance, and this now keeps me in right standing with God at all times. As soon as I did this, I became strong and was no longer easily offended. I don't just forgive people, but I am now a forgiving person. A forgiving person has settled it in their heart to forgive any wrong done to them in advance. If you choose to live this way, you will be like God, who forgave you over 2000 years ago when Jesus died on the cross for your sins.

God forgave you before you were born when Jesus died on the cross. When you repent, you enter into the forgiveness of God. Since God forgave you of your sins, why wouldn't you forgive others? Living and walking in forgiveness is the best way to live. Bitter people invite many troubles, heartaches, and sickness into their life. Yes, sickness, because unforgiveness can make you unhealthy. When you walk in the forgiveness of God, you can access the healing power of God and keep yourself healthy.

I hope this secret helps you when it comes to forgiving others. We never want to be in a position of not being forgiven by God. By forgiving people in advance, you always stay right with God. The devil cannot get a foothold into your heart when you live this way. You will also be able to offer the *Prayer of Faith*, which is speaking to the mountain and making it move at your command.

In conclusion, God has to hear your prayers for you to win the war of words. When God hears your prayers, you have the authority to speak to mountains. When you speak to these mountains, they will move if you are in right standing with God. The *Law of Faith* demands that you forgive others for you to be in right standing with God. A person in right standing with God can speak to any mountain and make it move because God will hear them.

CHAPTER 14

LAW #8

A PURE CONSCIENCE

Understanding the importance of a pure conscience is vital for the *Law of Faith* and speaking to mountains. This chapter will get into what your conscience is, why it is vital to keep your conscience pure, and what it means to sear your conscience and become reprobate. I will also help you understand why your conscience is not always right, but it is never right to go against it. Finally, we will reveal the purpose of the conscience when it comes to the New Covenant.

To start, let's define what your conscience is. The conscience is an inner feeling or voice that guides someone if what they are saying or doing is right or wrong. The conscience is the moral sense of right and wrong found in the heart of all humankind. The conscience is also the inner mechanism located in the heart of humankind that God uses by His Spirit to speak to and guide people. The conscience is not the Holy Spirit but is used by the Holy Spirit when God is talking to His people. People who are not Christians and do not have the Spirit of God indwelling in them still have a conscience, but it is not regenerated.

Now, let's look at what it means to sear your conscience. The word sear means to scorch the surface of something with sudden and intense heat. When the Bible speaks of a seared conscience or talks about searing the conscience, it refers to when someone hears and feels in their conscience not to do something and goes ahead and does it anyway. This person knows in their heart what they are about to say or do is wrong and still goes ahead and says or does it. Anytime someone does this, according to the Bible, they are searing or burning their conscience with a hot iron. When someone does this repeatedly, they completely burn their conscience where it will not speak to them anymore about right or wrong.

> **1 Timothy 4:1-2 (KJV)**
> *1 Now the Spirit speaketh expressly, that in the latter times **some shall depart from the faith,** giving heed to seducing spirits, and doctrines of devils; 2 Speaking lies in hypocrisy; **having their conscience seared with a hot iron;***

A seared conscience is burned to the point where it cannot feel anything concerning right or wrong. What I mean by *cannot feel anything* is that the person with the seared conscience can wrong the moral code of their conscience to the point where they do not feel bad about doing evil before the Lord. This type of person did not want to retain the knowledge of God in their mind, and they were turned over to a reprobate mind. A reprobate mind is a mind void of the judgments and Laws of God. A reprobate is someone who has completely rejected God, His Word, and His Laws. They seared their conscience over and over to the point where it is dead. A reprobate person can do all sorts of evil and not feel bad on the inside of their heart and conscience anymore. If you feel bad about sin, it is a sign you are not a reprobate.

Romans 1:28-32 (KJV)

*28 **And even as they did not like to retain God in their knowledge, God gave them over to a reprobate mind,** to do those things which are not convenient; 29 Being filled with all unrighteousness, fornication, wickedness, covetousness, maliciousness; full of envy, murder, debate, deceit, malignity; whisperers, 30 Backbiters, haters of God, despiteful, proud, boasters, inventors of evil things, disobedient to parents, 31 Without understanding, covenant breakers, without natural affection, implacable, unmerciful: 32 Who knowing the judgment of God that they which commit such things are worthy of death, not only do the same but have pleasure in them that do them.*

With this understanding of the conscience and what it means to be a reprobate, you can see why listening to and obeying your conscience is vital. If you want to be close to God and go to Heaven, you must listen to your conscience and keep it pure. A pure conscience is of high value before the Lord.

Let's look at some Scriptures that talk about a pure conscience.

1 Timothy 3:8-10 (KJV)

*8 Likewise must the deacons be grave, not double-tongued, not given to much wine, not greedy of filthy lucre; 9 Holding the mystery of the faith in **a pure conscience.** 10 And let these also first be proved; then let them use the office of a deacon, being found blameless.*

2 Timothy 1:3 (KJV)

*3 I thank God, whom I serve from my forefathers with **pure conscience,** that without ceasing I have remembrance of thee in my prayers night and day;*

Titus 1:15 (KJV)

*15 **Unto the pure all things are pure:** but unto them that are defiled and unbelieving is nothing pure; **but even their mind and conscience is defiled.***

The word pure means clean, unsoiled, and legal cleanness. Someone who has a pure conscience is spiritually clean. They are free from spiritual pollution and the guilt of sin. They are sincere, upright, and void of evil. This person walks by the moral code of their conscience and does not do anything they feel wrong about. The Spirit of God is also leading them through the voice of their conscience.

A clean and pure conscience is of great value. There is no better feeling than knowing you are in right standing with God and going to Heaven. No money could pay for you to be in this place. A pure conscience is worth more than all the money in the world. I also want to add that having a pure conscience doesn't mean you are perfect. It just means you are living up to the moral code of your own heart and mind. As a Christian, your conscience will grow as you grow in your knowledge of the Lord.

Now that you understand your conscience better, I want to explain why your conscience may not always be right, but it is never right to go against it. To understand this truth, we will look at what was happening to the Church in Corinth.

The Church of Corinth was living in the middle of the Roman pagan society. The Romans were heathens and worshipped many false gods. They even went so far as to sacrifice the meat they ate to false gods, a common practice during this time. The early Christian Church knew there was only One God, and that Jesus Christ was His Son sent from Heaven and didn't want anything to do with false gods.

However, the Church had to live and operate within the heathen society in which they lived. Let's read what the Apostle Paul had to say to the Corinthian Church considering this matter.

1 Corinthians 8:4-13 (KJV)
*4 **As concerning therefore the eating of those things that are offered in sacrifice unto idols**, we know that an idol is nothing in the world, **and that there is none other God but one.** 5 For though there be that are called gods, whether in Heaven or in earth, (as there be gods many, and lords many,) 6 **But to us there is but one God, the Father, of whom are all things, and we in him; and one Lord Jesus Christ, by whom are all things, and we by him.** 7 Howbeit there is not in every man that knowledge: **for some with conscience of the idol unto this hour eat it as a thing offered unto an idol; and their conscience being weak is defiled.** 8 But meat commendeth us not to God: for neither, if we eat, are we the better; neither, if we eat not, are we the worse. 9 But take heed lest by any means this liberty of yours become a stumbling block to them that are weak. 10 For if any man see thee which hast knowledge sit at meat in the idol's temple, **shall not the conscience of him which is weak be emboldened to eat those things which are offered to idols; 11 And through thy knowledge shall the weak brother perish, for whom Christ died?** 12 But when ye sin so against the brethren, **and wound their weak conscience,** ye sin against Christ. 13 Wherefore, if meat make my brother to offend, I will eat no flesh while the world standeth, lest I make my brother to offend.*

The Apostle Paul told them not to eat the meat sacrificed to an idol if they had a conscience about it. But he also stated that an idol is nothing and that eating this food offered to an idol was not a problem if you didn't have a conscience about it. However, if someone didn't have a conscience about it, they shouldn't eat the meat offered to an idol if it would weaken the conscience of someone who didn't have such knowledge. They had to protect the weak conscience of every believer.

In this passage, you can see an interesting fact that the conscience was not always right, but it is not right to go against it. A weak conscience could be sinned against, and it would be a sin against Christ. So, now you have a scenario in the New Testament where it is okay for one person to do something, and it is not okay for another person to do something. This is all based upon their conscience, but they still had to watch out for others in love so as not to embolden one of their fellow Christians to go against their conscience.

There is another passage in the Book of Romans where we can see this same truth, and it ties in with your faith. Your faith is connected to your conscience and the Laws of God written in your heart and mind.

Romans 14:1-6 (KJV)

1 Him that is weak in the faith receive ye, but not to doubtful disputations. 2 For one believeth that he may eat all things: another, who is weak, eateth herbs. 3 Let not him that eateth despise him that eateth not; and let not him which eateth not judge him that eateth: for God hath received him. 4 Who art thou that judgest another man's servant? to his own master he standeth or falleth. Yea, he shall be holden up: for God is able to make him stand. 5 One man esteemeth one day above another: another esteemeth every day alike. Let every man be fully persuaded in his own mind. 6 He that regardeth the day, regardeth it unto the Lord; and he that regardeth not the day, to the Lord he doth not regard it. He that eateth, eateth to the Lord, for he giveth God thanks; and he that eateth not, to the Lord he eateth not, and giveth God thanks.

The Apostle Paul, in this chapter, is saying that some Christians feel okay to eat all things and others only feel okay with eating herbs. He also gets into some feeling good about esteeming one day above another or not. This could be about the Holy Days found in the Old Testament and the Sabbath. Either way, each person had to be fully persuaded in their mind, and they had to walk by the moral compass found in their own heart, mind, and conscience. This was called living by faith. Another way to say it is that they had to live by what they believed to be right or wrong. They could not go against their own moral code, or it would be a sin to them. The teaching of faith and conscience played an important role in the lives of early believers. This was one of Apostle Paul's primary teachings. The Apostle Paul had to teach Gentile believers how to live in a pagan world without wounding their conscience.

I also want to add here that although people were to live by their own moral code in the New Testament, they were also called to protect the conscience and faith of their fellow believers. Meaning, if one of their fellow believers was weak in their faith, they had to watch what they did around them, so they would not wound their weak conscience. This means they may feel okay about eating meat sacrificed to idols, but if their fellow believer didn't believe this was right, they shouldn't eat the meat. You don't do certain things because it could embolden the weak in faith Christian to do something against their conscience and sin against the Laws of God written on their heart and mind.

Romans 14:14-17 (KJV)

14 I know, and am persuaded by the Lord Jesus, that there is nothing unclean of itself: but to him that esteemeth any thing to be unclean, to him it is unclean. 15 But if thy brother be grieved with thy meat, now walkest thou not charitably. Destroy not him with thy meat, for whom Christ died. 16 Let not then your good be evil spoken of: 17 For the kingdom of God is not meat and drink; but righteousness, and peace, and joy in the Holy Ghost.

We are called to love, help, and support our fellow believers. But with all of this being said, we can see a basic understanding of the conscience. The conscience may not always be right, but it is never right to sin against it. You, also, shouldn't sin against the weak conscience of your fellow believer.

The conscience is also tied to the faith of the believer. Faith has everything to do with what you believe. So if someone doesn't believe they should do something, they shouldn't do it. A critical Scripture that makes up one of the most fundamental truths that Christians should live by is in the Book of Habakkuk Chapter 2.

Habakkuk 2:4 (KJV)

*4 Behold, his soul which is lifted up is not upright in him: **but the just shall live by his faith.***

The just are called to live by faith. Faith has everything to do with what you believe and makes up the foundation of the whole Christian walk. Faith is a big word that encompasses the whole life of a New Testament believer. Faith is how we are saved. Faith is how we speak to mountains. Faith is how we get anything from God, and faith is how we live. Faith is also tied directly into your conscience.

Let's look at how the 14th chapter of Romans ties in with faith and your conscience.

Romans 14:20-23 (KJV)

20 For meat destroy not the work of God. All things indeed are pure; but it is evil for that man who eateth with offence. 21 It is good neither to eat flesh, nor to drink wine, nor any thing

whereby thy brother stumbleth, or is offended, or is made weak.
*22 **Hast thou faith?** have it to thyself before God. **Happy is he***
that condemneth not himself in that thing which he alloweth.
23 And he that doubteth is damned if he eat, because he eateth
not of faith: for whatsoever is not of faith is sin.

Romans Chapter 14 ends by saying that whatsoever is not of faith is sin. This means if you eat or don't eat things you feel good about or not feel good about, it is all based upon your faith. This goes for everything you do in life. If you don't feel good about something, don't do it. Your faith and belief system are constantly working with your conscience. Your conscience, however, may not be 100% right. Your conscience is only working with data and the amount of the Laws of God it knows about. Either way, you should never sin against your conscience or belief system by going against it. You should also never sin against a fellow believer's weak conscience.

These passages pose an interesting thought because sin is now varying based upon the individual's conscience. To understand what is going on here, you have to dig into the New Covenant. We know that the Old Covenant was based upon the Laws that God gave to Moses. The Jews were called to adhere to these Laws to be right with God. Jesus, however, fulfilled all of these Laws and established the New Covenant through His death, burial and resurrection.

Let's look at the passage found in the Book of Jeremiah to see what God says about the New Covenant.

Jeremiah 31:31-34 (KJV)
31 Behold, the days come, saith the Lord, that I will make a new
covenant with the house of Israel, and with the house of Judah:
*32 **Not according to the covenant that I made with their fathers***

*in the day that I took them by the hand to bring them out of the land of Egypt; **which my covenant they brake**, although I was an husband unto them, saith the Lord: 33 **But this shall be the covenant that I will make with the house of Israel;** After those days, saith the Lord, **I will put my law in their inward parts, and write it in their hearts**; and will be their God, and they shall be my people. 34 And they shall teach no more every man his neighbour, and every man his brother, saying, **Know the Lord: for they shall all know me, from the least of them unto the greatest of them, saith the Lord:** for I will forgive their iniquity, and I will remember their sin no more.*

Here we see the New Covenant was not according to the Old Covenant God made with them in the wilderness during the time of Moses. In the New Covenant, the Laws of God would be written on their inward parts and their hearts. In the New Testament, we find that He is talking about the conscience. Let's go to the Book of Hebrews to see how these Laws being written on the heart and mind tie into the conscience.

Hebrews 10:15-22 (KJV)

*15 Whereof the Holy Ghost also is a witness to us: for after that he had said before, 16 **This is the covenant that I will make with them after those days, saith the Lord, I will put my laws into their hearts, and in their minds will I write them;** 17 **And their sins and iniquities will I remember no more.** 18 Now where remission of these is, there is no more offering for sin. 19 Having therefore, brethren, boldness to enter into the holiest by the blood of Jesus, 20 By a new and living way, which he hath consecrated for us, through the veil, that is to say, his flesh; 21 And having an high priest over the house of God; 22 **Let us draw near with a*** *true heart in full assurance of faith, having our hearts sprinkled from an evil conscience,* and our bodies washed with pure water.

When someone accepts Jesus Christ into their heart and confesses Him as their Lord, Jesus' Blood cleanses their evil conscience. The Blood of Jesus is sprinkled on their heart, and their evil conscience is revived. This is another way of saying the Laws of God are written on their heart. A sign of a new born again believer is they will not want to sin anymore. Their conscience is revived, and God's Laws are written on their heart. Your conscience takes the newly written Laws of God on your heart and convicts you of right and wrong by His Spirit.

This is also another way to say they know God and don't need anyone to teach them anymore. This doesn't mean we do away with the five-fold ministry of the apostles, prophets, evangelists, pastors, and teachers. This means that everyone can know God and His Laws on their own. The five-fold ministry is sent to help people understand the New Covenant better and know God for themselves. They are sent to teach people the truth of the New Covenant and the Laws of God being written on their hearts and minds.

This is the New Covenant that Jesus established the night before He was crucified.

Matthew 26:26-28 (KJV)

*26 And as they were eating, Jesus took bread, and blessed it, and brake it, and gave it to the disciples, and said, Take, eat; this is my body. 27 And he took the cup, and gave thanks, and gave it to them, saying, Drink ye all of it; 28 **For this is my blood of the new testament, which is shed for many for the remission of sins.***

Jesus died on the cross so we could be restored to God by the remission and forgiveness of sins. Our sins were purged by the blood of Jesus. When the blood of Jesus is applied to our hearts and conscience, our evil conscience is revived to obey God.

Now you can see the importance of not sinning against your conscience. The very Laws of God are written on your heart, and your conscience is there to help you do what is right before God. The conscience works with the Laws of God written on your heart. Therefore, your conscience must be listened to, obeyed, and protected at all costs. Jesus paid a heavy price for your heart to have the Laws of God written upon it. When the blood of Jesus is applied to your heart at salvation, the Spirit of God writes the Laws of God upon your heart.

> ### 2 Corinthians 3:2-6 (KJV)
> *2 Ye are our epistle written in our hearts, known and read of all men: 3 **Forasmuch as ye are manifestly declared to be the epistle of Christ ministered by us, written not with ink, but with the Spirit of the living God; not in tables of stone, but in fleshy tables of the heart.** 4 And such trust have we through Christ to God-ward: 5 Not that we are sufficient of ourselves to think any thing as of ourselves; but our sufficiency is of God; 6 **Who also hath made us able ministers of the new testament; not of the letter, but of the spirit: for the letter killeth, but the spirit giveth life.***

A Christian becomes a law unto themselves. Meaning they no longer need just to read the Law of Moses, but they become the Law of Moses. God's Law is written on their heart. Your conscience takes the Laws of God and reminds you of them when you are faced with any decision. I also want to point out that your conscience can grow as you mature as a Christian. God by His Spirit will start teaching you more about His Laws and continually help you understand His ways.

This is why your conscience is not always right, but it is never right to go against it. A mature Christian understands the importance of listening to their conscience in everything. Your conscience will help protect your walk with God. Your conscience helps you live the moral code of God from the inside out. You don't need anyone to tell you what is wrong anymore; your own heart and conscience will convict you of right and wrong. Living by your conscience is one of the most powerful ways for a Christian to live. Your conscience can be your best friend if you obey it and your worst nightmare if you disobey it.

The Laws of God that are written upon the heart and mind is how God will judge people on Judgement Day. Your conscience is here to help guide you until you die and face God on Judgement Day.

> ### *Romans 2:12-16 (KJV)*
> *12 **For as many as have sinned without law shall also perish without law: and as many as have sinned in the law shall be judged by the law;** 13 (For not the hearers of the law are just before God, but the doers of the law shall be justified. 14 For when the Gentiles, which have not the law, do by nature the things contained in the law, these, **having not the law, are a law unto themselves: 15 Which shew the work of the law written in their hearts, their conscience also bearing witness, and their thoughts the mean while accusing or else excusing one another;)** 16 **In the day when God shall judge the secrets of men by Jesus Christ according to my gospel.***

On Judgment Day, God will judge people based upon the Laws written upon their hearts. The Judgement will be based upon if you listened to your conscience or not. Your own heart will either excuse you or accuse you based upon if you listened and obeyed the moral code inside of yourself. This will make Judgment Day very fair. God will be looking to see who obeyed their conscience.

Now that we understand the importance of living by your conscience, I want to turn your attention to how this applies to your faith and speaking to mountains. When someone lives by their conscience, they have boldness with their faith because their heart is not condemning them. When your heart condemns you, you become weak, and your prayers are not answered. To move mountains and have your prayers answered, you have to have confidence before God, and you can only have this confidence if your conscience is pure.

Let's look at a vital verse that helps to understand this truth.

> *1 John 3:19-22 (KJV)*
> *19 And hereby we know that we are of the truth, **and shall assure our hearts before him.** 20 **For if our heart condemn us,** God is greater than our heart, and knoweth all things. 21 **Beloved, if our heart condemn us not, then have we confidence toward God.** 22 **And whatsoever we ask, we receive of him, because we keep his Commandments, and do those things that are pleasing in his sight.***

This passage of Scripture says that if your heart does not condemn you, you have confidence before God. When you keep God's Commandments and do those things that are pleasing in His sight, you can ask God for things, and you will receive them. Praying to God and moving mountains has everything to do with God hearing your prayer. You have to have a pure conscience to have boldness before God, and this confidence only comes if your heart does not condemn you. Your heart will not condemn you if you are always obeying the moral compass of your conscience.

Now you can see how important it is to live by your conscience. The New Covenant is based upon the Laws of God being written upon your heart and you obeying those Laws. Your conscience is given to you to help you obey and keep the Laws of God. The Holy Spirit works with your conscience and speaks to you through your conscience to keep you pure before God. Jesus died on the cross so you could have and live by a pure conscience.

As we conclude this chapter, let's tie all of this together. Your faith has everything to do with how you live, speak, and believe. Your faith is linked to what you believe, and to live by faith, you must be living by what you believe to be true. You cannot live by faith and violate your conscience. Your conscience was given to you to help you know the difference between right and wrong. If you violate your conscience, you violate your faith. If you violate your faith, you won't have the authority to speak to mountains and make them move, and you will lose the war of words.

To speak to mountains and win the war of words, your conscience must be pure before God. You can only have a pure conscience by the Blood of Jesus and by obeying the Laws of God written on your heart. When you live by a pure conscience, you have confidence before God. When you have confidence before God, your prayers can be answered. Therefore, your faith can move mountains when you speak to them by living by a pure conscience.

Finally, you must have a pure conscience to win the war of words. The devil does not want you to understand this truth. The truth of living by your conscience will set you free and simplify your walk with God. All you have to do to be right with God is keep your conscience pure as you grow in your wisdom and understanding of God and His Word. The *Law of Faith* only works with a pure conscience. Your conscience, however, will grow in time as you learn more of God's Word, but until then, never disobey your conscience. Your conscience will always help you stay right with God as you learn His Laws and ways.

CHAPTER 15

LAW #9

KEEP THE COMMANDMENTS OF GOD

Keeping the Commandments of God is crucial to winning the war of words and living within the *Laws of Faith*. In the last chapter, I taught the importance of keeping your conscience pure. In this chapter, you will learn about keeping the Commandments of God and how it applies to the *Law of Faith*. Living by faith means living by God's Laws and keeping the Commandments of God. You cannot live by faith if you don't understand the importance of keeping God's Commandments.

Many people believe the Great Commission that Jesus gave to the Church before He left this earth is about getting people baptized into water and being saved. However, the Great Commission is about getting people saved and baptized in water and teaching people to observe everything Jesus Commanded us. The Commands of Jesus play an important role in the salvation of the believer and the preaching of the Gospel.

Let's look at what Jesus said was the Great Commission in the Book of Matthew about His Commands before He left the earth to be with His Father.

Matthew 28:18-20 (KJV)

*18 And Jesus came and spake unto them, saying, All power is given unto me in Heaven and in earth. 19 Go ye therefore, **and teach all nations,** baptizing them in the name of the Father, and of the Son, and of the Holy Ghost: 20 **Teaching them to observe all things whatsoever I have commanded you**: and, lo, I am with you always, even unto the end of the world. Amen.*

The Commands of Jesus have and will always play a big part in the preaching of the Gospel and the salvation of all humanity. Jesus did not come to earth, die on the cross, and have people believe and do whatever they wanted. Instead, Jesus expected His disciples who call Him Lord to follow and obey His Commands. Calling Jesus Lord means you do the things which He says.

Luke 6:46 (KJV)

46 And why call ye me, Lord, Lord, and do not the things which I say?

Jesus also said in the Book of John that those who loved Him would keep His Commandments. If you don't keep the Commands of Jesus, you don't love Him. We love Jesus by keeping His Word and His Commandments. The Words and Commandments Jesus taught came from our Heavenly Father.

John 14:21-24 (KJV)

21 He that hath my Commandments, and keepeth them, he it is that loveth me: and he that loveth me shall be loved of my

*Father, and I will love him, and will manifest myself to him. 22 Judas saith unto him, not Iscariot, Lord, how is it that thou wilt manifest thyself unto us, and not unto the world? 23 **Jesus answered and said unto him, If a man love me, he will keep my words**: and my Father will love him, and we will come unto him, and make our abode with him. 24 **He that loveth me not keepeth not my sayings: and the word which ye hear is not mine, but the Father's which sent me.***

The Words Jesus was speaking came directly from God the Father. It is important to note that Jesus didn't just randomly say anything He wanted to. All of Jesus' Words were of extreme importance coming from the heart of our Heavenly Father. There is a prophecy found in the Old Testament about the coming of the **Prophet** and that we were to take heed to all of the Words that He spoke, and those that didn't, God would require it of them.

Let's look at this prophecy to better understand the importance of obeying all of the Words that Jesus spoke.

Deuteronomy 18:15-19 (KJV)

*15 The Lord thy God will raise up unto thee a Prophet from the midst of thee, of thy brethren, like unto me; unto him ye shall hearken; 16 **According to all that thou desiredst of the Lord thy God in Horeb in the day of the assembly, saying, Let me not hear again the voice of the Lord my God, neither let me see this great fire any more, that I die not.** 17 And the Lord said unto me, They have well spoken that which they have spoken. 18 I will raise them up a **Prophet** from among their brethren, like unto thee, **and will put my words in his mouth; and he shall speak unto them all that I shall command him.** 19 And it shall come* *to pass, that whosoever will not hearken unto my words which he shall speak in my name, I will require it of him.*

In this passage, we see that God refers back to the people asking not to hear God's voice on the day God spoke the Ten Commandments from Mount Horeb. Verse 16, *According to all that thou desiredst of the Lord thy God in Horeb in the day of the assembly, saying, Let me not hear again the voice of the Lord my God, neither let me see this great fire anymore, that I die not.* This verse refers to one of the most amazing and powerful days on planet earth.

God spoke the Ten Commandments audibly from a mountain called Mount Sinai. Mount Sinai is also known as Horeb, the Mountain of God. The event was so terrifying that the children of Israel removed themselves and stood afar off. Then they asked Moses to speak to them and not God because they thought they would die if they continued to hear God speak. God's voice was so powerful they couldn't handle it. Moses told them that God had come to prove them and that His fear would be before their faces that they sin not.

Let's look at this event where God spoke audibly from Heaven found in Deuteronomy and spoke the Ten Commandments to the children of Israel.

Deuteronomy 5:1-29 (KJV)

*1 And Moses called all Israel, and said unto them, Hear, O Israel, the statutes and judgments which I speak in your ears this day, that ye may learn them, and keep, and do them. 2 The Lord our God made a covenant with us in Horeb. 3 The Lord made not this covenant with our fathers, but with us, even us, who are all of us here alive this day. 4 **The Lord talked with you face to face in the mount out of the midst of the fire,** 5 (I stood between the*

Lord and you at that time, to shew you the word of the Lord: for ye were afraid by reason of the fire, and went not up into the mount;) saying, 6 I am the Lord thy God, which brought thee out of the land of Egypt, from the house of bondage. 7 Thou shalt have none other gods before me. 8 Thou shalt not make thee any graven image, or any likeness of any thing that is in Heaven above, or that is in the earth beneath, or that is in the waters beneath the Earth: 9 Thou shalt not bow down thyself unto them, nor serve them: for I the Lord thy God am a jealous God, visiting the iniquity of the fathers upon the children unto the third and fourth generation of them that hate me, 10 And shewing mercy unto thousands of them that love me and keep my Commandments. 11 Thou shalt not take the name of the Lord thy God in vain: for the Lord will not hold him guiltless that taketh his name in vain. 12 Keep the sabbath day to sanctify it, as the Lord thy God hath commanded thee. 13 Six days thou shalt labour, and do all thy work: 14 But the seventh day is the sabbath of the Lord thy God: in it thou shalt not do any work, thou, nor thy son, nor thy daughter, nor thy manservant, or thy maidservant, nor thine ox, nor thine ass, nor any of thy cattle, nor thy stranger that is within thy gates; that thy manservant and thy maidservant may rest as well as thou. 15 And remember that thou wast a servant in the land of Egypt, and that the Lord thy God brought thee out thence through a mighty hand and by a stretched out arm: therefore the Lord thy God commanded thee to keep the sabbath day. 16 Honour thy father and thy mother, as the Lord thy God hath commanded thee; that thy days may be prolonged, and that it may go well with thee, in the land which the Lord thy God giveth thee. 17 Thou shalt not kill. 18 Neither shalt thou commit adultery. 19 Neither shalt thou steal. 20 Neither shalt thou bear false witness against thy neighbour. 21 Neither shalt thou desire thy neighbour's wife, neither shalt thou covet thy neighbour's house, his field, or his manservant, or his maidservant, his ox, or his ass, or any thing that is thy neighbour's. 22 **These words the Lord spake unto all your assembly in the mount out of the midst of the fire, of the cloud, and of the thick darkness, with a great voice: and he added no more.** *And he wrote them in two tables of stone, and delivered them unto me. 23* **And it came to pass, when ye heard the voice out of the midst of the darkness, (for the mountain did burn with fire,) that ye came near unto me, even all the heads of your tribes, and your elders; 24 And ye said, Behold, the Lord our God hath shewed us his glory and his greatness, and we have heard his voice out of the midst of the fire: we have seen this day that God doth talk with man, and he liveth.** *25 Now therefore why should we die? for this great fire will consume us:* **if we hear the voice of the Lord our God any more, then we shall die. 26 For who is there of all flesh, that hath heard the voice of the living God speaking out of the midst of the fire, as we have, and lived? 27 Go thou near, and hear all that the Lord our God shall say: and speak thou unto us all that the Lord our God shall speak unto thee; and we will hear it, and do it.** *28 And the Lord heard the voice of your words, when ye spake unto me; and the Lord said unto me, I have heard the voice of the words of this people, which they have spoken unto thee: they have well said all that they have spoken. 29 O that there were such an heart in them, that they would fear me, and keep all my Commandments always, that it might be well with them, and with their children for ever!*

Many people don't understand that Jesus was sent as the ***Prophet*** to come to finish what God had started speaking from the Mountain of

God that day. The children of Israel didn't want God to speak directly to them. They wanted Moses to hear from God and come and tell them what God was saying. God listened to what they requested and stopped speaking from Heaven. It wasn't until the time of Jesus that God started speaking audibly from Heaven again.

To fully grasp the significance of God speaking from Heaven, let's look at the history of God speaking audibly with His voice on the earth. The first instance is obviously in the beginning during creation. So let's look at the first recorded instance where God spoke with His creative voice in the Bible found in the first chapter of Genesis.

Genesis 1:1-3 (KJV)
*1 In the beginning God created the Heaven and the earth. 2 And the Earth was without form, and void; and darkness was upon the face of the deep. And the Spirit of God moved upon the face of the waters. 3 **And God said, Let there be light: and there was light.***

The next rerecorded time we know of God speaking on the earth was when He went to meet with Adam in the cool of the day after Adam and Eve sinned by eating of the Tree of Knowledge of Good and Evil. After Adam and Eve sinned, they realized they were naked and became afraid of God. When they heard God's voice, they were afraid and hid.

Genesis 3:8-10 (KJV)
*8 **And they heard the voice of the Lord God walking in the garden in the cool of the day: and Adam and his wife hid themselves from the presence of the Lord God amongst the trees of the garden.** 9 And the Lord God called unto Adam, and said unto him, Where art thou? 10 And he said, **I heard thy voice in the garden, and I was afraid, because I was naked; and I hid myself.***

The next time we find God speaking from the earth audibly was when He spoke the Ten Commandments from Horeb, the Mountain of God, as I mentioned before.

> **Deuteronomy 5:2-4 (KJV)**
> *2 **The Lord our God made a covenant with us in Horeb.** 3 The Lord made not this covenant with our fathers, but with us, even us, who are all of us here alive this day. 4 **The Lord talked with you face to face in the mount out of the midst of the fire,***

We don't have any record of God speaking on the earth again after He spoke the Ten Commandments until the time of Christ. God heard what they requested and stopped speaking on the earth. The next recorded instance we know of God speaking on the earth again was at the baptism of Christ by John the Baptist

> **Matthew 3:13-17 (KJV)**
> *13 **Then cometh Jesus from Galilee to Jordan unto John, to be baptized of him.** 14 But John forbad him, saying, I have need to be baptized of thee, and comest thou to me? 15 And Jesus answering said unto him, Suffer it to be so now: for thus it becometh us to fulfil all righteousness. Then he suffered him. 16 And Jesus, when he was baptized, went up straightway out of the water: and, lo, the Heavens were opened unto him, and he saw the Spirit of God descending like a dove, and lighting upon him: 17 **And lo a voice from Heaven, saying, This is my beloved Son, in whom I am well pleased.***

God spoke from Heaven once again and proclaimed that Jesus is His beloved Son, in whom He was well pleased. Now let's read the following account of God speaking on the earth during the ministry of Jesus. God says something similar to what He spoke from Heaven at

Jesus' Baptism but adds something extra. What God adds is very important to take note of. The next event of God speaking from Heaven is at the event known as the Mount of Transfiguration.

Mark 9:1-8 (KJV)

1 And he said unto them, Verily I say unto you, That there be some of them that stand here, which shall not taste of death, till they have seen the kingdom of God come with power. 2 And after six days Jesus taketh with him Peter, and James, and John, and leadeth them up into an high mountain apart by themselves: and he was transfigured before them. 3 And his raiment became shining, exceeding white as snow; so as no fuller on earth can white them. 4 And there appeared unto them Elias with Moses: and they were talking with Jesus. 5 And Peter answered and said to Jesus, Master, it is good for us to be here: and let us make three tabernacles; one for thee, and one for Moses, and one for Elias. 6 For he wist not what to say; for they were sore afraid. 7 ***And there was a cloud that overshadowed them: and a voice came out of the cloud, saying, This is my beloved Son: hear him.*** *8 And suddenly, when they had looked round about, they saw no man any more, save Jesus only with themselves.*

This time when God the Father spoke from Heaven saying that Jesus was His beloved Son, He added, *hear Him.* It was not only crucial that God wanted people to know that Jesus was His beloved Son, but the importance of listening to the Words He spoke. Jesus is that **Prophet** to come. Therefore, it is imperative for our salvation that we accept Him as our Savior, listen to, and obey all of His Words.

Now let's look at the final recorded time that God spoke from Heaven. This account occurred later on in the ministry of Jesus, and then we will get back into the importance of the Words Jesus spoke and the importance of us obeying what He said.

John 12:27-30 (KJV)

*27 Now is my soul troubled; and what shall I say? Father, save me from this hour: but for this cause came I unto this hour. 28 Father, glorify thy name. **Then came there a voice from Heaven, saying, I have both glorified it, and will glorify it again.** 29 The people therefore, that stood by, and heard it, said that it thundered: others said, An angel spake to him. 30 **Jesus answered and said, This voice came not because of me, but for your sakes.***

The Father honored His Son Jesus by speaking from Heaven during His ministry. It is interesting to note that God's voice sounded like thunder and that some people thought it was an angel speaking to Him. Jesus, however, revealed that God speaking from Heaven was for their sake, but it showed how incompatible people had become with God's voice.

Now that we have read about all of the Biblical recorded times God spoke audibly from Heaven, let's tie it all together and what it means for us today. After God spoke the Ten Commandments, we know that the children of Israel didn't want to hear God's voice anymore. They requested that Moses hear from God and tell them what God said. Later, Moses prophesied that a **Prophet** would come and speak to them all that God spoke to Him, and everything that He spoke God would require it of them.

From the Scriptures and Biblical history, we know that Jesus was that **Prophet** to come. When Jesus started His earthly ministry, He went to John the Baptist to be baptized. While He was being baptized, the Holy Spirit ascended upon Him like a dove and God the Father spoke from Heaven. First, the Father said that Jesus was His beloved Son. Next, God spoke to

Peter, James, and John on the Mount of Transfiguration, saying that Jesus was His beloved Son and for them to hear Him.

We can conclude that the Father is sending a strong message for people to hear His Son. Jesus is the **Prophet** to come, and all of His Words are of utmost importance. Most Bibles even print all of the Words of Christ in red. All of Jesus' Words must be read, memorized, studied, and most importantly, obeyed. I cannot express enough in this book the importance of adhering to all the Commands and Words of Jesus the Christ.

Now, I want to turn your attention to what Jesus had to say about His own Words.

John 5:24 (KJV)
*24 Verily, verily, I say unto you, **He that heareth my word, and believeth on him that sent me, hath everlasting life,** and shall not come into condemnation; but is passed from death unto life.*

John 6:63 (KJV)
*63 It is the spirit that quickeneth; the flesh profiteth nothing: **the words that I speak unto you, they are spirit, and they are life.***

John 7:14-19 (KJV)
*14 Now about the midst of the feast Jesus went up into the temple, and taught. 15 And the Jews marvelled, saying, How knoweth this man letters, having never learned? 16 Jesus answered them, and said, **My doctrine is not mine, but his that sent me.** 17 If any man will do his will, he shall know of the doctrine, whether it be of God, **or whether I speak of myself.** 18 **He that speaketh of himself seeketh his own glory: but he that seeketh his glory that sent him, the same is true, and no unrighteousness is in him.** 19 Did not Moses give you the law, and yet none of you keepeth the law? Why go ye about to kill me?*

John 8:26 (KJV)

*26 **I have many things to say and to judge of you:** but he that sent me is true; **and I speak to the world those things which I have heard of him.***

John 8:31-32 (KJV)

*31 Then said Jesus to those Jews which believed on him, **If ye continue in my word, then are ye my disciples indeed;** 32 And ye shall know the truth, and the truth shall make you free.*

John 8:51 (KJV)

*51 Verily, verily, I say unto you, **If a man keep my saying, he shall never see death.***

John 10:27-28 (KJV)

*27 **My sheep hear my voice, and I know them, and they follow me:** 28 And I give unto them eternal life; and they shall never perish, neither shall any man pluck them out of my hand.*

John 12:48-50 (KJV)

*48 **He that rejecteth me, and receiveth not my words, hath one that judgeth him: the word that I have spoken, the same shall judge him in the last day. 49 For I have not spoken of myself; but the Father which sent me, he gave me a commandment, what I should say, and what I should speak.** 50 And I know that his commandment is life everlasting: **whatsoever I speak therefore, even as the Father said unto me, so I speak.***

John 14:10 (KJV)

*10 Believest thou not that I am in the Father, and the Father in me? **the words that I speak unto you I speak not of myself:** but the Father that dwelleth in me, he doeth the works.*

John 14:21 (KJV)
21 He that hath my Commandments, and keepeth them, he it is that loveth me: and he that loveth me shall be loved of my Father, and I will love him, and will manifest myself to him.

John 15:3 (KJV)
3 Now ye are clean through the word which I have spoken unto you.

In the teachings of Jesus, He said that He would not judge us, but the very Words He spoke would judge us on Judgment Day. The Words of Christ will be what you are accountable for on Judgment Day. God will require of you if you listened to and obeyed the Words of Christ or not. Jesus went on to say many more things about His Words and that Heaven and earth would pass away, but His Words will never pass away.

Matthew 24:35 (KJV)
35 Heaven and Earth shall pass away, but my words shall not pass away.

To bring this all together, it is imperative that if you profess Jesus as your Lord, you must adhere to and obey all that He has said. God will require the whole world to give an account of how they handled the Words of Christ in their life. ***NO ONE CAN ESCAPE THIS FACT!***

To win the war of words and walk in the *Law of Faith*, you must obey all the Words of Christ. The Words of Christ will save your eternal soul if obeyed. All of Jesus' Words were spoken from the heart of the Father, who only desires the best for His children. God has many important things to say to His people that were spoken by Jesus the Christ that are imperative for them to hear to be saved and be prepared for the time to come.

With all this being said, the Words of Jesus Christ cannot be underestimated in the life of a believer. We need to study them, obey them, pray over them, and adhere to them in every area of our life. Our very lives depend upon them.

> *1 John 3:22 (KJV)*
> *22 And whatsoever we ask, we receive of him, because we keep his Commandments, and do those things that are pleasing in his sight.*

Those who obey the Words of Christ will be able to eat of the Tree of Life and gain access to the eternal city of God, the New Jerusalem.

> *Revelation 22:14 (KJV)*
> *14 Blessed are they that do his Commandments, that they may have right to the tree of life, and may enter in through the gates into the city.*

In conclusion, we have seen in this chapter the importance of obeying the Commands of Christ. Jesus spoke Words directly from the Father. The Words of Christ will save our soul and protect us from eternal damnation if obeyed. Jesus' Words will also help you win the war of words while on this earth. His Words have power and are the strongest Words on the planet. Walking in the *Law of Faith* will require that you read and obey everything Christ spoke. We, as Christians, must keep the Commandments of God.

CHAPTER 16

———•●•——

LAW #10
FAITH WITHOUT WORKS IS DEAD

F aith without works is dead because your faith is meaningless if you are unwilling to back your faith with action. Corresponding actions reinforce true faith. Faith is powerful, and when works back your faith, it becomes an unstoppable force that pleases God. Faith can move mountains, raise the dead, heal the sick, calm storms, cast out devils, and change lives. Faith can turn failure into victory and death into life. In this chapter, we will explore the truth of how faith must be backed by works to be genuine before God.

In the Book of James, we find the famous verse, *Faith without works is dead.*

> **James 2:20 (KJV)**
> *20 But wilt thou know, O vain man, that **faith without works is dead?***

We know that faith has to do with what you believe and speak out of your mouth. Faith, however, is a **Big** and all-encompassing word in the Christian life. Faith has a deeper meaning than just what we believe and speak. You can spend years learning all there is to know about true Biblical Faith and barely scratch the surface of all there is to know about it. God intended the whole Christian experience to be based upon our faith. This is why He said in the Book of Habakkuk, *The just shall live by his faith.*

Habakkuk 2:4 (KJV)
*4 Behold, his soul which is lifted up is not upright in him: **but the just shall live by his faith.***

To understand what God means by faith, we have to go to the chapter in the Book of Hebrews dedicated to nothing but examples of Old Testament saints who had what God calls faith. The people found in the 11th chapter of Hebrews are considered **Heroes of Faith**. This chapter can also be called the **Faith Hall of Fame**. Let's study this exciting chapter together and see how these **Heroes of Faith** combined their faith with their works to please God.

Hebrews 11:1-2 (KJV)
*1 Now faith is the substance of things hoped for, the evidence of things not seen. 2 **For by it the elders obtained a good report.***

The elders or the **Heroes of Faith** obtained a good report by their faith. A good report means to testify to the truth of what one has seen, heard, or knows about God. These **Heroes of Faith** used their faith to testify what they knew to be true about the invisible God. They had faith in things not seen, which gave them a good report.

Hebrews 11:3 (KJV)
*3 **Through faith we understand that the worlds were framed by the word of God,** so that things which are seen were not made of things which do appear.*

The first example we have of faith is God Himself. God used His faith to create and frame the worlds. Faith has its original roots in God Himself.

God is a God of faith, and He lives by the same faith He expects His children to live by. God believes, speaks, creates, works, and wars all by His faith. God is the **GREATEST** example of faith you will ever find, and He backs His faith with works. This is why you cannot please God without faith.

Hebrews 11:6 (KJV)
*6 **But without faith it is impossible to please him:** for he that cometh to God **must believe** that he is, and that he is a rewarder of them that diligently seek him.*

Now, let's look at some examples of people who had faith in God and showed it by their actions in this great chapter.

Hebrews 11:4 (KJV)
*4 **By faith Abel offered unto God a more excellent sacrifice than Cain,** by which he obtained witness that he was righteous, God testifying of his gifts: and by it he being dead yet speaketh.*

Abel's act of faith was to offer God a more excellent sacrifice than Cain.

Hebrews 11:7 (KJV)
*7 **By faith Noah, being warned of God of things not seen as yet, moved with fear, prepared an ark** to the saving of his house; by the which he condemned the world, and became heir of the righteousness which is by faith.*

Noah's work of faith was to build an ark before the flood came.

Hebrews 11:8-10 (KJV)
*8 **By faith Abraham, when he was called to go out into a place which he should after receive for an inheritance, obeyed;** and he went out, not knowing whither he went. 9 By faith he sojourned*

in the land of promise, as in a strange country, dwelling in tabernacles with Isaac and Jacob, the heirs with him of the same promise: 10 For he looked for a city which hath foundations, whose builder and maker is God.

Abraham's work of faith was to obey God to leave where he was and go to a place where he didn't know where he was going.

Hebrews 11:17 (KJV)
*17 **By faith Abraham, when he was tried, offered up Isaac:** and he that had received the promises offered up his only begotten son,*

Abraham's most remarkable work of faith was to offer up his son Isaac to die on an altar as a sacrifice in obedience to God.

James 2:20-22 (KJV)
*20 **But wilt thou know, O vain man, that faith without works is dead? 21 Was not Abraham our father justified by works, when he had offered Isaac his son upon the altar?** 22 Seest thou how faith wrought with his works, **and by works was faith made perfect?***

Abraham is called the father of our faith because he was one of the first to obey God and lay it all on the line when it came to his faith in God. Abraham was willing to sacrifice his son on the altar in obedience to God. This is faith and works being displayed at the highest level. But the story does not end there; Abraham believed that if Isaac died and was burned on the altar, God would raise him from the dead because he was the promised seed.

Hebrews 11:17-19 (KJV)

*17 By faith Abraham, when he was tried, **offered up Isaac: and he that had received the promises offered up his only begotten son,** 18 Of whom it was said, That in Isaac shall thy seed be called: 19 **Accounting that God was able to raise him up, even from the dead; from whence also he received him in a figure.***

Abraham believed in God in a profound and personal way by being willing to lay his son at the altar of God. Because of Abraham's great faith, he was called the friend of God.

James 2:23 (KJV)

*23 And the Scripture was fulfilled which saith, Abraham believed God, and it was imputed unto him for righteousness: **and he was called the Friend of God.***

You, too, can be called a friend of God if you have faith like Abraham.

Hebrews 11:20-21 (KJV)

*20 **By faith Isaac blessed Jacob and Esau** concerning things to come. 21 **By faith Jacob, when he was a dying, blessed both the sons of Joseph;** and worshipped, leaning upon the top of his staff.*

Sometimes the work of faith is to bless others with your words as Jacob did.

Hebrews 11:23 (KJV)

*23 **By faith Moses, when he was born, was hid three months of his parents,** because they saw he was a proper child; and they were not afraid of the king's commandment.*

The mother of Moses' work of faith was to hide her son and not fear the king's commandment to kill all male children.

Hebrews 11:24-27 (KJV)
24 By faith Moses, when he was come to years, refused to be called the son of Pharaoh's daughter; 25 Choosing rather to suffer affliction with the people of God, than to enjoy the pleasures of sin for a season; 26 Esteeming the reproach of Christ greater riches than the treasures in Egypt: for he had respect unto the recompence of the reward. 27 By faith he forsook Egypt, not fearing the wrath of the king: for he endured, as seeing him who is invisible.

Moses' work of faith was to refuse to be called the son of Pharaoh's daughter and suffer affliction with God's people. He also showed his faith by leaving Egypt and not fearing the king's wrath.

Hebrews 11:28-29 (KJV)
28 Through faith he kept the passover, and the sprinkling of blood, lest he that destroyed the firstborn should touch them. 29 By faith they passed through the Red sea as by dry land: which the Egyptians assaying to do were drowned.

By faith, Moses kept the Passover and the sprinkling of blood so the angel wouldn't kill their firstborn. They also walked on dry land when passing through the Red Sea.

Hebrews 11:30 (KJV)
30 By faith the walls of Jericho fell down, after they were compassed about seven days.

We know that the work of faith for the children of Israel was to stay silent for six days and shout on the seventh day to bring down the walls of Jericho. Sometimes your work of faith is not to do something. God told them to be silent, but they marched around the walls of Jericho for six days and seven times on the seventh day. The walls of Jericho came down in their obedience to God when they shouted.

Hebrews 11:31 (KJV)
31 By faith the harlot Rahab perished not with them that believed not, when she had received the spies with peace.

Rahab, the harlot, revealed her faith in her action when she hid the Israelite spy's from the king of Jericho when they came into her city.

James 2:25-26 (KJV)
25 Likewise also was not Rahab the harlot justified by works, when she had received the messengers, and had sent them out another way? 26 For as the body without the spirit is dead, so faith without works is dead also.

God can take a sinner, and if they show an act of faith, He will save them. But, faith must be combined with actions. If you say you believe in God, you will be required to do something. Faith being alone is dead. But, if you really believe in God, you will show your faith with a work of faith. Faith does have works, but it's not the works of the Law.

1 Thessalonians 1:3 (KJV)
3 Remembering without ceasing your work of faith, and labour of love, and patience of hope in our Lord Jesus Christ, in the sight of God and our Father;

2 Thessalonians 1:11 (KJV)
11 Wherefore also we pray always for you, that our God would count you worthy of this calling, and fulfil all the good pleasure of his goodness, and the work of faith with power:

We don't do works to go to Heaven or to get God to hear us. We do works of faith because of all that God has done for us. We respond in works of faith because we believe in God and have faith in the finished work of Christ. Our works are only in response to all that God has done for us.

Ephesians 2:8-10 (KJV)

*8 For by grace are ye saved through faith; and that not of yourselves: it is the gift of God: 9 Not of works, lest any man should boast. 10 **For we are his workmanship, created in Christ Jesus unto good works, which God hath before ordained that we should walk in them.***

Salvation and all answers to prayers are a gift from God that works cannot earn. But, because of all that God has done, we respond in good works. God has ordained us to walk in good works because of His kindness He has shown us in Christ.

To win the war of words, you must have faith, and actions must back this faith. What good is it if you have faith and don't have any actions or works to back your faith? Faith is tangible and has substance. Our faith can be seen by our words and actions. Sometimes your faith is speaking to a mountain, or it may be something God requires you to do. You may be asked to go somewhere like Abraham was or called to sacrifice something. If you have faith, it will show up in some action.

To conclude this chapter, let's ponder upon the truth that faith without works is dead. The Bible is filled with examples of **Heroes of Faith** that said or did something because they believed. Jesus, Himself, showed His faith by coming to this cursed world and dying on a cross. His faith also caused God to raise Him from the dead. God is the God of all faith, and Jesus is the most remarkable example of faith in action. Thanks be to God for all that He has done for us with His faith.

CHAPTER 17

LAW #11

Meditation + Confession
= Possession

Meditation and confession are two of the most powerful tools in the Christian's arsenal. Any Christian who uses these tools as weapons has a significant advantage in winning the war of words. Meditation gets into what you are thinking, whereas confession gets into what you are saying. When your thoughts and speech align, you can possess great answers to your prayers from God. In this chapter, I will teach you great secrets from the Word of God about the power of meditation and confession.

To start with, let's look at Joshua, one of the most outstanding men found in the Old Testament. Joshua was Moses' assistant and had seen all of God's miracles against the Egyptians. Joshua continually stayed in the Tabernacle of the Lord, even many times after Moses left. He was also one of the faithful spies who returned with a good report from the *Promised Land*. Joshua was very devoted to God and given the responsibility to lead the children of Israel into the *Promised Land* after the death of Moses.

Before Joshua went into the *Promised Land*, God gave him some charges, so he would prosper and be successful. A charge is a mandate, commandment, requirement, responsibility, or duty. Let's look at a famous verse where God charges Joshua, and let's see what this charge is.

> **Joshua 1:8 (KJV)**
> 8 **This Book of the law shall not depart out of thy mouth; but thou shalt meditate therein day and night,** *that thou mayest observe to do according to all that is written therein: for then thou shalt make thy way prosperous, and then thou shalt have good success.*

God told Joshua that the Law should not depart from out of his mouth for him to succeed. Joshua was instructed to meditate on God's Law, day and night. This meant that God's Law had to be what he thought and spoke of all day. When we read the Book of Joshua, we see that Joshua was successful, so he must have done this. At this time, the Law of Moses had only been around in the last 40 years during the wandering of the children of Israel in the wilderness. Joshua is now entering the *Promised Land.* Joshua will need the Law of God to be successful because the heart and mind of God is in all its pages. By meditating on the Law of Moses, Joshua could learn the mind and will of God.

Let's look at what the word meditation means. Meditation means to ponder in your mind over and over again. Biblical meditation is where you muse in your mind over and over the Word of God. To muse means to rotate over and over. When meditating on the Word of God, you stay focused and don't let any other thoughts in. This is very important for success because the devil likes to flood people's minds with ungodly thoughts. The devil's thoughts are of fear, doubt, and unbelief. When you practice Biblical meditation, you keep your mind and heart focused only on God, His Word, and His thoughts.

Let's look at what King David wrote about meditation in the Psalms.

Psalm 1:1-3 (KJV)
*1 Blessed is the man that walketh not in the counsel of the ungodly, nor standeth in the way of sinners, nor sitteth in the seat of the scornful. 2 **But his delight is in the law of the Lord; and in his law doth he meditate day and night. 3 And he shall be like a tree planted by the rivers of water, that bringeth forth his fruit in his season; his leaf also shall not wither; and whatsoever he doeth shall prosper.***

King David said that the man who didn't walk in the counsel of the ungodly, and didn't stand in the way of sinners, or sit in the seat of the scornful but instead meditated on God's Law day and night would prosper in whatever he does. A godly man stays far away from the thoughts and speech of wicked people. He constantly meditates on God's Laws. The devil can use sinful people to bring his thoughts to a person so they will think and speak his demonic thoughts. We must resist the devil, and he will flee. How do you do this? By meditation and using God's Words to combat ungodly speech. This is one way you can win the war of words.

Let's look at more verses on meditation from the Book of Psalms:

Psalm 77:12 (KJV)
*12 **I will meditate also of all thy work, and talk of thy doings.***

Psalm 119:48 (KJV)
*48 My hands also will I lift up unto thy Commandments, which I have loved; **and I will meditate in thy statutes.***

Psalm 119:78 (KJV)

*78 Let the proud be ashamed; for they dealt perversely with me Without a cause: but **I will meditate in thy precepts**.*

Psalm 119:148 (KJV)

*148 Mine eyes prevent the night watches; that **I might meditate in thy word**.*

Meditation on God's Word played a big part in the lives of Jews in the Old Testament. Let's now look into the New Testament and see what it says about meditation.

1 Timothy 4:14-15 (KJV)

*14 Neglect not the gift that is in thee, which was given thee by prophecy, with the laying on of the hands of the presbytery. 15 **Meditate upon these things; give thyself wholly to them; that thy profiting may appear to all**.*

The Apostle Paul told Timothy to meditate and give himself wholly to the gift given to him by prophecy and laying on of hands by the presbytery. Paul said that his profiting would appear to all if he did this. Or, in other words, everyone would see how this meditation changed him for the better.

I have also learned a secret that I call *Holy Spirit Meditation*. This is where I find a quiet place to focus on Scriptures, things God has said to me, or questions I have for Him about the Bible. I have found that if I can connect with the Holy Spirit during this time in my spirit, He will start to talk with me and lead me down a path of thought as He brings answers to me. I have done this many times, and the revelations that God has given me have greatly helped me. Because these times are so precious, I try to have them as much as possible. Another thing I do during this time is to stay still and listen to God

Psalm 46:10 (KJV)

*10 **Be still, and know that I am God:** I will be exalted among the heathen; I will be exalted in the earth.*

The word *still* here can also mean to relax. When you quiet your soul and the voices around you and get still before God, He can talk to you. The more you do this, the more acquainted you will become with His voice. It works well whenever you have a question or a thought. He can take you down a path of thinking and bring answers to your questions. You must learn how to meditate even when at work. Meditation can also be all of the thoughts flowing through your mind. You can only think one thing at a time, so it is vital to stay focused on God and His Word. God also says that those who keep their minds on Him would be kept in perfect peace because they trust Him.

Isaiah 26:3 (KJV)

*3 Thou wilt keep him in **perfect peace, whose mind is stayed on thee**: because he trusteth in thee.*

You have to force your mind to stay in God's Word and His thoughts. The devil comes in to distract and pull you away from God's inner thoughts and peace. Some of the most significant attacks on Christians come from distractions. If the devil can get you to think other thoughts than what God wants you to think, he can dominate you.

To conclude the subject on meditation, be conscious that you are in a war of words, and it begins with your thought life. You have to take control of your thoughts and stay focused on: God, His Word, and the things He has prophesied over you. The more you practice meditating on these things; your mind will get stronger. The stronger your mind gets, the easier it becomes to focus and have quiet time with God. Meditation is a big step to success in winning the war of words.

Now, let's turn our attention to confession. Meditation has to do with your thought life, whereas confession has to do with the words coming out of your mouth. Let's go back to Joshua 1:8 to understand this better.

Joshua 1:8 (KJV)

*8 **This Book of the law shall not depart out of thy mouth;** but thou shalt meditate therein day and night, that thou mayest observe to do according to all that is written therein: for then thou shalt make thy way prosperous, and then thou shalt have good success.*

God told Joshua that the Law of God had to stay in his mouth for him to be prosperous and have good success. We know he did this because he was successful. We just finished exploring the power of meditation and keeping your mind on God. Now, we have to see the power of speaking God's Word all day long. The devil wants to get God's people to say the thoughts he gives them. The devil's thoughts have to do with fear, lack, doubt, and defeat. Ephesians 6:13 says to stand in these evil days. The devil comes in like a flood and tries to get God's people off track.

One of the great promises of God concerning His Word being in our mouth is in the Book of Isaiah. Let's look at this verse together.

Isaiah 59:21 (KJV)

*21 As for me, this is my covenant with them, saith the Lord; My spirit that is upon thee, **and my words which I have put in thy mouth, shall not depart out of thy mouth, nor out of the mouth of thy seed, nor out of the mouth of thy seed's seed,** saith the Lord, from henceforth and forever.*

God made a covenant that His Word would not depart out of the mouth of those He was in covenant with and their seed after them. For His people to be successful and win the war of words, God knows they would need to put His Word in their mouths. The devil cannot touch or defeat a Christian who has God's Word not only in their thoughts but coming out of their mouth. Keep notice whenever you are under a spiritual attack, you get flooded with negative thoughts of fear. At that moment, you have a choice of what you are going to do. You can back off and live in that fear, or you can stand up and fight by taking God's Word and speaking it out of your mouth.

I don't care what you are facing. If you allow God's Word to flow out of your mouth and believe it with your heart, you will win! Many people don't know this, but Jesus not only came to save us from our sins, but He also came to teach us what to confess. Your confession will have everything to do with your victory on the day of your attack of words. Let's look at this truth of Jesus being the Apostle and High Priest of our confession found in the Book of Hebrews.

Hebrews 3:1 (KJV)
1 Wherefore, holy brethren, partakers of the Heavenly calling, ***consider the Apostle and High Priest of our profession, Christ Jesus;***

The word profession means confession in Greek. Apostle means sent one, so He is saying that Jesus was sent as an Apostle and High Priest of our confession. The word confession means to say the same thing. This means we are to say the same thing Jesus is saying and say it over and over again. You have to say what Jesus is saying, and you have to keep saying it over and over. It's not good enough to make a bold confession and then later violate that confession by saying something different.

When someone starts to grow in their faith and get answers from God, they will find their thoughts and words align with God's thoughts and Words. A person of great faith will know they have the answer even before it manifests. The real battle is when you believe and repeatedly speak God's Word while waiting for the manifestation of the promise. Some Christian minds are weak, so they cannot maintain saying what God is saying while under attack. But we as Christians must hold fast to our confession and never back off.

> *Hebrews 4:14 (KJV)*
>
> *14 Seeing then that we have a great high priest, that is passed into the Heavens, Jesus the Son of God, **let us hold fast our profession.***

The word profession here also means confession in Greek. So we fight the good fight of faith by holding to our confession.

> *1 Timothy 6:12 (KJV)*
>
> *12 **Fight the good fight of faith,** lay hold on eternal life, whereunto thou art also called, **and hast professed a good profession before many witnesses.***

Your good confession (profession) will bring possession of what you are believing God for. Keeping your mouth filled with the Word of God is the key. The fight of faith is in your mouth. Your words have to battle the words of the devil until you prevail. You have to maintain this good confession (profession) with a bold fierceness until you win.

Here are some confessions you can speak straight from the Word of God to help you when you are in a battle of words.

> *Philippians 4:13 (KJV)*
>
> *13 I can do all things through Christ which strengtheneth me.*

Philippians 4:19 (KJV)

19 But my God shall supply all your need according to his riches in glory by Christ Jesus.

Psalm 91:2-4 (KJV)

2 I will say of the Lord, He is my refuge and my fortress: my God; in him will I trust. 3 Surely he shall deliver thee from the snare of the fowler, and from the noisome pestilence. 4 He shall cover thee with his feathers, and under his wings shalt thou trust: his truth shall be thy shield and buckler.

Psalm 23:1 (KJV)

1 The Lord is my shepherd; I shall not want.

3 John 1:2 (KJV)

2 Beloved, I wish above all things that thou mayest prosper and be in health, even as thy soul prospereth.

Psalm 118:17 (KJV)

17 I shall not die, but live, and declare the works of the Lord.

Matthew 6:33 (KJV)

33 But seek ye first the kingdom of God, and his righteousness; and all these things shall be added unto you.

Psalm 37:25 (KJV)

25 I have been young, and now am old; yet have I not seen the righteous forsaken, nor his seed begging bread.

Hebrews 13:5-6 (KJV)

5 Let your conversation be without covetousness; and be content with such things as ye have: for he hath said, I will never leave thee, nor forsake thee. 6 So that we may boldly say, The Lord is my helper, and I will not fear what man shall do unto me.

There are so many verses we can use to confess over our lives. These are just a few. You can take any Scripture with a promise from God in it and turn it into a confession. The key is to keep speaking the Word of God over your life all day long. Use your mouth for God, and never speak any thoughts from the devil. This is the secret to winning the war of words and prospering in everything you do. God's Word in your mouth is like a two-edged sword. It will slice, dice, and cut out everything the devil has spoken to you. This battle will take everything you have, but you will win every time without fail when you are committed to God and His Word. All of God's promises are sure and steadfast.

Now, let's look at what Jesus had to say about your confession and speaking to mountains in Mark 11.

> ### Mark 11:22-24 (KJV)
> *22 And Jesus answering saith unto them, **Have faith in God.** 23 For verily I say unto you, That whosoever **shall say** unto this mountain, Be thou removed, and be thou cast into the sea; and shall not doubt in his heart, but shall believe that those things which **he saith** shall come to pass; he shall have whatsoever **he saith**. 24 Therefore I say unto you, What things soever ye desire, when ye pray, believe that ye receive them, and ye shall have them.*

Jesus said three times that you have to say it. The mountain needs to hear you say it over and over. There is a famous story about Elijah when he prayed for it to rain, and James connects this story to receiving healing by the *Prayer of Faith* being offered by Church elders. Let's look at this passage of Scripture together.

James 5:14-18 (KJV)

*14 Is any sick among you? **let him call for the elders of the Church;** and let them pray over him, anointing him with oil in the name of the Lord: 15 **And the Prayer of Faith shall save the sick,** and the Lord shall raise him up; and if he have committed sins, they shall be forgiven him. 16 Confess your faults one to another, and pray one for another, that ye may be healed. The effectual fervent prayer of a righteous man availeth much. 17 **Elias was a man subject to like passions as we are**, and he prayed earnestly that it might not rain: and it rained not on the earth by the space of three years and six months. 18 **And he prayed again, and the Heaven gave rain, and the earth brought forth her fruit.***

When we go back and look into the story of Elijah praying for it to rain, we see that he sent his servant seven times to the ocean to look for a storm. Elijah kept praying over and over. We know that the *Prayer of Faith* that saves the sick is a spoken word over the person with the sickness. Someone has to command them to be healed. Now, we know that God already healed them, but to get it to manifest, someone has to speak directly to the problem and keep speaking to it until it manifests. The sick person should also talk to the sickness and be in agreement. This is how you get miracles to manifest. Let's take a deeper look at Elijah's story in the Old Testament praying for rain and see how it ties in with people getting healed by the *Prayer of Faith.*

1 Kings 18:42-44 (KJV)

*42 So Ahab went up to eat and to drink. And Elijah went up to the top of Carmel; and he cast himself down upon the earth, and put his face between his knees, 43 And said to his servant, Go up now, look toward the sea. And he went up, and looked, and said, There is nothing. And he said, **Go again seven times. 44 And it came to***

pass at the seventh time, that he said, Behold, there ariseth a
little cloud out of the sea, like a man's hand. And he said, Go
up, say unto Ahab, Prepare thy chariot, and get thee down that
the rain stop thee not.

Elijah maintained his confession seven times before the rain manifested. Elijah would have kept his confession going longer if he had to, but seven confessions were all it took. When you are in a war of words, you may have to keep your confession going for a while. It all depends on how many evil words you are up against. However, a person of great faith will understand the battle and lock in with their confession until the promise of God manifests, no matter how long it takes.

In the next chapter, I will discuss how patience plays a big part in the *Law of Faith*. Some battles take time to win, but we must persevere through faith and patience to inherit the promises. We are in a war of words and what we confess regularly plays a big part in us winning the war of words. Our confession comes from within our hearts, where we should be meditating on God and His Word all day long. Those who meditate on God's Word all day long and confess what God says will always win the war of words.

In conclusion, Christians must maintain their meditation and confession on God's Word to win the war of words. God sent His Word to save, heal and deliver us. We may not see God with our natural eyes during our lifetime, but we do have His written Word. God's Word was given to us to meditate on and speak. Through meditation, we can understand God and His will in a greater way. We can overcome the devil and win the war of words by confessing what we have meditated on in God's Word. The devil comes to stop this whole process and get you to think and speak his words. Now that you understand where the battle is, you will be better equipped to face the war of words and win every time.

CHAPTER 18

LAW #12
Patience and Faith
Inherits the Promises

P atience is one of the most important virtues to have as a Christian. Patience is also one of the most important things to understand regarding your faith, inheriting promises, and winning the war of words. We are going to dig deep into this subject in this chapter, and in the end, you will see why it is essential to have faith and patience when inheriting the promises of God.

Patience is defined as having long-endurance, perseverance, and the ability to remain strong in the face of delays or trouble without getting upset and staying calm when dealing with problems or difficult people. Finally, patience is also defined as keeping your faith by never losing your trust in God while waiting for Him to answer your prayers or to fulfill a promise.

The Book of James says that when you let patience have its perfect work, you will be perfect and entire wanting nothing.

James 1:4 (KJV)
4 But let patience have her perfect work, that ye may be perfect and entire, wanting nothing.

The Book of Hebrews says for us not to be slothful but to follow those who inherit the promises through faith and patience.

Hebrews 6:12 (KJV)
12 That ye be not slothful, but followers of them who through faith and patience inherit the promises.

The Book of Hebrews goes on to say that you need patience and that after you have done the will of God, you might receive the promise.

Hebrews 10:36 (KJV)
36 For ye have need of patience, that, after ye have done the will of God, ye might receive the promise.

We are also to look to Jesus and run with patience the race set before us.

Hebrews 12:1-2 (KJV)
*1 Wherefore seeing we also are compassed about with so great a cloud of witnesses, let us lay aside every weight, and the sin which doth so easily beset us, **and let us run with patience the race that is set before us,** 2 Looking unto Jesus the author and finisher of our faith; who for the joy that was set before him endured the cross, despising the shame, and is set down at the right hand of the throne of God.*

Many Christians understand that they have to have faith but sometimes fall into discouragement when they think an answer to their prayer is taking too long or may not come. Some Christians give up and start speaking in fear, doubt, and unbelief when they don't see a promise from God fulfilled right away. They fail to see that when they put their faith to work, things go into motion immediately in the spirit world. The spirit world is unseen to us but is very seen to God.

The Bible was written to help us see into the unseen world. Let's look at some stories in the Bible that will help us see into the unseen world and why it was important for people to keep their faith while believing God for an answer to their prayer. For the first story, let's look at the birth of John the Baptist. Zacharias and Elisabeth, the parents of John the Baptist, had prayed for a child for many years. We see this when the angel Gabriel appears to Zacharias in the Temple of God.

> ### Luke 1:13 (KJV)
> *13 But the angel said unto him, Fear not, Zacharias: **for thy prayer is heard;** and thy wife Elisabeth shall bear thee a son, and thou shalt call his name John.*

Zacharias and Elisabeth were now past the age of having kids, but they must have prayed for a child when they were younger.

> ### Luke 1:18 (KJV)
> *18 And Zacharias said unto the angel, **Whereby shall I know this? for I am an old man, and my wife well stricken in years.***

Zacharias and his wife prayed and believed God for a child when they were younger but did not realize that God had a bigger plan in the timing of the birth of their son John the Baptist. Jesus said, later in His ministry, that John the Baptist was the greatest prophet of those born of women. What an honor!

Luke 7:28 (KJV)

*28 For I say unto you, **Among those that are born of women there is not a greater prophet than John the Baptist:** but he that is least in the kingdom of God is greater than he.*

Zacharias and Elisabeth didn't realize that God had a plan far more significant than they could ever imagine. Although they had to wait, they had the privilege of getting in on the ministry of the Son of God through the birth of their son. Zacharias also had the honor of the angel Gabriel appearing and talking with him. Very few people ever see or speak with an angel of God in their lifetime.

The Bible says that Jesus came in the fullness of time. Therefore, God needed John to be born at the perfect time to be a forerunner of Jesus and prepare the children of Israel for His ministry. You may not understand why you are waiting for an answer to your prayer but hold on because God makes all things perfect in His time. There may be a reason for a delay much more significant than you realize.

Ecclesiastes 3:11 (KJV)

*11 **He hath made every thing beautiful in his time:** also he hath set the world in their heart, so that no man can find out the work that God maketh from the beginning to the end.*

When Zacharias heard the angel speak this great news to him, he either forgot his prayer or lost all hope about having a child because of his age. As a result, Zacharias ended up in unbelief, so the angel had to shut his mouth. This part of the story is amazing when considering all we have learned about the war of words. The angel shut Zacharias' mouth until the birth of his son John because he didn't want him to say anything that would stop or hinder the miracle of God. This shows us how important words are when it comes to faith, getting answers from

God, and winning the war of words. God, actually, shut the mouth of Zacharias until his son John was born.

> ### Luke 1:18-20 (KJV)
> *18 And Zacharias said unto the angel, Whereby shall I know this? for I am an old man, and my wife well stricken in years. 19 And the angel answering said unto him, I am Gabriel, that stand in the presence of God; and am sent to speak unto thee, and to shew thee these glad tidings. 20 **And, behold, thou shalt be dumb, and not able to speak, until the day that these things shall be performed, because thou believest not my words, which shall be fulfilled in their season.***

Let's look at another famous story in the Bible where someone needed patience with their faith while waiting on God in prayer. Daniel was a man greatly beloved by God and would pray three times a day. As a result, Daniel had many visitations from God and Heavenly beings. He received deep prophetic insight concerning kingdoms and the plan of God through the centuries. Daniel was shown what was going to happen with the nations of the world.

One time, while Daniel was praying, he had a visitation, but it was taking some time for him to get an answer from God. We gain insight into the spirit world and why his answer took so long during this Heavenly visitation. This insight will help you when you are praying and not immediately seeing an answer to your prayer.

> ### Daniel 10:12-14 (KJV)
> *12 Then said he unto me, Fear not, Daniel: **for from the first day that thou didst set thine heart to understand, and to chasten thyself before thy God, thy words were heard, and I am come for thy words. 13 But the prince of the kingdom of Persia***

withstood me one and twenty days: but, lo, Michael, one of the chief princes, came to help me; and I remained there with the kings of Persia. 14 Now I am come to make thee understand what shall befall thy people in the latter days: for yet the vision is for many days.

Daniel did not know this, but his prayer was heard from the first day he prayed, but a demonic spirit hindered the Heavenly messenger from getting through to Daniel. Michael, an archangel of God, had to come in and help fight against this Persian demonic force stopping the messenger. The unseen realm operates in ways we don't understand. That is why we need the Bible to help us see into the unseen supernatural world. This story shows us once again about the war of words. The messenger came because of the words of Daniel. God heard his word as soon as he started praying, but there was a fight for Daniel to get his answer. If Daniel had lost patience and given up, he would not have received his answer.

You must understand that when God speaks, His Words don't return to Him void, but they accomplish what He sent them to do. His Word may take some time to manifest in the natural, but one thing is for sure, God's Word will always come to pass. The same is true with us when we speak God's Word. When God speaks through us, or when we put the Word of God in our mouth, it comes to pass every time. It may take some time, but it will come to pass.

Isaiah 55:10-11 (KJV)

10 For as the rain cometh down, and the snow from Heaven, and returneth not thither, but watereth the earth, and maketh it bring forth and bud, that it may give seed to the sower, and bread to the eater: 11 So shall my word be that goeth forth out of my mouth: it shall not return unto me void, but it shall accomplish that which I please, and it shall prosper in the thing whereto I sent it.

We need patience because some things take time for God to work. Your patience is so important because God needs you to stay strong in faith while He is working things out for you in the unseen realm. God's Word is the final authority, and if you have faith and will be patient, you will see His Word accomplished in your life.

A person with patience is powerful because they have the inner strength to keep believing without giving up while God is working in the unseen world on their behalf. Faith can see into the unseen world and stay strong while God does His perfect work. Patience is the ability to remain strong. When you are going through these trials, your faith is being tested; but the trying of your faith works patience.

James 1:2-3 (KJV)

*2 My brethren, count it all joy when ye fall into divers temptations; 3 Knowing this, **that the trying of your faith worketh patience.***

I also want to bring up something the children of Israel thought about God and the fulfillment of His Word. Ezekiel dealt with this issue; let's see what God had to say through Ezekiel about the timing of His Word coming to pass.

Ezekiel 12:21-25 (KJV)

21 And the word of the Lord came unto me, saying, 22 Son of man, what is that proverb that ye have in the land of Israel, saying, The days are prolonged, and every vision faileth? 23 Tell them therefore, Thus saith the Lord God; I will make this proverb *to cease, and they shall no more use it as a proverb in Israel; **but say unto them, The days are at hand, and the effect of every vision.** 24 For there shall be no more any vain vision nor flattering divination within the house of Israel. 25 **For I am the Lord: I will speak, and the word that I shall speak shall come to pass; it shall be no more prolonged:** for in your days, **O rebellious house, will I say the word, and will perform it, saith the Lord God.***

The children of Israel were trying to say that God's Word was prolonged, but God wanted them to know that His Word wouldn't be prolonged, but He was going to perform it. So, we see here they were trying to accuse God of prolonging His Word, but this is just not true. We have to stay patient because God is good and working things out for us in the unseen world. We have to have faith and patience in this war of words. Your words of faith keep God working on your behalf. If you give up on your faith and lose patience, you could lose the answer to your prayer.

Now let's look at a parable Jesus spoke concerning the timing of prayers being answered.

Luke 18:1-8 (KJV)

*1 **And he spake a parable unto them to this end, that men ought always to pray, and not to faint;** 2 Saying, There was in a city a judge, which feared not God, neither regarded man: 3 And there was a widow in that city; and she came unto him, saying, Avenge me of mine adversary. 4 **And he would not for a while:** but afterward he said within himself, Though I fear not God, nor regard man; 5 Yet because this widow troubleth me, I will avenge her, **lest by her continual coming she weary me.** 6 And the Lord said, Hear what the unjust judge saith. 7 **And shall not God*** *avenge his own elect, which cry day and night unto him, though he bear long with them? 8 I tell you that he will avenge them speedily. Nevertheless when the Son of man cometh, shall he find faith on the earth?*

Jesus told this parable about the unjust judge and the persistency of the widow. This is how God wants us to be with our prayers of faith. We are never to faint, and if an unjust judge will answer this widow for bugging him, how much more our Heavenly Father answers our prayers? The key is to mix your faith with your patience and never give up. Jesus is telling us in this passage to bug God until you get your answer. Your patience keeps your faith alive and invokes God to work in the unseen world to answer your prayer.

In conclusion, we can see the importance of staying strong in our faith while patiently waiting for God to answer our prayers. God works all things out in His timing. There are many unknown factors to us but known to God when He is answering our prayers. These factors determine when you receive answers to your prayers. God will always come through for you if you have faith and patience. Don't be a person who gives up. You need to understand the importance of Biblical patience if you are going to win the war of words. Genuine faith never gives up but remains faithful to the end.

—●◆●—

CHAPTER 19

LAW #13

Prayer and Fasting

P rayer and fasting played an essential role in the life and ministry of Jesus Christ. Jesus, and the Bible, have a lot to say when it comes to prayer and fasting. This chapter will explore what Jesus and the Bible say about prayer and fasting and how they tie into the *Law of Faith* and winning the war of words. To win the war of words, you must understand the significance of prayer and fasting.

As much as Jesus was a man of prayer and fasting, He taught His disciples to pray and fast in private. During the time of Jesus, the religious leaders made a great show to everyone with their prayer and fasting. Jesus called them hypocrites because prayer and fasting were to be done in secret before God. Jesus taught His disciples if they prayed and fasted in secret, their Heavenly Father would reward them openly. Prayer and fasting were never meant to be religious acts that people did to show off how spiritual they were.

Let's look at what Jesus had to say about these subjects from the Bible. We will first start with prayer.

Matthew 6:5-8 (KJV)

*5 **And when thou prayest, thou shalt not be as the hypocrites are:** for they love to pray standing in the synagogues and in the corners of the streets, that they may be seen of men. Verily I say unto you, They have their reward. 6 **But thou, when thou prayest,** enter into thy closet, and when thou hast shut thy door, **pray to thy Father which is in secret; and thy Father which seeth in secret shall reward thee openly.** 7 But when ye pray, use not vain repetitions, as the heathen do: for they think that they shall be heard for their much speaking. 8 Be not ye therefore like unto them: for your Father knoweth what things ye have need of, before ye ask him.*

Jesus taught His followers that prayer was something to be done in secret between you and your Heavenly Father. When your Heavenly Father saw you pray in secret, He would reward you openly. The reward would be that He heard you and answered your prayer. You were also not to use vain repetitions. Your Heavenly Father is a real person, and you can talk to Him from your heart. But, we are not to go to God in fear, doubt, or unbelief. Instead, we are to pray and speak to Him in faith.

Now, let's see what Jesus had to say about fasting.

Matthew 6:16-18 (KJV)

*16 **Moreover when ye fast, be not, as the hypocrites, of a sad countenance:** for they disfigure their faces, that they may appear unto men to fast. Verily I say unto you, They have their reward. 17 But thou, when thou fastest, anoint thine head, and wash thy face; 18 That thou appear not unto men to fast, but unto thy Father which is in secret: **and thy Father, which seeth in secret, shall reward thee openly.***

Jesus taught His followers that fasting was also always to be done in secret. You are not even to appear that you are fasting when you are fasting. If you are fasting and want God, the Father, to hear you, you must fast in secret. The purpose of fasting is to set yourself apart to get closer to God and have Him listen to you. You are shutting down your appetite to draw closer to God. Jesus said any fasting done to be seen by man and not God was hypocritical. Jesus confronted religious hypocrisy whenever He could.

In the Scriptures, I want to point out that we read many things Jesus had to say about fasting, but we don't read much about Jesus fasting. You don't read much about Jesus fasting because He practiced what He preached. Jesus was fasting in secret. Jesus was not a spiritual hypocrite; He had a real and living relationship with His Heavenly Father. Jesus spent a lot of time in secret fasting and praying to His Heavenly Father.

We read about Jesus fasting during His forty days of temptation in the wilderness. Jesus was led by the Holy Spirit into this fast for forty days. This is the only recorded time we read about Jesus fasting, but it doesn't mean He wasn't fasting a lot during His ministry.

Matthew 4:1-2 (KJV)
*1 **Then was Jesus led up of the Spirit** into the wilderness to be tempted of the devil. 2 **And when he had fasted forty days and forty nights,** he was afterward an hungred.*

Jesus was set apart for forty days while He spent time with His Heavenly Father. When He reached the end of His forty-day fast, He was hungry, and this is when the devil came to tempt Him. Jesus, however, overcame every test the devil placed before Him. Jesus then came out of the wilderness and started operating in the Anointing of the Holy Spirit. By the Anointing of the Spirit, Jesus began to heal people and do signs, wonders, and miracles.

Luke 4:14-15 (KJV)

*14 **And Jesus returned in the power of the Spirit into Galilee:** and there went out a fame of him through all the region round about. 15 And he taught in their synagogues, being glorified of all.*

Jesus had fasted and prayed in secret, and the Father rewarded Him with a powerful public ministry. During Jesus' ministry, He cast out many devils, healed the sick, and performed many miracles. Jesus was also teaching His disciples to do the same. One time, however, His disciples could not cast a demon out. When Jesus came on the scene, He cast the devil out. The disciples came to Jesus and asked why they could not cast the devil out. Let's look at this story together and see what Jesus said about why they could not cast the devil out.

Matthew 17:14-21 (KJV)

*14 And when they were come to the multitude, there came to him a certain man, kneeling down to him, and saying, 15 Lord, have mercy on my son: for he is lunatick, and sore vexed: for ofttimes he falleth into the fire, and oft into the water. 16 **And I brought him to thy disciples, and they could not cure him.** 17 Then Jesus answered and said, O faithless and perverse generation, how long shall I be with you? how long shall I suffer you? bring him hither to me. 18 And Jesus rebuked the devil; and he departed out of him: and the child was cured from that very hour. 19 **Then came the disciples to Jesus apart, and said, Why could not we cast him out?** 20 And Jesus said unto them, Because of your unbelief: for verily I say unto you, If ye have faith as a grain of mustard seed, ye shall say unto this mountain, Remove hence to yonder place; and it shall remove; and nothing shall be* *impossible unto you. 21 **Howbeit this kind goeth not out but by** **prayer and fasting.***

Jesus emphasized that this type of demon would not come out unless you spent time praying and fasting. Therefore, Jesus must have already been fasting and praying, and that is why He was able to cast this devil out successfully. I also want to add how prayer and fasting help you speak to a mountain. Jesus taught that it took faith to move mountains, but in this case, it took prayer, fasting, and faith. Therefore, prayer and fasting play a vital role in the *Law of Faith*.

When you spend time praying and fasting, you set yourself apart to God. You are quieting your flesh from all the pulls of this life. You are shutting your appetite down so you can hear from God and get the answer to your prayer. When you are in a heavy battle of the war of words, prayer and fasting can help you get into deeper contact with God.

Your words have power and can move mountains, but you sometimes face strong demonic power. You might also be facing more evil words that were spoken that you have to come against. Either way, when you pray, fast, and offer the *Prayer of Faith*, God will hear you, grant you your request, and the mountain will move.

Prayer and fasting were also early Church practices in the Book of Acts.

Acts 13:1-3 (KJV)
*1 Now there were in the Church that was at Antioch certain prophets and teachers; as Barnabas, and Simeon that was called Niger, and Lucius of Cyrene, and Manaen, which had been brought up with Herod the tetrarch, and Saul. 2 **As they ministered to the Lord, and fasted,** the Holy Ghost said, Separate me Barnabas and Saul for the work whereunto I have called*

*them. 3 **And when they had fasted and prayed,** and laid their hands on them, they sent them away.*

Prayer and fasting play a vital role in the New Testament believer's life. Prayer is spending alone time in secret with your Heavenly Father. Fasting is the absence of eating food for a period of time. Fasting is to be done in such a way so that you don't let people know you are fasting. Sometimes, however, it can't be hidden from those you live with or are in close contact with. Either way, you are not showing off to people that you are some great spiritual person because you are praying and fasting.

Now, I want to turn your attention to another form of fasting. This form of fasting is not taught very often from the pulpit but is very important to God. God revealed through the prophet Isaiah this form of fasting. It is found in the 58th chapter of Isaiah. Let's go through some of the verses in this chapter together and see what God says about the fast He chooses.

Isaiah 58:1-3 (KJV)
*1 Cry aloud, spare not, lift up thy voice like a trumpet, and shew my people their transgression, and the house of Jacob their sins. 2 Yet they seek me daily, and delight to know my ways, as a nation that did righteousness, and forsook not the ordinance of their God: they ask of me the ordinances of justice; they take delight in approaching to God. 3 **Wherefore have we fasted, say they, and thou seest not? wherefore have we afflicted our soul, and thou takest no knowledge?** Behold, in the day of your fast ye find pleasure, and exact all your labours.*

God is calling out their transgression. Interestingly, these people sought God daily and were delighted to know God's ways. They did righteousness, didn't forsake the ordinance of God, asked God for the ordinances of justice, and they took delight approaching God. They were even fasting. God, however, pointed out their transgression. So let's see what God had against them.

Isaiah 58:4-5 (KJV)

*4 Behold, ye fast for strife and debate, and to smite with the fist of wickedness: **ye shall not fast as ye do this day, to make your voice to be heard on high. 5 Is it such a fast that I have chosen?** a day for a man to afflict his soul? is it to bow down his head as a bulrush, and to spread sackcloth and ashes under him? wilt thou call this a fast, and an acceptable day to the Lord?*

God told them that they were fasting for strife and debate. They were also hitting people with the fist of wickedness. God said they would not be heard with this type of fast. Let's see what God's fast is.

Isaiah 58:6-7 (KJV)

*6 **Is not this the fast that I have chosen?** to loose the bands of wickedness, to undo the heavy burdens, and to let the oppressed go free, and that ye break every yoke? 7 Is it not to deal thy bread to the hungry, and that thou bring the poor that are cast out to thy house? when thou seest the naked, that thou cover him; and that thou hide not thyself from thine own flesh?*

God's fast is to loose people from the bands of wickedness. God's fast is also to get people to repent, undo their heavy burdens, help the oppressed go free and break every yoke they are under. This is where you help people and help them get out of their problems and bondages. You also feed the hungry and bring the poor into your house. You clothe the naked and help people just like you would want to be helped if you were in that situation.

In the ministry and teachings of Jesus, you will find that He had great compassion for the poor. Jesus also taught His early Church to have compassion for the poor, and they carried this ministry on after His ascension into Heaven. People laid gifts at the apostle's feet in the Book of Acts, and distribution was made to help those in need.

> ### Acts 4:34-35 (KJV)
> *34 **Neither was there any among them that lacked:** for as many as were possessors of lands or houses sold them, and brought the prices of the things that were sold, 35 And laid them down at the apostles' feet: **and distribution was made unto every man according as he had need.***

The early Church carried on the teachings and ministry of Jesus when it came to prayer and fasting. The early Church also practiced the truths found in Isaiah 58. Now, let's look at the promises God made in Isaiah 58 for those who chose the fast of the Lord.

> ### Isaiah 58:8-12 (KJV)
> *8 **Then shall thy light break forth as the morning, and thine health shall spring forth speedily: and thy righteousness shall go before thee; the glory of the Lord shall be thy reward. 9 Then shalt thou call, and the Lord shall answer; thou shalt cry, and he shall say, Here I am.** If thou take away from the midst of thee the yoke, the putting forth of the finger, and speaking vanity; 10 And if thou draw out thy soul to the hungry, and satisfy the afflicted soul; **then shall thy light rise in obscurity, and thy darkness be as the noon day: 11 And the Lord shall guide thee continually, and satisfy thy soul in drought, and make fat thy bones: and thou shalt be like a watered garden, and like a spring of water, whose waters fail not.** 12 And they that shall be of thee shall build the old waste places: thou shalt raise up the foundations of many generations; and thou shalt be called, The repairer of the breach, The restorer of paths to dwell in.*

God promised that your light would break forth as the morning, and you would be healthy if you kept His fast. You will call upon the Lord, and He will answer you. You will cry, and God will say, here I am. The Lord will guide you continually and satisfy your soul in a drought. God makes many promises to the person who chooses the fast of helping the poor, weak, the naked, and people in bondage.

The whole point of praying and fasting is to get God to hear you. In this passage of Scripture, He is not only promising to listen to you but be quick about hearing you when you cry out to Him. Helping the poor and needy is a big deal to God. Feeding and taking care of the poor is on God's heart, and He will bless anyone who helps them.

> ### Proverbs 19:17 (KJV)
> *17 He that hath pity upon the poor lendeth unto the Lord; and that which he hath given will he pay him again.*

> ### Proverbs 22:9 (KJV)
> *9 He that hath a bountiful eye shall be blessed; for he giveth of his bread to the poor.*

The Apostle Paul was also eager to help the poor.

> ### Galatians 2:10 (KJV)
> *10 Only they would that we should remember the poor; the same which I also was forward to do.*

We as Christians should always be eager to help the poor at every chance we can get. Jesus taught that when we help the poor, we are helping Him, which is the fast that He has chosen. Let's look at a powerful parable Jesus taught to understand better the importance of helping others.

Matthew 25:34-40 (KJV)

*34 Then shall the King say unto them on his right hand, **Come,
ye blessed of my Father, inherit the kingdom prepared for you
from the foundation of the world:** 35 For I was an hungred, and
ye gave me meat: I was thirsty, and ye gave me drink: I was a
stranger, and ye took me in: 36 Naked, and ye clothed me: I was
sick, and ye visited me: I was in prison, and ye came unto me.*
*37 Then shall the righteous answer him, saying, Lord, when saw
we thee an hungred, and fed thee? or thirsty, and gave thee drink?
38 When saw we thee a stranger, and took thee in? or naked, and
clothed thee? 39 Or when saw we thee sick, or in prison, and
came unto thee? 40 And the King shall answer and say unto them,
**Verily I say unto you, Inasmuch as ye have done it unto one of
the least of these my brethren, ye have done it unto me.***

The ministry to the poor, naked, sick, and imprisoned is very close to
the heart of God. Let's see what else God has to say in Isaiah 58 about
His fast.

Isaiah 58:13-14 (KJV)

*13 If thou turn away thy foot from the sabbath, from doing thy
pleasure on my holy day; and call the sabbath a delight, the holy
of the Lord, honourable; and shalt honour him, not doing thine
own ways, nor finding thine own pleasure, **nor speaking thine
own words:** 14 Then shalt thou delight thyself in the Lord; and I
will cause thee to ride upon the high places of the earth, and feed
thee with the heritage of Jacob thy father: for the mouth of the
Lord hath spoken it.*

I want to point out how He says not speaking your own words. Too many
people speak their own words, which is why they have no power with God.
If you want God to hear you when you fast and pray, you must have the

heart to help others and speak God's Word. You can tell the difference between a real man or woman of God by how much they do in secret and how much they care for the poor.

If you are going to win the war of words, God must hear your words and prayers. God will listen to you if you reach out and help those in need around you. A genuine Christian spends a lot of alone time with God and helping others in secret. God loves to hear and answer our prayers when we pray in faith. When this faith is mixed with a secret life of prayer, fasting, and helping the poor, it has more power with God. This is true religion before God, according to the Book of James.

James 1:26-27 (KJV)
*26 If any man among you seem to be religious, and bridleth not his tongue, but deceiveth his own heart, this man's religion is vain. 27 **Pure religion and undefiled before God and the Father is this, To visit the fatherless and widows in their affliction,** and to keep himself unspotted from the world.*

Pure religion helps those in need. What good is it if you say you have faith but don't help people? God hates that kind of religion. God has called His Church to help the poor. God has chosen the poor to be rich in faith. We are not called to just speak words of faith over the poor, but we need to help them in their time of need as much as we can. If your faith only speaks to mountains but never helps people, what good is your faith?

James 2:14-17 (KJV)
*14 What doth it profit, my brethren, though a man say he hath faith, and have not works? can faith save him? 15 If a brother or sister be naked, and destitute of daily food, 16 And one of you say unto them, **Depart in peace, be ye warmed and filled; notwithstanding ye give them not those things which are***

needful to the body; what doth it profit? *17 Even so faith, if it hath not works, is dead, being alone.*

Jesus also taught that we were to give our alms or gifts to the poor in secret.

Matthew 6:1-4 (KJV)

1 Take heed that ye do not your alms before men, to be seen of them: otherwise ye have no reward of your Father which is in Heaven. 2 Therefore when thou doest thine alms, do not sound a trumpet before thee, as the hypocrites do in the synagogues and in the streets, that they may have glory of men. *Verily I say unto you, They have their reward. 3 But when thou doest alms, let not thy left hand know what thy right hand doeth: 4 **That thine alms may be in secret: and thy Father which seeth in secret himself shall reward thee openly.***

We are in a war of words but helping the poor is very important. We must have actions to back our words of faith. If you are going to win the war of words, you need God to hear you. God has promised to listen to you if you help the poor, naked, and destitute. What you do with the poor and needy plays a big part in winning the war of words. This is the fast that God has chosen.

I know this chapter went in a different direction than you may have expected. But there are great secrets revealed in this chapter that can help you with your walk with God. God loves for us to pray, fast, and help the poor. But He wants it to be done in secret before Him. God will hear you and reward you openly if you do these things in secret. These are the true *Laws* and *Ways* of God. This chapter is a great revealing of the *Law of Faith* being done by secret actions.

CHAPTER 20

LAW #14
FAITH WORKS BY LOVE

God is love and oversees the vastness of all that He created from His loving heart. It was by God's faith that He created everything, and He runs His Kingdom by love. However, God's love is not like man's love. God's love is far more reaching and sometimes misunderstood by humankind. This chapter will show from the Holy Scriptures how God describes His love and how faith works by love. If we are to speak to mountains and win the war of words, we need to understand God's love.

Many people declare that they know God, but the Bible is clear that the only people who know God and are born of God are the ones who know how to love.

1 John 4:7-8 (KJV)
*7 Beloved, let us love one another: for love is of God; **and every one that loveth is born of God, and knoweth God. 8 He that loveth not knoweth not God; for God is love.***

God is the essence and definition of love. Understanding what the word love means should be high on the list of every believer because God is love. To better understand love, we need to understand what the word love means. The English language only has one word for love, whereas the Greek language has multiple words for love. People who speak English use the word love for many things. English-speaking people say they love their wife, child, pet, food, and many other things with the same word. However, we know that the love for food is much different from the love for a spouse or a child. Let's look at some of the Greek language's words for love, and then we will get into the Biblical definition of God's love.

Below are some of the Greek words used for different types of love:

1. **EROS:** This is romantic, passionate love between lovers, husbands, and wives.
2. **PHILEO:** This is a love between friends and is also called brotherly love.
3. **STORGE:** This is a love for family members and parents towards their children.
4. **PHILAUTIA:** This is self-love that has to do with having a healthy self-esteem.
5. **AGAPE:** This is an unconditional and selfless love for others.

When the Bible says God is love, it uses the Greek word, *Agape*. The Greek word *Agape* is the most powerful word you can use to describe God and His love. It is through this love that God operates and runs the universe. His love works by His loving faith. For example, God lovingly created humanity and came back to die on a cross to save humanity from their sins. Everything that God does is out of His *Agape* love for others.

Let's read one of the most famous verses that tell us of God's *Agape* sacrificial love.

John 3:16 (KJV)
*16 **For God so loved the world, that he gave his only begotten Son,** that whosoever believeth in him should not perish, but have everlasting life.*

Let's dig a little deeper into this word *Agape* and its actual definition to understand who God is. The Greek word *Agape* gets into having favor, goodwill, and benevolence towards not only your neighbor but also your enemies. God's love is so deep that He even loves His enemies. Jesus died for everyone, yes, including the wretched sinners who have fallen away from God. God desires that everyone be saved and go to Heaven. God sent His Son to save the world because He loves the people of the world and does not want any of them to perish.

1 Timothy 2:1-4 (KJV)
*1 I exhort therefore, that, first of all, supplications, prayers, intercessions, and giving of thanks, be made for all men; 2 For kings, and for all that are in authority; that we may lead a quiet and peaceable life in all godliness and honesty. 3 For this is good and acceptable in the sight of God our Saviour; 4 **Who will have all men to be saved, and to come unto the knowledge of the truth.***

Until the time of Jesus, most people only loved themselves, their children, family, and friends. However, Jesus introduced a love that went far beyond natural understanding. Jesus taught His disciples to not only love their family and friends but also to love their enemies. This type of love was unheard of in the world up to this point, and indeed it shows God's heart and His *Agape* love for humankind.

> ### Matthew 5:43-48 (KJV)
>
> *43 Ye have heard that it hath been said, Thou shalt love thy neighbour, and hate thine enemy. 44 **But I say unto you, Love your enemies,** bless them that curse you, **do good to them that hate you, and pray for them which despitefully use you, and persecute you;** 45 That ye may be the children of your Father which is in Heaven: for he maketh his sun to rise on the evil and on the good, and sendeth rain on the just and on the unjust. 46 **For if ye love them which love you, what reward have ye? do not even the publicans the same?** 47 And if ye salute your brethren only, what do ye more than others? do not even the publicans so? 48 Be ye therefore perfect, even as your Father which is in Heaven is perfect.*

Jesus was introducing a revolutionary love that changed the world. It is important to understand that the Bible says we love God because He first loved us. We would not know how to truly love with the *Agape* love of God if God didn't show us how to.

> ### 1 John 4:19 (KJV)
>
> *19 **We love him, because he first loved us.***

God loved us when we were enemies to Him and showed us what real *Agape* love is. Let's look at a beautiful Scripture in the Book of Romans to better understand God's amazing *Agape* love for us.

> ### Romans 5:6-10 (KJV)
>
> *6 For when we were yet without strength, **in due time Christ died for the ungodly.** 7 For scarcely for a righteous man will one die: yet peradventure for a good man some would even dare to die.*

*8 **But God commendeth his love toward us, in that, while we were yet sinners, Christ died for us.** 9 Much more then, being now justified by his blood, we shall be saved from wrath through him. 10 For if, when we were enemies, we were reconciled to God by the death of his Son, much more, being reconciled, we shall be saved by his life.*

God did not have to send Jesus to save humanity and have Him die on a cross. He could have left us in our sins and been tormented in everlasting hell away from Him. However, God's very loving nature could not let this happen. He knew the only solution to save humankind from the fall of Adam was to send His only begotten Son, Jesus, to die on the cross. Jesus' death on the cross was the most sacrificial and highest form of *Agape* love ever demonstrated in the history of the world. Jesus went to great lengths to save us, and He gave up everything to do it.

God revealed what true *Agape* love is. *Agape* love will sacrifice and lay down one's life for another. *Agape* love is far more than just emotional love: it will forgive the worst of sinners and do everything to help them. This love and help go all the way to the point of death and is unconditional and given without reservation. God's one requirement to receive His love is to believe. To receive God's love, you have to believe and receive what God did for you in the death, burial, and resurrection of Jesus Christ.

When someone believes that God raised Jesus from the dead and confesses Jesus as their Lord, they become Christians. Once someone becomes a Christian, they know God and the ones who truly know God will love others with the same *Agape* love that God showed them. A genuine Christian who has been forgiven of their sins will love others in the same way God loved them. God revealed to all humanity how to love when He sent Jesus to the earth to die for our sins.

We also know that we are called to walk by faith when we get saved. Just like Abraham did, we are also called to live by faith.

Habakkuk 2:4 (KJV)
4 Behold, his soul which is lifted up is not upright in him: **but the just shall live by his faith.**

Faith is believing in our hearts and speaking with our mouths.

2 Corinthians 4:13 (KJV)
13 We having the same spirit of faith, according as it is written, **I believed, and therefore have I spoken; we also believe, and therefore speak;**

The point of this book is to reveal how to win the war of words with your faith. I have gone into great detail about speaking to mountains and all of the Laws that govern faith. But, if you don't have the *Agape* love in your heart and operate out of God's love, what good is it? We are not here to be mean to people and use our words for selfish gain. Jesus used His faith to speak to people's mountains and help them in their time of need. Our faith must work by love, and this *Agape* love is for everyone.

Galatians 5:6 (KJV)
6 For in Jesus Christ neither circumcision availeth anything, nor uncircumcision; **but faith which worketh by love.**

Your faith must be motivated by operating and working in *Agape* love. This love is unconditional and seeks not its own. God dedicated a whole chapter in the Book of first Corinthians to help us better understand His

Agape love. Let's walk through this chapter and see what God says about His amazing *Agape* love. The word charity used in this chapter for love is the same word for *Agape* in the Greek language. Charity is the word used by the people who translated the King James Bible from Greek to English for the word *Agape*.

1 Corinthians 13:1-3 (KJV)

*1 Though I speak with the tongues of men and of angels, **and have not charity**, I am become as sounding brass, or a tinkling cymbal. 2 And though I have the gift of prophecy, and understand all mysteries, and all knowledge; and though I have all faith, so that I could remove mountains, **and have not charity**, I am nothing. 3 And though I bestow all my goods to feed the poor, and though I give my body to be burned, **and have not charity**, it profiteth me nothing.*

If you have faith to move mountains but don't have the *Agape* love of God, it doesn't do you any good. Everything a New Testament Christian does must be motivated out of the *Agape* love of God. God, however, isn't just into good works; you must do good works out of love. Jesus died and rose again so that He could place His love in your heart. The love of God changes us from the inside out. Let's continue to see how this chapter describes and defines the *Agape* love of God in the following verses.

1 Corinthians 13:4-8 (KJV)

*4 **Charity suffereth long, and is kind; charity envieth not; charity vaunteth not itself, is not puffed up, 5 Doth not behave itself unseemly, seeketh not her own, is not easily provoked, thinketh no evil; 6 Rejoiceth not in iniquity, but rejoiceth in the truth; 7 Beareth all things, believeth all things, hopeth all things, endureth all things. 8 Charity never faileth:** but whether* *there be prophecies, they shall fail; whether there be tongues, they shall cease; whether there be knowledge, it shall vanish away.*

These are some of the best verses in the Bible that reveal the Love of God. God is love, and Jesus died for us in love. His actions show that He wants us to walk in this same type of love. This passage should be read and internalized by every believer in Christ. If you fall short in any area of these verses, you need to repent and allow God to work His perfect love in your heart. Who cares if you can speak to a mountain and make it move if you don't have the *Agape* love of God in your heart?

On the night that Jesus was betrayed, He spoke to His disciples about having this love for each other. Lets' see what Jesus had to say before He was betrayed and crucified. This is a significant passage of Scripture.

John 13:1 (KJV)
*1 Now before the feast of the passover, when Jesus knew that his hour was come that he should depart out of this world unto the Father, **having loved his own which were in the world, he loved them unto the end.***

On the night Jesus was betrayed, He gave His disciples a new commandment to love one another. Jesus taught them that people would know they were His disciples if they loved one another.

John 13:34-35 (KJV)
*34 **A new commandment I give unto you, That ye love one another; as I have loved you, that ye also love one another. 35 By this shall all men know that ye are my disciples, if ye have love one to another.***

A true mark of what a New Testament disciple was is to love the brethren with this new *Agape* love that Jesus was revealing to them. This was a love that obeyed the Commands of God, was willing to lay down their lives for God and loved any disciple of Jesus. It was also a love that loved their enemies.

> *John 15:12-14 (KJV)*
> *12 **This is my commandment, That ye love one another, as I have loved you. 13 Greater love hath no man than this, that a man lay down his life for his friends. 14 Ye are my friends, if ye do whatsoever I command you.***

Jesus taught His disciples how to love each other with God's love. In just a few hours, Jesus was betrayed and the next day crucified. Jesus came and demonstrated God's great sacrificial love. Jesus was the most loving God/Man who has ever been born into this planet. Faithful Christians who have been born again understand this love and are changed by God's love. Only God can take the hardest sinner and transform them into a beautiful Christian full of God's love. God's love is amazing in how it can change people.

Let's go back and finish reading about the *Agape* love of God in 1 Corinthians 13.

> *1 Corinthians 13:9-11 (KJV)*
> *9 For we know in part, and we prophesy in part. 10 But when that which is perfect is come, then that which is in part shall be done away. 11 **When I was a child, I spake as a child, I understood as a child, I thought as a child: but when I became a man, I put away childish things.***

We are supposed to teach our children how to love when they are young. But unfortunately, most babies are born very selfish and self-centered. A newborn babe requires the attention of a mother and father continually. Everything is about them eating and getting their sleep. If they don't get their way or their needs met, they will cry and continue to cry until they get what they want and need. When someone grows up, they are supposed to grow out of this state and learn to love others. Children whose parents showed and taught them love are better able to love others and quit being selfish.

1 Corinthians 13:12-13 (KJV)
*12 For now we see through a glass, darkly; but then face to face: now I know in part; but then shall I know even as also I am known. 13 And now abideth faith, hope, **charity, these three; but the greatest of these is charity.***

You are never the same once you experience God's *Agape* love. God came to reveal His love through Jesus Christ. It doesn't matter how much you know or how much stuff you end up with if you don't receive God's love into your heart. What does a man profit if he gains the whole world and loses his soul? Or what shall a man give in exchange for his soul? We have all heard of stories of wealthy people who were greedy and died alone in their greed. Life is much better when you experience God's love and learn how to love others. This type of life is very rewarding.

One of the most powerful ways of showing love is helping our fellow Christians in need.

1 John 3:16-18 (KJV)
*16 **Hereby perceive we the love of God,** because he laid down his life for us: and we ought to lay down our lives for the brethren.*

*17 But whoso hath this world's good, and seeth his brother have need, and shutteth up his bowels of compassion from him, **how dwelleth the love of God in him? 18 My little children, let us not love in word, neither in tongue; but in deed and in truth.***

To conclude, we are called to reveal the *Agape* love of God to this lost and dying world. Everything God does is out of love, and He works His faith by love. This love is not like worldly human love. God has called us as Christians to experience this love and give this experience to others. We are called to move mountains by faith and win the war of words, but this is to be done in the *Agape* love of God. Faith plays a vital role in the believer's life, but God always meant for this faith to operate and work by love. The *Agape* love of God has the power to change the world. All of the *Laws of Faith* work by love. Keep yourself in the love of God!

Jude 1:21 (KJV)
*21 **Keep yourselves in the love of God,** looking for the mercy of our Lord Jesus Christ unto eternal life.*

CHAPTER 21

LAW #15

THE NAME OF JESUS CHRIST OF NAZARETH

The Scriptures refer to God by many names. Each of God's names was revealed for us to know and understand who God is and what He can do. One name could never fully describe all that God is and all that He can do. God is big, powerful, mighty, and wonderful; therefore, He needs many names to help us understand the full measure of who He is. In this chapter, I will reveal the significance of God's Names, the significance of people's names in the Bible, and finally, the power of **The Name of the Lord Jesus Christ of Nazareth**.

From the Scriptures, we can see that God placed importance on people's names. God used people's names to reveal an aspect of Himself and a person's God-given destiny. In some cases, God named people before they were born to represent what they were called to do. In other cases, God changed people's names after they were born because their original name didn't fully represent who He called them to be or what He called them to do.

Here is a list of people from the Bible who God changed their names to better suit what they were called to do:

1. **ABRAM** (Exalted Father) to **ABRAHAM** (Father of a Multitude) – Genesis 17:5
2. **SARAI** (My Princes) to **SARAH** (Mother of Many Nations) – Genesis 17:15
3. **JACOB** (Supplanter, Deceiver) to **ISRAEL** (Prince with God) – Genesis 32:27-28
4. **SIMON** (To Hear) to **PETER** (A Stone, Rock) – John 1:41-42; Matthew 16:17-18

All of these people played an essential role in the plan of God. God changed their names to match who they were called to be while fulfilling His will on the earth. If you study the names of people God used in the Bible who didn't have their name changed, you will find their name already represented them correctly for who they were and what they were called to do. Their parents knowingly or unknowingly named them correctly in God's eyes.

Here is a list of some people God named in the Bible before they were born and what their names mean.

1. **ISHMAEL** (God Will Hear) – Genesis 16:11
2. **ISAAC** (Laughter) – Genesis 17:19
3. **SOLOMON** (Peace) – 1 Chronicle 22:9
4. **JOSIAH** (God Supports and Heals) – 1 Kings 13:2

5. JOHN (Jehovah Has Been Gracious and Shown Favor) – Luke 1:13

6. JESUS (God Is Salvation) – Matthew 1:21

As you can see, a person's name is important to God. Jesus will give the overcomers who go to Heaven a stone that has a new name written on it that only they will know.

Revelation 2:17 (KJV)

*17 He that hath an ear, let him hear what the Spirit saith unto the Churches; To him that overcometh will I give to eat of the hidden manna, **and will give him a white stone, and in the stone a new name written, which no man knoweth saving he that receiveth it.***

Now let's look at some of the important Names of God found in the Old Testament. God revealed each of His names throughout the history of the Bible for a reason. Each of God's names represented who He is and what He does or will do. God did not reveal all of His Names at once. Some of His Names were revealed at specific times in Biblical history for specific reasons.

1. ELOHIM: God, Supreme One, Mighty One, God the Creator (Genesis 1:1)

2. EL-SHADDAI: God Almighty, All-Sufficient One (Genesis 17:1)

3. I AM THAT I AM (YAHWEH): The Self Existing One, Eternal God (Exodus 3:14)

4. JEHOVAH: I Am The One Who Is (Exodus 6:3)

5. **JEHOVAH JIREH:** The LORD our Provider (Genesis 22:14)

6. **JEHOVAH RAPHA:** The LORD our Healer (Exodus 15:26)

7. **JEHOVAH NISSI:** The LORD our Banner (Exodus 17:15)

8. **JEHOVAH SHALOM:** The LORD our Peace (Judges 6:24)

9. **JEHOVAH RAAH:** The LORD our Shepherd (Psalms 23:1)

10. **JEHOVAH TSIDKENU:** The LORD our Righteousness (Jeremiah 23:6)

11. **JEHOVAH SHAMMAH:** The LORD is Here (Ezekiel 48:35)

It is essential to know and understand the Names of God. God has revealed Himself through all of these Holy Names so we can understand who He is and what He can do for us. God cannot be understood or described in just one Name because He is too wonderfully *Big!* We will be spending all of eternity getting to know how *Big* God is.

Now that we understand the importance of names and God's Names, let's get into the real purpose of this chapter. This chapter is about **The Name of the Lord Jesus Christ of Nazareth.**

> *Luke 1:30-33 (KJV)*
> *30 And the angel said unto her, Fear not, Mary: for thou hast found favour with God. 31 And, behold, thou shalt conceive in thy womb, and bring forth a son, **and shalt call his name Jesus.** 32 He shall be great, and shall be called the Son of the Highest: and the Lord God shall give unto him the throne of his father David: 33 And he shall reign over the house of Jacob for ever; and of his kingdom there shall be no end.*

God gave Jesus His Name through the angel Gabriel before Jesus was born. Jesus' Name means ***Savior or God is Salvation***. Jesus is our

Savior. God specifically Named His Son Jesus because He would be the *Savior* of the world, and anyone who called upon the Name of Jesus would be saved.

Now you have to ask yourself, what is He saving us from? This is very important to ask yourself. First, Jesus saves us from whatever problem we face; this includes problems we face in this life and, yes, saving us from going to hell. To understand this truth of Jesus the Christ saving us from problems we face during this life and not just saving us from hell, we have to look at what Jesus was anointed to do in Isaiah 61. Christ means *Anointed One*.

> ### *Isaiah 61:1-3 (KJV)*
> *1 The Spirit of the Lord God is upon me; because the Lord hath anointed me to preach good tidings unto the meek; he hath sent me to bind up the brokenhearted, to proclaim liberty to the captives, and the opening of the prison to them that are bound; 2 To proclaim the acceptable year of the Lord, and the day of vengeance of our God; to comfort all that mourn; 3 To appoint unto them that mourn in Zion, to give unto them beauty for ashes, the oil of joy for mourning, the garment of praise for the spirit of heaviness; that they might be called trees of righteousness, the planting of the Lord, that he might be glorified.*

When God anointed Jesus through John the Baptist, He went about doing good and healing all that the devil oppressed. Jesus quoted this verse from Isaiah 61 when He went back to His hometown of Nazareth after He was baptized and tempted in the wilderness by the devil.

> ### *Luke 4:16-20 (KJV)*
> *16 And he came to Nazareth, where he had been brought up: and, as his custom was, he went into the synagogue on the sabbath*

*day, and stood up for to read. 17 And there was delivered unto him the Book of the prophet Esaias. And when he had opened the book, he found the place where it was written, 18 **The Spirit of the Lord is upon me, because he hath anointed me to preach the gospel to the poor; he hath sent me to heal the brokenhearted, to preach deliverance to the captives, and recovering of sight to the blind, to set at liberty them that are bruised, 19 To preach the acceptable year of the Lord.** 20 And he closed the book, and he gave it again to the minister, and sat down. And the eyes of all them that were in the synagogue were fastened on him.*

During the ministry of Jesus, He saved people from blindness, demons, death, storms, fevers, poverty, and sicknesses. Finally, He went to the cross and rose again to save people from their sins and restore people to God so they could go to Heaven. Therefore, Jesus is **The Savior** of the world, and His Name is **Great** for all those who call upon Him. Because Jesus came to this earth, humbled Himself, and died on the cross, God made His Name greater than any other name. Therefore, every tongue will confess that Jesus Christ is Lord.

Philippians 2:5-11 (KJV)

*5 Let this mind be in you, which was also in Christ Jesus: 6 Who, being in the form of God, thought it not robbery to be equal with God: 7 But made himself of no reputation, and took upon him the form of a servant, **and was made in the likeness of men: 8 And being found in fashion as a man, he humbled himself, and became obedient unto death, even the death of the cross. 9 Wherefore God also hath highly exalted him, and given him a name which is above every name: 10 That at the name of Jesus every knee should bow, of things in Heaven, and things in*** *earth, and things under the earth; 11 And that every tongue should confess that Jesus Christ is Lord, to the glory of God the Father.*

Jesus will forever be our **Savior**, He granted us everlasting life, and it is because of Him we can be saved from curses that torment us today. But, we have to believe God raised Jesus from the dead and confess with our mouth that Jesus is Lord, and then we will be saved. If you call upon The Name of the Lord Jesus Christ, you will be saved.

Romans 10:11-13 (KJV)

*11 For the Scripture saith, Whosoever believeth on him shall not be ashamed. 12 For there is no difference between the Jew and the Greek: **for the same Lord over all is rich unto all that call upon him. 13 For whosoever shall call upon the name of the Lord shall be saved.***

When we call upon the Name of Jesus, we are calling upon all that His name represents and all He has done for us. We have spoken a lot about the *Law of Faith* in this book, but the *Law of Faith* only works because of Jesus. These are not just laws and things we do. These laws reveal how to work with a living **Savior** and how to call upon His Name tangibly. When you call upon the Name of Jesus, you are calling upon all that He said He would be for you. Everything has to submit to the authority of His Name and who He is. So, when you call upon the Name of the Lord, He will be there for you in all of His glory and might to save you.

Jesus taught that when we pray, we are to pray in His Name if we want an answer from God.

John 14:12-14 (KJV)

12 Verily, verily, I say unto you, He that believeth on me, the works that I do shall he do also; and greater works than these *shall he do; because I go unto my Father. 13 **And whatsoever ye shall ask in my name, that will I do,** that the Father may be glorified in the Son. 14 **If ye shall ask any thing in my name, I will do it.***

John 15:16 (KJV)

*16 Ye have not chosen me, but I have chosen you, and ordained you, that ye should go and bring forth fruit, and that your fruit should remain: **that whatsoever ye shall ask of the Father in my name, he may give it you.***

John 16:24 (KJV)

*24 **Hitherto have ye asked nothing in my name: ask, and ye shall receive, that your joy may be full.***

Jesus taught His disciples to use His Name when praying to God the Father. Our Father in Heaven honors the Name of Jesus. When you speak the Name of Jesus, you call upon God and His covenant. He will answer you. Let's look at the Scripture where Peter used the Name of Jesus to heal someone.

Acts 3:1-7 (KJV)

*1 Now Peter and John went up together into the temple at the hour of prayer, being the ninth hour. 2 And a certain man lame from his mother's womb was carried, whom they laid daily at the gate of the temple which is called Beautiful, to ask alms of them that entered into the temple; 3 Who seeing Peter and John about to go into the temple asked an alms. 4 And Peter, fastening his eyes upon him with John, said, Look on us. 5 And he gave heed unto them, expecting to receive something of them. 6 **Then Peter said, Silver and gold have I none; but such as I have give I thee: In the name of Jesus Christ of Nazareth rise up and walk.** 7 And*

*he took him by the right hand, and lifted him up: and immediately
his feet and ankle bones received strength.*

Peter testified that faith in Christ's Name made the man strong and
whole.

Acts 3:16 (KJV)
*16 **And his name through faith in his name hath made this man
strong,** whom ye see and know: yea, the faith which is by him
hath given him this perfect soundness in the presence of you all.*

Acts 4:10 (KJV)
*10 Be it known unto you all, and to all the people of Israel, **that
by the name of Jesus Christ of Nazareth,** whom ye crucified,
whom God raised from the dead, even by him doth this man stand
here before you whole.*

Do you see how Peter was specific in saying Jesus Christ of Nazareth?
Peter said His Name, title, and location where He was from. The
Apostle Peter added the city of Nazareth because other people were
named Jesus during this time, and he wanted the man to be certain
whose name he was calling upon. Naming the location where Jesus was
from made everyone know for sure the *Person* and Name He was
calling upon to bring healing. You must be specific when calling upon
God's Name. Even when demons came into contact with Jesus, they
named what city He was from.

Mark 1:23-25 (KJV)
*23 And there was in their synagogue a man with an unclean
spirit; and he cried out, 24 **Saying, Let us alone; what have we
to do with thee, thou Jesus of Nazareth?** art thou come to destroy*

us? I know thee who thou art, the Holy One of God. 25 And Jesus rebuked him, saying, Hold thy peace, and come out of him.

Before Jesus left to be with His Father, He gave a *Great Commission* to the early Church. He told them to cast out devils in His Name.

Mark 16:15-18 (KJV)

15 And he said unto them, Go ye into all the world, and preach the gospel to every creature. 16 He that believeth and is baptized shall be saved; but he that believeth not shall be damned. 17 And these signs shall follow them that believe; **In my name shall they cast out devils;** *they shall speak with new tongues; 18 They shall take up serpents; and if they drink any deadly thing, it shall not hurt them; they shall lay hands on the sick, and they shall recover.*

When you are walking in your proper position as a child of God, you have every right to call upon the Name of Jesus Christ of Nazareth. When you call upon the Name of Jesus Christ of Nazareth, God will respond by delivering you or the person you are praying for. Another way of saying Jesus Christ of Nazareth, is **The Anointed Saviour from Nazareth**. Jesus came from Nazareth and was anointed to save people.

Let's look at what the Book of Proverbs has to say about the Name of the Lord.

Proverbs 18:10 (KJV)

10 **The name of the Lord is a strong tower: the righteous runneth into it, and is safe.**

God's Name is a strong tower, and when you call upon the Name of Jesus, He will be there for you to protect you. He will do for you all that His Name represents. When you apply your faith and speak the Name of Jesus Christ of Nazareth, God will deliver you. Calling upon the

Name of Jesus invokes God to keep His Covenant. The devil runs in fear of Jesus and those who call upon His Name. The Father honors the Name of Jesus and listens to the prayers offered by faith in His Name.

I put calling upon **The Name of the Lord Jesus Christ of Nazareth** as a *Law of Faith* because it is probably one of the highest of all Laws. When you call upon the Name of Jesus Christ of Nazareth, you are calling upon the *Lawgiver*. Jesus is the one who makes all the Laws of the universe and can create any Law He wants to. He is the King of the seen and unseen world. Therefore, everything must submit to His Laws, Authority, and His Name.

Just say His Name if you ever find yourself in a situation and don't know what to do. Many people have been saved and delivered from terrible circumstances by calling upon the Name of Jesus Christ of Nazareth. God gave us Jesus and the power of His Name to save us from whatever we might face in this life.

In winning the war of words, the Name of Jesus is the greatest thing you can speak out of your mouth. If you say His Name in faith, He will be there for you. There is no other significant Name you can say or call upon. **The Name of the Lord Jesus Christ** is the sum of all that He is and has done for us. He is the faithful *Savior* of the entire world. It is sad that so many people say His Name in vain or use it as a curse word. They do not realize the danger by taking His Name in vain. God commanded us to not take His Name in vain. Let's look at this commandment together.

Exodus 20:7 (KJV)
7 Thou shalt not take the name of the Lord thy God in vain; for the Lord will not hold him guiltless that taketh his name in vain.

If you have ever spoken the Name of Jesus Christ in vain, you need to repent to God immediately and vow you will never do it again. Jesus Christ of Nazareth is to be honored in the highest way possible. God's Name is hallowed, holy, set apart, and worthy of all respect.

Matthew 6:9 (KJV)
9 After this manner therefore pray ye: Our Father which art in Heaven, Hallowed be thy name.

God's Name is not to be taken lightly. His Name is holy, mighty, powerful, and wonderful. Therefore, I thank God the Father for sending Jesus Christ of Nazareth to be the Savior of the world. He is the gift of all gifts and has a Name above all other names.

2 Corinthians 9:15 (KJV)
15 Thanks be unto God for his unspeakable gift.

In conclusion, you can see how important the Name of Jesus Christ of Nazareth is. The Name of Jesus is critical when it comes to the *Law of Faith* and winning the war of words. If you ever find yourself in a war of words, call on **The Name of the Lord Jesus Christ of Nazareth,** and He will be there every time in power and strength. His Name was given for us to use in our times of need. No devil can remain, and no words can withstand His Name. Jesus is the Name above all names. So, to win the war of words, call upon **The Name of the Lord Jesus Christ,** and you will win every time without fail.

CHAPTER 22

LAW #16

THANKSGIVING

I placed thanksgiving as the last *Law of Faith* in this book, but it is not the least important. Thanksgiving is, in fact, one of the most important *Laws of Faith*. Thanksgiving is a powerful way to declare your faith and get your prayers answered by the Lord. This chapter will explain the importance of thanksgiving and how it works with your faith.

To start, let's define thanksgiving. Thanksgiving is an expression of gratitude to someone for what they have said or done for you. It acknowledges any favor or benefits you received from someone and shows appreciation for what they have done. We can see why it is so important to thank God because of all He has done for us. He created us, sent Jesus to die for us, and freely gives us all things that pertain to life and godliness.

Now I want to explain why thanksgiving is so important for our prayers being answered. In one of the earlier chapters, I talked about time and how God is eternal and not connected to time like we are. Therefore, when you are talking to God and want an answer to your prayer, it is essential to understand how your speech is important and how you use your words regarding time. Some people, when they pray, pray in the future tense of wanting God to do something. But, from God's perspective, whatever you are asking for is already done. This is where faith and thanksgiving come together. When you learn the secret of this truth, you will know you have already won your war of words before you even start the war. Therefore, the answer to your prayer is actually in the past.

To better understand this, let me ask you a question. When do we usually thank someone for doing something for us? We typically thank them after they have done it. This is why thanksgiving is so important when it comes to God. It is a sign of faith that we believe we have received what we asked for. When you thank God in advance, you declare by faith and agree that God already answered your prayer before you asked.

Let's look at a critical verse that shows this point, and then we will tie it in with the teachings of Jesus.

>*Philippians 4:6-7 (KJV)*
>*6 Be careful for nothing; **but in every thing by prayer and supplication with thanksgiving** let your requests be made known unto God. 7 And the peace of God, which passeth all understanding, shall keep your hearts and minds through Christ Jesus.*

When we go to God in prayer, we are to offer our requests with thanksgiving. We are to thank God in advance when we are offering a supplication. This thankfulness is a sign that we know God already answered our prayer, and this is how we can have the peace of God before the manifestation of the answer.

With this thought in mind, let's look at what Jesus had to say about prayer in the Book of Mark, Chapter 11.

Mark 11:24 (KJV)
*24 Therefore I say unto you, What things soever ye desire, when ye pray, **believe that ye receive them, and ye shall have them.***

Thanksgiving is one of the highest forms of believing you have received an answer from God when you pray. You fully understand by faith that God made provision for your prayer before you even prayed.

TESTIMONY

I learned the power of thanksgiving when I was very young and about to have my first child. I was in a situation where I would be the only one working after my son was born. I knew that my income would not be enough to provide for my son. I was a P.E. teacher for a Christian school and taught first through sixth grade.

I went to the school principal, let him know my situation, and asked for a raise. He, unfortunately, told me that the school was not able to give me a raise at that time. So, I let him know that I would have to go and find another job. He understood, and I started looking for a new job.

As I started to look, I could not find any job that would pay me more than what I was making. I was young and did not have a lot of skill sets. Once I realized this, I knew I needed to seek God for help. My son would be born in about six months, so I knew I had a few months to ask God and believe Him for a miracle. I knew and had faith that if I asked God and prayed hard enough, God would help me.

I started praying day and night from this point on, and I mean day and night. My back was against a wall, and I needed help from God. So, I would pray in the morning before I went to work, on my lunch, and when I got home. I also prayed any other time I could. I had read Smith Wigglesworth books and knew I could get an answer from God by faith. Smith

Wigglesworth was a faith healer during the early '20s and '40s, and he saw many miracles during his ministry.

After about a month of praying like this, God spoke to me and said, "If you believe I heard you, wouldn't you just ask me one time, and I would answer you." I said, "Yes, but what do I do with my mind during the day when it is freaking out?" God answered me, "Just thank Me during that time." I agreed and said I would ask one more time and then turn my prayer into thanksgiving.

I went from praying and asking God all day long to thanking God all day long. I thanked God morning, noon, and night. Finally, after a short while of intensely thanking God, something happened to me on the inside. What happened to me is what you can call the cross-over point. This is where you cross over in your soul from fear to believing you have the answer. I knew that I knew that I knew that I knew, that I knew that God had heard me, and I had my answer. If you ever reach this level of cross-over faith, you will know what I am talking about.

I crossed over into a level of faith I had never experienced before. It didn't matter what happened in the natural anymore. I had received my answer by faith from God and knew I had it. It was so wonderful to cross over into this level of believing God, where I was free from fear, doubt, and unbelief. What happened next was so wonderful, but I can't say it surprised me because I was in high levels of faith.

The school principal came to me and said he didn't want to lose me. So he brought me into his office and asked how much I needed. He ended up giving me a promotion and a raise. I was now going to run the after-school sports program and be the P.E. Teacher. After this, someone in my Church, who didn't know my situation, said they heard from God and gave me some money. I cannot tell you enough how thankful I am to God for answering my prayer and teaching me the power of thanksgiving. This experience changed my life forever.

After my son was born, I was an assistant pastor at a Church and lived entirely by faith. Jesus knew and operated in the power of thanking God. Our Church ended up going to a revival meeting in Oakland, CA. I didn't have enough money to buy my family lunch at that time. The Church was a Church of faith, and we had all agreed only to ask God for our needs and not man. If we told someone our situation, we could not let them give it to us. It had to be genuine faith and direct answers from God.

Too many people tell people their problems and don't go directly to God, and then when the person they went to has compassion on them, they give to them. The person who asked will sometimes say they had a miracle from God when all they had was an answer from another person and not God. The Bible says to let your requests be made known to God and not man. Your Father in Heaven knows what you need even before you ask.

Matthew 6:7-8 (KJV)

*7 But when ye pray, use not vain repetitions, as the heathen do: for they think that they shall be heard for their much speaking. 8 Be not ye therefore like unto them: **for your Father knoweth what things ye have need of, before ye ask him.***

At lunchtime, I went outside and prayed the *Prayer of Faith* with thanksgiving for God to provide for my family at this convention. I prayed to God once and thanked Him for the answer. I then went back inside the auditorium to be with my family. Within no less than five minutes, a woman came up to us from out of nowhere and said she had heard from God to give us a pear. That one pear fed my whole family. It was like God multiplied and filled us up with that pear. Since that time, I have used the secret of thanksgiving to receive many answers from God, and it works every time.

Those were my early days of learning how to believe God for answers. I have been in many tight places throughout my life, and I have seen God faithfully answer my thankful prayers. Let's look at the story of Lazarus in the Bible and how Jesus thanked the Father before Lazarus was raised from the dead.

> ### John 11:39-42 (KJV)
> *39 Jesus said, Take ye away the stone. Martha, the sister of him that was dead, saith unto him, Lord, by this time he stinketh: for he hath been dead four days. 40 Jesus saith unto her, Said I not unto thee, that, if thou wouldest believe, thou shouldest see the glory of God? 41 Then they took away the stone from the place where the dead was laid.* **And Jesus lifted up his eyes, and said, Father, I thank thee that thou hast heard me.** *42 And I knew that thou hearest me always: but because of the people which stand by I said it, that they may believe that thou hast sent me.*

Jesus thanked the Father in advance for hearing Him. Jesus knew and operated in the power of thanking God. He believed He received, and all that was left to do was speak to the mountain, and Lazarus was raised from the dead.

> ### John 11:43-44 (KJV)
> *43 And when he thus had spoken,* **he cried with a loud voice, Lazarus, come forth.** *44 And he that was dead came forth, bound hand and foot with graveclothes: and his face was bound about with a napkin. Jesus saith unto them, Loose him, and let him go.*

Thanksgiving is one of the most powerful *Laws of Faith*. Besides, who wants to bless an ungrateful person? Jesus healed ten lepers once, and only one came back to thank Him.

> ### Luke 17:11-19 (KJV)
> *11 And it came to pass, as he went to Jerusalem, that he passed through the midst of Samaria and Galilee. 12 And as he entered into a certain village, there met him ten men that were lepers, which stood afar off: 13 And they lifted up their voices, and said, Jesus, Master, have mercy on us. 14 And when he saw them, he said unto them, Go shew yourselves unto the priests. And it came to pass, that, as they went, they were cleansed. 15 **And one of them, when he saw that he was healed, turned back, and with a loud voice glorified God, 16 And fell down on his face at his feet, giving him thanks:** and he was a Samaritan. 17 And Jesus answering said, **Were there not ten cleansed? but where are the nine? 18 There are not found that returned to give glory to God, save this stranger.** 19 And he said unto him, Arise, go thy way: thy faith hath made thee whole.*

Thanksgiving is your faith speaking out, and it is true faith if you can thank God in advance before the manifestation of the prayer. God will pass over a million people to find someone of faith. It is only by faith we can please Him. You will please God with your faith when you learn to thank Him in advance.

> ### Hebrews 11:6 (KJV)
> *6 **But without faith it is impossible to please him:** for he that cometh to God must believe that he is, and that he is a rewarder of them that diligently seek him.*

I now want to bring up a powerful truth about thanksgiving that you don't hear preached much about. Did you know that the Bible not only teaches us to be thankful in prayer but to be thankful for *all* things? It is the will of God that you are thankful in *all* things, and I mean *all* things. Let's look at a verse that teaches this truth.

> *1 Thessalonians 5:18 (KJV)*
> *18 In every thing give thanks: for this is the will of God in Christ Jesus concerning you.*

One of the devil's biggest lies is to get people to believe that God is not good. If you don't believe God is inherently good, how could you trust Him? God is good, and there is nothing mean, evil, or unkind in Him. There is always more to the story if you are going through something. Sometimes, there are unseen forces at work, and you can't blame God for anything. The Bible says all things work together for good to those who love God and are called to His purpose.

> *Romans 8:28 (KJV)*
> *28 And we know that **all things work together for good to them that love God, to them who are the called according to his purpose.***

If you are going through something and don't understand the reason, start thanking God. When I am in those situations, I just shelf the issue and never lay a charge at the feet of Jesus. God is beyond good. He sent His dearly beloved Son to die for us and rise from the dead. One thing is for sure; if you thank God during your moment of grief or sorrow, God will at some point reveal what was going on in the background. It could be as simple as this book is teaching. There could have been things spoken you have no idea about. But God sees all and hears all. This book was written to help you understand the war of words and what is going on in the unseen realm. Never lay a charge at the feet of God for anything. He is only to be thanked and praised for all of His goodness.

So, if you find yourself in a war of words and don't understand why you are under attack, just know that God is good. Begin to thank God, and He will be with you. Thanksgiving is one of the best ways to offer up a sacrifice to God. To win the war of words, the sacrifice of praise must continually be offered from our lips. We do this by giving thanks to His Name.

> **Hebrews 13:15 (KJV)**
> *15 By him therefore let us offer the sacrifice of praise to God continually, that is, **the fruit of our lips giving thanks to his name.***

The Psalms are filled with thanksgiving to God. Let's look at some of these Psalms together.

> **Psalm 69:30 (KJV)**
> *30 I will praise the name of God with a song, **and will magnify him with thanksgiving.***

> **Psalm 75:1 (KJV)**
> *1 **Unto thee, O God, do we give thanks, unto thee do we give thanks**: for that thy name is near thy wondrous works declare.*

> **Psalm 79:13 (KJV)**
> *13 **So we thy people and sheep of thy pasture will give thee thanks for ever:** we will shew forth thy praise to all generations.*

> **Psalm 95:2 (KJV)**
> *2 **Let us come before his presence with thanksgiving,** and make a joyful noise unto him with psalms.*

Psalm 100:4 (KJV)
4 Enter into his gates with thanksgiving, and into his courts
with praise: be thankful unto him, and bless his name.

Thanksgiving is the only way to enter into God's holy presence. God is good and greatly to be praised. He has never failed anyone. If you learn the secret to thanksgiving and the *Laws of Faith*, you will find God ready to help you in your time of need. It is only through ignorance and ungratefulness that people miss out on the great promises of God.

The Bible teaches that people will be unthankful as we move into the *Last Days*.

2 Timothy 3:1-5 (KJV)
*1 This know also, that in the **last days** perilous times shall come.*
2 For men shall be lovers of their own selves, covetous, boasters,
*proud, blasphemers, disobedient to parents, **unthankful,** unholy,*
3 Without natural affection, trucebreakers, false accusers,
incontinent, fierce, despisers of those that are good, 4 Traitors,
heady, high-minded, lovers of pleasures more than lovers of God;
5 Having a form of godliness, but denying the power thereof:
from such turn away.

The war of words will intensify as we near the *Last Days*. It is imperative that we don't give in to the devil's lies and become ungrateful. If you can learn the secret of the law of thanksgiving, you will overcome any obstacle and keep your heart free from the evil traps of the devil. No one likes being around an ungrateful person. They poison everything they touch and speak to. You are called to be a shining light in a dark ungrateful world. Your testimony, positive attitude, and thankfulness have the power to change the world and win the war of words.

In conclusion, to win the war of words and walk in all the *Laws of Faith*, we must learn to be thankful at all times and for all things. If you can learn to be thankful for everything, your life will be blessed. You will win the war of words, and please God as you thank God in advance for your prayers being answered. God is good and has never wronged anyone. We can only thank Him, even when we do not understand what is going on. You can always trust that God is good and works all things out for the good to those who love Him and are the called according to His purpose. Thanks be unto God for His unspeakable gift in Christ.

CHAPTER 23

———•◦•———

SPEAK NO EVIL

This chapter will cover an area most people don't completely understand regarding the war of words. It is just as important to understand what to say as what not to say. When we were created in God's image, we were not designed to use our voices to speak *ANY* evil. Our voices were created for speaking good and blessings to God, people, and things. Our voices were only to speak a pure flow of love, peace, and goodwill. This chapter will touch on evil words that should never be spoken out of our mouths. Until you stop and control evil from coming out of your mouth, you can't master the art of speech and win the war of words.

Your mouth is a powerful conduit that can cause good things or evil things to come to pass. If you are going to climb higher and access a greater entrance into God's Kingdom, your mouth must be cleaned out of any evil speech. Evil speaking comes in many different forms. David asked God to put a watch over his mouth and keep the door of his lips. David understood the importance of what he spoke and wanted to ensure he didn't say anything wrong or evil before God.

Psalm 141:3 (KJV)
3 Set a watch, O Lord, before my mouth; keep the door of my
lips.

David also said that he wanted his words and meditation of his heart to
be acceptable to God.

Psalm 19:14 (KJV)
14 Let the words of my mouth, and the meditation of my heart,
be acceptable in thy sight, O Lord, my strength, and my
redeemer.

For us to be right with God, we must be diligent in discerning thoughts
from our hearts and using wisdom before saying anything. The New
Testament also has a lot to say about what we speak. One verse sums
up what we shouldn't allow coming out of our mouths. Let's look at
this verse from the New Testament and gain insight from these verses.

Ephesians 4:29-32 (KJV)
29 Let no corrupt communication proceed out of your mouth,
but that which is good to the use of edifying, that it may minister
grace unto the hearers. 30 And grieve not the Holy Spirit of
God, whereby ye are sealed unto the day of redemption. 31 Let
all bitterness, and wrath, and anger, and clamour, and evil
speaking, be put away from you, with all malice: 32 And be ye
kind one to another, tenderhearted, forgiving one another, even
as God for Christ's sake hath forgiven you.

We are not to allow any corrupt communication or evil speech to flow
out of our mouths because the Holy Spirit is grieved when we do. As
Christians, we are called to be like a pure river where only blessings

come from our mouths. We are also called to bless and not curse those that do us evil. When we do this, we are like our Father in Heaven.

Matthew 5:43-45 (KJV)

*43 Ye have heard that it hath been said, Thou shalt love thy neighbour, and hate thine enemy. 44 **But I say unto you, Love your enemies, bless them that curse you,** do good to them that hate you, and pray for them which despitefully use you, and persecute you; 45 **That ye may be the children of your Father which is in Heaven:** for he maketh his sun to rise on the evil and on the good, and sendeth rain on the just and on the unjust.*

Jesus taught His disciples to bless those that persecuted them. The Apostle Paul also taught this truth.

Romans 12:14 (KJV)

*14 **Bless them which persecute you: bless, and curse not.***

James Chapter 3 is one of the most powerful Scriptures about this subject. So let's look at what James, the brother of Jesus, had to say about your mouth.

James 3:8-12 (KJV)

*8 **But the tongue can no man tame; it is an unruly evil, full of deadly poison.** 9 Therewith bless we God, even the Father; and therewith curse we men, which are made after the similitude of God. 10 **Out of the same mouth proceedeth blessing and cursing. My brethren, these things ought not so to be. 11 Doth a fountain send forth at the same place sweet water and bitter? 12 Can the fig tree, my brethren, bear olive berries? either a vine, figs? so can no fountain both yield salt water and fresh.***

We, as Christians, cannot have a flow of blessing and cursing coming out of the same mouth. When you got saved, God called you to be a *Blesser* with a clean flow of fresh Holy Spirit water of words coming out of your mouth. A clean and pure mouth is one of the signs that you are a true Christian. It is a beautiful thing to watch a mature Christian stay in positive love, even in the midst of a crooked and perverse society that hurls insults at them. We are not called to curse anyone, even if they curse at us. The fact is that an evil person will eventually bring down a curse upon themselves out of their own mouth.

Now, let's look at some critical areas to remove any evil communication from our tongues. The key is to allow the leading of the Holy Spirit to help you in these areas and for God to place a watch over our mouths. By doing so, it will be pleasing in God's sight, and your voice will increase in authority upon the earth. Below, I listed nine areas to watch and prevent any corrupt communication from flowing out of our mouths.

1. SPEAKING EVIL OF GOVERNMENTAL LEADERS
2. SLANDER AND GOSSIPING
3. CUSSING AND SWEARING
4. COMPLAINING
5. JESTING OR DEROGATORY JOKES
6. TAKING GOD'S NAME IN VAIN
7. LYING
8. A CONTENTIOUS SPIRIT AND ARGUING
9. PROUD BOASTING

If you speak any evil words, you need to repent immediately and get right with God. All this evil speaking grieves the precious Holy Spirit, in which you were sealed until the Day of Judgment. Your mouth should be only glorifying God and speaking good things.

Let's look at the nine detailed examples from the Bible in the areas of evil speech to avoid, so we can learn what not to say and cleanse our lips from all forms of evil speaking.

1. SPEAKING EVIL OF GOVERNMENTAL LEADERS

The Bible says we are to pray for kings and all that are in authority, that we may lead a quiet and peaceable life. God also wants us to pray for our governmental leaders' salvation.

> *1 Timothy 2:1-4 (KJV)*
> *1 **I exhort therefore, that, first of all, supplications, prayers, intercessions, and giving of thanks, be made for all men; 2 For kings, and for all that are in authority; that we may lead a quiet and peaceable life** in all godliness and honesty. 3 For this is good and acceptable in the sight of God our Saviour; 4 **Who will have all men to be saved, and to come unto the knowledge of the truth.***

We are not called to speak evil of any leader. God has put them in their place of authority, and He alone will have them give an account for their actions on Judgment Day.

2. SLANDER AND GOSSIPING

Slandering and gossiping about others is one of the evilest things someone can do to someone else. Slander and gossip can ruin someone's reputation in a heartbeat. If someone has done something harmful to you or another person, you are to go directly to that person and confront them. I am not excusing anyone's bad behavior, nor am I saying people shouldn't be held accountable for what they have said or done. I am referring to someone going around and just speaking evil about another person to other people.

Titus 3:2 (KJV)
*2 **To speak evil of no man**, to be no brawlers, but gentle, shewing all meekness unto all men.*

Let's see what the Bible has to say about slander.

Proverbs 10:18
*18 He that hideth hatred with lying lips, **and he that uttereth a slander, is a fool.***

1 Timothy 3:10-11 (KJV)
*10 And let these also first be proved; then let them use the office of a deacon, being found blameless. 11 Even so must their wives be grave, **not slanderers,** sober, faithful in all things.*

The mouth of the slanderer and gossiper must be stopped. Slander and gossiping have been some of the biggest evils to be done on the earth. We should do unto others as we would want to be done unto us. Nobody wants other people speaking badly about them to someone else. So, if you don't have anything good to say, don't say anything at all.

I also want to add the danger of cursing someone in covenant with God. Anyone that is in Christ is walking in the *Covenant of Abraham.* One of the promises God made to Abraham is that He would bless them that blessed him, and curse those who cursed him.

Genesis 12:3 (KJV)
*3 **And I will bless them that bless thee, and curse him that curseth thee:** and in thee shall all families of the Earth be blessed.*

You can invoke a curse upon yourself if you curse someone who is a Christian walking in the *Covenant of Abraham*. It is never good to speak and slander against one of God's children. It is just better to leave them alone. Anyone who curses someone walking in the *Abrahamic Covenant* will bring a curse upon themselves.

3. CUSSING AND SWEARING

Cussing and swearing are cursing. Cuss words are evil. When you cuss and swear, you are condemning something. All foul words have a curse behind them. Those who cuss have allowed their mouth to bring down curses on themselves, other people, or things. Cussing may seem harmless to some people, but they don't realize those cuss words are usually spoken when someone is in anger or has a heart full of hatred.

On the night Peter denied Christ, we know that he began to curse and swear. This is because his heart was not fully converted, and nasty words flowed out of his mouth. Later, he repented and got right with God, but the cursing and swearing showed where he was spiritually. He cursed in his denial of knowing Jesus.

> ### *Matthew 26:69-75 (KJV)*
> *69 Now Peter sat without in the palace: and a damsel came unto him, saying, Thou also wast with Jesus of Galilee. 70 But he denied before them all, saying, I know not what thou sayest. 71 And when he was gone out into the porch, another maid saw him, and said unto them that were there, This fellow was also with Jesus of Nazareth. 72 And again he denied with an oath, I do not know the man. 73 And after a while came unto him they that stood by, and said to Peter, Surely thou also art one of them; for thy speech bewrayeth thee. 74 **Then began he to curse and to swear,** saying, I know not the man. And immediately the cock crew. 75*

*And Peter remembered the word of Jesus, which said unto him, Before the cock crow, thou shalt deny me thrice. **And he went out, and wept bitterly.***

4. COMPLAINING

I cannot teach enough about the curse you can bring on yourself by complaining. A chronic complainer has nothing good to say and continually expresses dissatisfaction about everything. Complaining is the beginning stage of betrayal. Complaining is the opposite of being thankful. Complainers can turn something extraordinary into something terrible with just their mouths. Complaining displeases the Lord and angers Him.

> ### Numbers 11:1 (KJV)
> *1 **And when the people complained, it displeased the Lord: and the Lord heard it; and his anger was kindled;** and the fire of the Lord burnt among them, and consumed them that were in the uttermost parts of the camp.*

Complaining and murmuring are some of the biggest reasons the children of Israel did not go into the Promised Land during the time of Moses. God hates complaining. God has called you to see the good in all things and for you to be thankful. Remember, thankfulness is one of the 16 *Laws of Faith*.

5. JESTING OR DEROGATORY JOKES

I have never seen anyone who jokes around too much have any type of real anointing. The joy of the Lord and having pure fun is different than jesting. Jesting has to do with being rude, crude, or unkind in your joking. Some people have bad motives behind their joking. They say mean things and then laugh it off and say they were just joking. They curse people and then laugh as if everyone sees it as a joke, or they make fun of people and put them down through subtlety within their jokes.

Proverbs 26:18-19 (KJV)
*18 As a mad man who casteth firebrands, arrows, and death, 19 So is the man that deceiveth his neighbour, and saith, **Am not I in sport?***

The Hebrew word for sport means to laugh, celebrate, rejoice, and mock. Therefore, as faithful saints of God, jesting is not to be once named among us.

Ephesians 5:3-4 (KJV)
*3 But fornication, and all uncleanness, or covetousness, let it not be once named among you, as becometh saints; 4 Neither filthiness, **nor foolish talking, nor jesting,** which are not convenient: **but rather giving of thanks.***

People who engage in jesting make light of everything. They even joke about the Holy things of God. As Christians, we are called to be serious about God and His Kingdom. The Gospel is nothing to joke about and make light of. Anointed people walk in holy reverence for God and the people of God. They have the joy of the Lord without any lightheartedness in their speech

6. TAKING GOD'S NAME IN VAIN

It is disgusting to hear anyone take God's name in vain or use the name of Jesus in a derogatory way. God has many names, and each of His names comes with unique and powerful revelations of who He is and what He does. Taking the Lord's name in vain is a very high offense that God spoke as one of the Ten Commandments for us not to do.

Exodus 20:7 (KJV)
7 Thou shalt not take the name of the Lord thy God in vain; for the Lord will not hold him guiltless that taketh his name in vain.

The Name of Jesus is so powerful that every knee will bow to His Name and confess that Jesus is Lord. EVERYONE!

Philippians 2:9-11 (KJV)
9 Wherefore God also hath highly exalted him, and given him a name which is above every name: 10 That at the name of Jesus every knee should bow, of things in Heaven, and things in Earth, and things under the Earth; 11 *And that every tongue should confess that Jesus Christ is Lord*, to the glory of God the Father.

7. LYING

Lying is a terrible sin that can keep you out of your inheritance and the Kingdom of God. God hates lying and the lying tongue. People lie for various reasons: some lie to protect themselves, some lie to gain money, and others lie to defame others so they can look better. But, some people lie just because they are habitual liars. They have such a habit of lying that they even believe their own lies.

The Bible has a lot to say about lying. The first and most important thing to understand is that those who lie are of their father, the devil. The devil is the father of all lies and liars.

John 8:44 (KJV)
44 Ye are of your father the devil, and the lusts of your father ye will do. He was a murderer from the beginning, and abode not in the truth, because there is no truth in him. *When he speaketh a lie, he speaketh of his own: for he is a liar, and the father of it.*

Every Christian should hate lying as much as God hates lying. A lying tongue hates those afflicted by it.

> *Proverbs 26:28 (KJV)*
> *28 **A lying tongue hateth those that are afflicted by it**; and a flattering mouth worketh ruin.*

A person who lies can never be trusted. It is amazing how many Christians lie. Those who lie have not put off the old man and are in danger of losing their salvation and not entering the Kingdom of God.

8. A CONTENTIOUS SPIRIT AND ARGUING

Some people like to argue and be contentious about everything. When they do this, they sow discord among people. Sowing discord among the brethren is one of the six things that God hates.

> *Proverbs 6:16-19 (KJV)*
> *16 **These six things doth the Lord hate: yea, seven are an abomination unto him:** 17 A proud look, a lying tongue, and hands that shed innocent blood, 18 An heart that deviseth wicked imaginations, feet that be swift in running to mischief, 19 A false witness that speaketh lies, **and he that soweth discord among brethren.***

If you ever find yourself in contention with others, the Bible says you are in pride.

> *Proverbs 13:10 (KJV)*
> *10 **Only by pride cometh contention:** but with the well advised is wisdom.*

So, what are we to do when it comes to arguing, contention, and sowing discord? First, just stop with the argument and only say something good.

Proverbs 17:14 (KJV)
*14 **The beginning of strife is as when one letteth out water: therefore leave off contention, before it be meddled with.***

The next thing to do is get away from the contentious person. The Bible calls them a scorner, and if they don't stop, get away from them.

Proverbs 22:10 (KJV)
*10 **Cast out the scorner, and contention shall go out;** yea, strife and reproach shall cease.*

9. PROUD BOASTING

Boasting is when someone speaks proudly about themselves, possessions, abilities, and accomplishments. The Bible says we should let someone else praise us and not our own lips.

Proverbs 27:2 (KJV)
*2 **Let another man praise thee, and not thine own mouth; a stranger, and not thine own lips.***

God hates every form of pride.

Proverbs 16:5 (KJV)
*5 **Every one that is proud in heart is an abomination to the Lord:** though hand join in hand, he shall not be unpunished.*

The Bible says that proud people stir up strife. Proud people start arguments.

Proverbs 28:25 (KJV)
*25 **He that is of a proud heart stirreth up strife:** but he that putteth his trust in the Lord shall be made fat.*

The tongue is a little member of the body, but it boasts great things. The Bible says that a boastful tongue is set on fire from hell.

James 3:5-6 (KJV)
*5 **Even so the tongue is a little member, and boasteth great things.** Behold, how great a matter a little fire kindleth! 6 And the tongue is a fire, a world of iniquity: so is the tongue among our members, that it defileth the whole body, and setteth on fire the course of nature; **and it is set on fire of hell.***

If you have spoken boastfully, the only thing you can do is repent and humble yourself before the Lord. But, first, you have to submit yourself to God. When you submit yourself before God, He will give you grace, and the devil will flee from you (James 4:7).

Anyone who allows these nine evil things to proceed out of their mouth doesn't fully understand the war they are in. How can you defeat evil and win the war of words if evil comes out of your mouth? To win the war of words, you not only have to speak the Holy Word of God, but you can't let any evil speech flow out of your mouth. God is watching everything you say *ALL* the time.

A fully mature Christian understands the war they are in and never allows their mouth to be used by the devil. The degree of your maturity in these areas is the degree from which God can impart authority into your words. For God to use you for His purposes, you must be 100% purely flowing in Holy Ghost communication from your mouth.

Jesus taught His disciples that it wasn't what entered people's mouths that defiled them, but what came out of their mouth is what defiled them.

> **Mark 7:15 (KJV)**
> *15 There is nothing from without a man, that entering into him can defile him: but the things which come out of him, those are they that defile the man.*

> **Mark 7:20-23 (KJV)**
> *20 And he said, **That which cometh out of the man, that defileth the man.** 21 For from within, out of the heart of men, proceed evil thoughts, adulteries, fornications, murders, 22 Thefts, covetousness, wickedness, deceit, lasciviousness, an evil eye, blasphemy, pride, foolishness: 23 All these evil things come from within, and defile the man.*

In conclusion, to win the war of words, you cannot allow evil speech to flow out of your mouth. Your mouth must be cleansed from all forms of evil speaking to win the war of words. As Christians, we must watch every word we say. Every word you speak is recorded in Heaven; therefore, be careful what you speak. Mature Christians set a guard over their mouth and only allow pure wholesome words to flow out of their mouth. Your speech is powerful, and every word you speak has eternal consequences; therefore, it is imperative that you only use your mouth to bless God and others. Never use your mouth to speak evil.

CHAPTER 24

---•◉•---

DAVID'S WORDS VS. GOLIATH'S WORDS

The epic story of David vs. Goliath has gone down in history as one of the most powerful displays of good conquering evil. When David faced Goliath, he was just a boy, but something happened to him before facing this giant that stacked the odds in his favor. In this chapter, we will see what happened to David before he faced Goliath head-on and how he was able to defeat this giant and win the war of words.

David was from the Tribe of Judah, which had a history of defeating giants. When the children of Israel first came into the Promised Land, Caleb from the Tribe of Judah asked Joshua for his mountain. Giants inhabited the mountain he asked for. These giants were called the Anakims and were some of the tallest giants in the Promised Land. So, David must have heard stories while growing up about his ancestors fighting large armies and defeating giants.

David grew up as a shepherd boy. While tending the sheep, he fought with a lion and a bear and defeated them with his bare hands. He was born with a warrior's heart. David, however, was the youngest in his family and was often overlooked. His brothers were enlisted in the armies of Israel, but David stayed behind, tending the sheep.

Samuel, the great prophet of Israel, had anointed Saul to be king during this time. Saul was very tall and from the tribe of Benjamin. Saul was the first Israelite to be made king. Up to this time, Israel had never had a king. Saul, however, disobeyed the Lord twice after being made king. As a result, God prophesied through the prophet Samuel that Saul's kingdom would not continue. Let's read this significant historical story from the Bible.

> ### 1 Samuel 13:13-14 (KJV)
> *13 And Samuel said to Saul, **Thou hast done foolishly: thou hast not kept the commandment of the Lord thy God, which he commanded thee: for now would the Lord have established thy kingdom upon Israel for ever. 14 But now thy kingdom shall not continue: the Lord hath sought him a man after his own heart, and the Lord hath commanded him to be captain over his people,** because thou hast not kept that which the Lord commanded thee.*

God sent the prophet Samuel to the house of Jesse, the father of David, to anoint a new king. Jesse had eight sons, but he only brought out seven to present before Samuel. None of them were chosen, so Samuel asked Jesse if he had more sons. Jesse said he had one more son that was feeding the sheep. So they sent for David, and when he came before Samuel, the Lord said, *Arise, anoint him: for this is he.*

> ### 1 Samuel 16:11-12 (KJV)
> *11 And Samuel said unto Jesse, Are here all thy children? And he said, There remaineth yet the youngest, and, behold, he keepeth the sheep. And Samuel said unto Jesse, Send and fetch him: for*

we will not sit down till he come hither. 12 And he sent, and brought him in. Now he was ruddy, and withal of a beautiful countenance, and goodly to look to. ***And the Lord said, Arise, anoint him: for this is he.***

Let's look at the rest of the passage and see what happens next.

1 Samuel 16:13 (KJV)
13 Then Samuel took the horn of oil, and anointed him in the midst of his brethren: and ***the Spirit of the Lord came upon David from that day forward.*** *So Samuel rose up, and went to Ramah.*

God anointed David as the next king of Israel, and the Spirit of God came upon him. We also know from Scripture that David also became a prophet and had the Word of the Lord in his mouth. David wrote and prophesied in many of the Psalms we read and sing today. The Psalms are filled with prophetic words, and many of these were fulfilled in the life and ministry of Jesus Christ.

Acts 2:29-30 (KJV)
29 Men and brethren, let me freely speak unto you of ***the patriarch David,*** *that he is both dead and buried, and his sepulchre is with us unto this day. 30* ***Therefore being a prophet,*** *and knowing that God had sworn with an oath to him, that of the fruit of his loins, according to the flesh, he would raise up Christ to sit on his throne;*

David was now anointed, and God was with him. This also meant that all of his words would come to pass as a prophet. David later became one of the most powerful warring kings in Israel and defeated many armies. He did this with the anointing from God he had received from the prophet Samuel.

Although David went on to become a great king, he wasn't king yet. Saul was still the king of Israel, and after David was anointed as the new king, Israel was getting ready to face one of its biggest tests. This test came in the form of Goliath of Gath, who was a mighty warring giant. Goliath stood over nine feet and nine inches tall. He had trained for war since he was a youth. His armor and weaponry that he wore weighed over 125 pounds. His spear was over 12 feet long and weighed about 33 pounds. This giant was no ordinary foe.

1 Samuel 17:4-6 (KJV)

4 And there went out a champion out of the camp of the Philistines, named Goliath, of Gath, whose height was six cubits and a span. 5 And he had an helmet of brass upon his head, and he was armed with a coat of mail; and the weight of the coat was five thousand shekels of brass. 6 And he had greaves of brass upon his legs, and a target of brass between his shoulders.

Goliath was the champion of the Philistines and was built for war. The Philistines had Goliath go down in the middle of the valley of Elah, stand between both armies, and put out a challenge. Goliath's challenge was that he would fight against any man that Israel chose one on one. Let's read this challenge he made to the Israelites from the Word of God.

1 Samuel 17:8-11 (KJV)

8 And he stood and cried unto the armies of Israel, and said unto them, Why are ye come out to set your battle in array? am not I a Philistine, and ye servants to Saul? choose you a man for you, and let him come down to me. 9 If he be able to fight with me, and to kill me, then will we be your servants: but if I prevail against him, and kill him, then shall ye be our servants, and serve us. 10 And the Philistine said, I defy the armies of Israel this day; give me a man, that we may fight together. 11 **When Saul and all Israel heard those words of the Philistine, they were dismayed, and greatly afraid.**

Goliath's words carried weight and power. His words made Saul and his whole army afraid. Goliath put out this challenge for forty days. Saul and the army of Israel knew this giant could back his words in battle. Israel was in a war of words with this giant, and he was winning for the moment.

This is the first time in recorded Biblical history that we read about one warrior challenging to stand and fight against another warrior of the other army to determine the whole war. Goliath knew his words were powerful because of his size, and he was using his words to put fear in the hearts of his enemies so that he could defeat them.

During this time, after David was anointed to be king, his father sent him down to the war against the Philistines to see how his brothers were doing. When David arrived on the scene, he heard how Goliath was defying the armies of Israel. This does not sit well with the newly anointed king, and David started asking what shall be done for the man who defeats Goliath. David puts himself in this war of words, and eventually, his words are told to King Saul.

1 Samuel 17:31-32 (KJV)
31 **And when the words were heard which David spake, they rehearsed them before Saul:** *and he sent for him. 32 And David said to Saul, Let no man's heart fail because of him; thy servant will go and fight with this Philistine.*

You must remember that David is no longer just speaking as a boy. He spoke as an anointed prophet of the Lord and the future king of Israel. These were not idle words. His words now had the power to change and affect things because of the anointing of the Spirit of the Lord upon him. He was speaking for God, and God Almighty now backed his words. Goliath had no idea what he was about to face. He ignorantly and proudly entered into a war of words with God Almighty, and God was soon going to reveal Himself through this young boy whose words were more powerful than Goliath's.

After Saul heard the words coming out of David's mouth, he was persuaded to let him go down and fight this giant. David was the only one speaking words of faith and courage. Let's see what David said to King Saul.

1 Samuel 17:33-37 (KJV)

*33 And Saul said to David, Thou art not able to go against this Philistine to fight with him: for thou art but a youth, and he a man of war from his youth. 34 And David said unto Saul, **Thy servant kept his father's sheep, and there came a lion, and a bear, and took a lamb out of the flock: 35 And I went out after him, and smote him, and delivered it out of his mouth: and when he arose against me, I caught him by his beard, and smote him, and slew him. 36 Thy servant slew both the lion and the bear: and this uncircumcised Philistine shall be as one of them, seeing he hath defied the armies of the living God.** 37 David said moreover, **The Lord that delivered me out of the paw of the lion, and out of the paw of the bear, he will deliver me out of the hand of this Philistine.** And Saul said unto David, Go, and the Lord be with thee.*

After this exchange of words, Saul offered David his armor and sword, but David chose to face this giant; with his staff, sling, five smooth stones, and most importantly, the Word of the Lord. Goliath was about to face his most powerful foe yet and didn't know it. Let's read this story together and see what they both say and prophesy to each other before they enter battle with each other.

> ### 1 Samuel 17:40-44 (KJV)
> *40 And he took his staff in his hand, and chose him five smooth stones out of the brook, and put them in a shepherd's bag which he had, even in a scrip; and his sling was in his hand: and he drew near to the Philistine. 41 And the Philistine came on and drew near unto David; and the man that bare the shield went before him. 42 And when the Philistine looked about, and saw David, he disdained him: for he was but a youth, and ruddy, and of a fair countenance. 43 And the Philistine said unto David, **Am I a dog, that thou comest to me with staves? And the Philistine cursed David by his gods. 44 And the Philistine said to David, Come to me, and I will give thy flesh unto the fowls of the air, and to the beasts of the field.***

Goliath cursed David by his gods and tried to prophesy his death. David, however, had no fear and entered into a war of words with this giant and prophesied the Word of the Lord. Let's read what God had to say through the mouth of His servant David to Goliath.

> ### 1 Samuel 17:45-47 (KJV)
> *45 Then said David to the Philistine, **Thou comest to me with a sword, and with a spear, and with a shield: but I come to thee in the name of the Lord of hosts, the God of the armies of Israel, whom thou hast defied. 46 This day will the Lord deliver thee into mine hand; and I will smite thee, and take thine head from***

thee; and I will give the carcases of the host of the Philistines this day unto the fowls of the air, and to the wild beasts of the earth; that all the earth may know that there is a God in Israel. 47 And all this assembly shall know that the Lord saveth not with sword and spear: for the battle is the Lord's, and he will give you into our hands.

David prophesied Goliath's death and how he would die. Goliath just thought he was facing a little shepherd boy and didn't realize he was facing the *Anointing* of the Prophet Samuel on David. David prophesied from the mouth of the Lord and went on to defeat Goliath. Precisely what he prophesied came to pass, because all the words of a true prophet come to pass. David used the prophetic Word of the Lord to defeat this disrespectful and wicked giant. Let's read the prophetic fulfillment of the Word of the Lord that David spoke to Goliath.

1 Samuel 17:48-54 (KJV)

48 And it came to pass, when the Philistine arose, and came, and drew nigh to meet David, that David hastened, and ran toward the army to meet the Philistine. 49 And David put his hand in his bag, and took thence a stone, and slang it, and smote the Philistine in his forehead, that the stone sunk into his forehead; and he fell upon his face to the earth. 50 So David prevailed over the Philistine with a sling and with a stone, and smote the Philistine, and slew him; but there was no sword in the hand of David. 51 Therefore David ran, and stood upon the Philistine, and took his sword, and drew it out of the sheath thereof, and slew him, and cut off his head therewith. And when the Philistines saw their champion was dead, they fled. 52 And the men of Israel and of Judah arose, and shouted, and pursued the Philistines, until thou come to the valley, and to the gates of

Ekron. And the wounded of the Philistines fell down by the way to Shaaraim, even unto Gath, and unto Ekron. 53 And the children of Israel returned from chasing after the Philistines, and they spoiled their tents. 54 And David took the head of the Philistine and brought it to Jerusalem, but he put his armor in his tent.

The Words of God flowing out of David's mouth prevailed over the words of Goliath. As big as Goliath was, his words were not big enough to face God's Word coming out of the mouth of David. You may find yourself in a battle that seems too big for you, but if you allow God's Word to flow out of your mouth, you will defeat whatever is facing you. God's Words *ALWAYS* prevail against the words of the enemy. You have to be bold like David to let God speak His Words through you for this to happen.

In conclusion, we can see it was the prophetic Word of the Lord flowing out of the mouth of David that prevailed over Goliath's words before he hit him with a stone. David spoke the Word of the Lord, and it came to pass. He spoke as a prophet before he went to war with this giant. David was in a prophetic war of words and prevailed. This story is a classic example of the power of God's Words. God has destined all his people to speak His Words and defeat all their enemies. If you are bold like David, you will defeat whatever giant is facing you, and you will win the war of words by the prophetic Word of God flowing out of your mouth.

CHAPTER 25

———◦●◦———

SOLOMON THE KING OF PEACE

K ing Solomon is one of the most fascinating characters to study in the Bible. King Solomon mastered the art of speech and winning the war of words through the wisdom given to him by God. Solomon's name means peace, and God gave peace to Solomon all the days of his life because he understood how to make peace with his words. This chapter will look at how Solomon ran his kingdom and shut down every adversary with wise words coming out of his mouth.

Once Solomon was anointed as the king of Israel, God came to him in a dream and asked him what he wanted. Solomon answered God by saying he wanted wisdom to judge the people of Israel. Solomon was very wise in how he answered God. Let's look at this special event in the Scriptures.

> *1 Kings 3:4-15 (KJV)*
> *4 And the king went to Gibeon to sacrifice there; for that was the great high place: a thousand burnt offerings did Solomon offer upon that altar. 5 In Gibeon the Lord appeared to Solomon in a dream by night: **and God said, Ask what I shall***

give thee. 6 And Solomon said, Thou hast shewed unto thy servant David my father great mercy, according as he walked before thee in truth, and in righteousness, and in uprightness of heart with thee; and thou hast kept for him this great kindness, that thou hast given him a son to sit on his throne, as it is this day. 7 And now, O Lord my God, thou hast made thy servant king instead of David my father: and I am but a little child: I know not how to go out or come in. 8 And thy servant is in the midst of thy people which thou hast chosen, a great people, that cannot be numbered nor counted for multitude. 9 ***Give therefore thy servant an understanding heart to judge thy people, that I may discern between good and bad: for who is able to judge this thy so great a people? 10 And the speech pleased the Lord, that Solomon had asked this thing.*** *11 And God said unto him, Because thou hast asked this thing, and hast not asked for thyself long life; neither hast asked riches for thyself, nor hast asked the life of thine enemies;* ***but hast asked for thyself understanding to discern judgment; 12 Behold, I have done according to thy words: lo, I have given thee a wise and an understanding heart; so that there was none like thee before thee, neither after thee shall any arise like unto thee. 13 And I have also given thee that which thou hast not asked, both riches, and honour: so that there shall not be any among the kings like unto thee all thy days.*** *14 And if thou wilt walk in my ways, to keep my statutes and my Commandments, as thy father David did walk, then I will lengthen thy days. 15 And Solomon awoke; and, behold, it was a dream. And he came to Jerusalem, and stood before the ark of the covenant of the Lord, and offered up burnt offerings, and offered peace offerings, and made a feast to all his servants.*

God answered his request and gave King Solomon a wise and understanding heart. He also added He would give Solomon riches and honor. God said that there would not be any other king like him. Solomon's speech pleased the Lord. Solomon woke up from his dream with great wisdom and understanding imparted to him by God.

The wisdom of God was so influential in King Solomon that the kings of the earth came from afar to hear his wisdom. His speech astounded people. King Solomon became wiser than all men, and his fame was in all nations around him. With this great, God imparted wisdom; Solomon wrote over 3,000 proverbs. A proverb is a short saying filled with counsel, advice, and wisdom.

> *1 Kings 4:29-34 (KJV)*
> *29 **And God gave Solomon wisdom and understanding exceeding much,** and largeness of heart, even as the sand that is on the sea shore. 30 And Solomon's wisdom excelled the wisdom of all the children of the east country, and all the wisdom of Egypt. 31 **For he was wiser than all men;** than Ethan the Ezrahite, and Heman, and Chalcol, and Darda, the sons of Mahol: **and his fame was in all nations round about.** 32 **And he spake three thousand proverbs**: and his songs were a thousand and five. 33 **And he spake of trees, from the cedar tree that is in Lebanon even unto the hyssop that springeth out of the wall: he spake also of beasts, and of fowl, and of creeping things, and of fishes. 34 And there came of all people to hear the wisdom of Solomon, from all kings of the earth, which had heard of his wisdom.***

King Solomon also spoke about trees, hyssop, beasts, fowls, creeping things, and fish. King Solomon was taking dominion over the earth with his words. He was ruling and reigning with powerful words. He also had peace and no wars during his time. With the wisdom of God, King Solomon won the war of words. He was so wise that no one wanted to go to war with him. All his potential enemies came to hear the wisdom that he received from God. King Solomon didn't just win the war of words; he shut down all wars before they even happened. Let's look at one of his Proverbs he wrote about when a man's ways please the Lord.

Proverbs 16:7 (KJV)

7 When a man's ways please the Lord, he maketh even his enemies to be at peace with him.

King Solomon's ways pleased the Lord, and it caused all of his enemies to be at peace with him. Moreover, Solomon so mastered the art of speech the kings of the earth came to hear him and gave him gifts.

2 Chronicles 9:22-24 (KJV)

22 And king Solomon passed all the kings of the earth in riches and wisdom. 23 And all the kings of the earth sought the presence of Solomon, to hear his wisdom, that God had put in his heart. 24 And they brought every man his present, vessels of silver, and vessels of gold, and raiment, harness, and spices, horses, and mules, a rate year by year.

God made King Solomon rich. The amount of gold and silver that came into his kingdom was astounding. He had so much gold he was making shields of gold, drinking from vessels of gold, and he overlaid his ivory throne with gold.

1 Kings 10:14-22 (KJV)

14 Now the weight of gold that came to Solomon in one year was six hundred threescore and six talents of gold, 15 Beside that he had of the merchantmen, and of the traffick of the spice merchants, and of all the kings of Arabia, and of the governors of the country. 16 **And king Solomon made two hundred targets of beaten gold:** *six hundred shekels of gold went to one target. 17* **And he made three hundred shields of beaten gold; three pound of gold went to one shield:** *and the king put them in the house of the forest of Lebanon. 18* **Moreover the king made a great throne of ivory, and overlaid it with the best gold.** *19 The throne had six steps, and the top of the throne was round behind: and there were stays on either side on the place of the seat, and two lions stood beside the stays. 20* **And twelve lions stood there on the one side and on the other upon the six steps:** *there was not the like made in any kingdom. 21* **And all king Solomon's drinking vessels were of gold, and all the vessels of the house of the forest of Lebanon were of pure gold;** *none were of silver: it was nothing accounted of in the days of Solomon. 22 For the king had at sea a navy of Tharshish with the navy of Hiram: once in three years came the navy of Tharshish, bringing gold, and silver, ivory, and apes, and peacocks.*

King Solomon ruled and reigned with the wisdom of God like never before seen on this earth. To get a deeper insight into this wisdom that God gave Solomon, you have to read what he wrote. The Book of Proverbs provides deeper insight into the wisdom that Solomon was walking in. When you read the Book of Proverbs, you begin to see how much King Solomon had to say about words. It is astounding how much he had to say about your mouth, tongue, lips, and the words that came out of your mouth. It is clear to see that a large portion of the wisdom that God gave to Solomon had everything to do with the words coming out of his mouth.

To put this in perspective, God did give Solomon wisdom, peace, and wealth, but the secret behind the wisdom was what God taught him about his speech. King Solomon was given wisdom in the power of his words. Solomon ran his kingdom with words of wisdom. He spoke the wisdom of God, and all of creation responded to him. He mastered the art of speech, and we can see it in all he said and accomplished.

I placed in this chapter some of the most important things that King Solomon had to say about wisdom from the Book of Proverbs. By learning and studying his sayings in Proverbs about the mouth, you too can walk in the wisdom of God and win the war of words. It cannot be underestimated how much Solomon had to say about wisdom and words. If you are going to have the success of King Solomon, you are going to have to learn the wisdom he taught about words.

As you read these Proverbs, you will understand the importance of speech and how it can bless your life or curse your life. One of the most famously quoted Proverbs is, *Death and life are in the power of the tongue: and they that love it shall eat the fruit thereof* (Proverbs 18:21 KJV). King Solomon's wisdom taught that your tongue could produce life and death.

I have copied many of the Proverbs that King Solomon wrote about that I believe are most important. You should, however, go to the Book of Proverbs and read all of them for yourself. Studying and applying the wisdom found in the Book Proverbs about your words will change your life. As you read over these Proverbs, meditate on them deeply and apply them to your life. Teach your tongue the wisdom of God from what these verses have to say.

Proverbs 4:23-24 (KJV)
23 Keep thy heart with all diligence; for out of it are the issues of life. 24 Put away from thee a froward mouth, and perverse lips put far from thee.

Proverbs 5:1-2 (KJV)

1 My son, attend unto my wisdom, and bow thine ear to my understanding: 2 That thou mayest regard discretion, and that thy lips may keep knowledge.

Proverbs 8:13 (KJV)

13 The fear of the Lord is to hate evil: pride, and arrogancy, and the evil way, and the froward mouth, do I hate.

Proverbs 10:6 (KJV)

6 Blessings are upon the head of the just: but violence covereth the mouth of the wicked.

Proverbs 10:11 (KJV)

11 The mouth of a righteous man is a well of life: but violence covereth the mouth of the wicked.

Proverbs 10:13 (KJV)

13 In the lips of him that hath understanding wisdom is found: but a rod is for the back of him that is void of understanding.

Proverbs 10:14 (KJV)

14 Wise men lay up knowledge: but the mouth of the foolish is near destruction.

Proverbs 10:19 (KJV)

19 In the multitude of words there wanteth not sin: but he that refraineth his lips is wise.

Proverbs 10:31 (KJV)

31 The mouth of the just bringeth forth wisdom: but the froward tongue shall be cut out.

Proverbs 10:32 (KJV)

32 The lips of the righteous know what is acceptable: but the mouth of the wicked speaketh frowardness.

Proverbs 11:9 (KJV)

9 An hypocrite with his mouth destroyeth his neighbour: but through knowledge shall the just be delivered.

Proverbs 12:6 (KJV)

6 The words of the wicked are to lie in wait for blood: but the mouth of the upright shall deliver them.

Proverbs 12:13 (KJV)

13 The wicked is snared by the transgression of his lips: but the just shall come out of trouble.

Proverbs 12:14 (KJV)

14 A man shall be satisfied with good by the fruit of his mouth: and the recompence of a man's hands shall be rendered unto him.

Proverbs 12:18 (KJV)

18 There is that speaketh like the piercings of a sword: but the tongue of the wise is health.

Proverbs 12:19 (KJV)

19 The lip of truth shall be established for ever: but a lying tongue is but for a moment.

Proverbs 13:2 (KJV)

2 A man shall eat good by the fruit of his mouth: but the soul of the transgressors shall eat violence.

Proverbs 13:3 (KJV)
3 He that keepeth his mouth keepeth his life: but he that openeth wide his lips shall have destruction.

Proverbs 14:3 (KJV)
3 In the mouth of the foolish is a rod of pride: but the lips of the wise shall preserve them.

Proverbs 14:7 (KJV)
7 Go from the presence of a foolish man, when thou perceivest not in him the lips of knowledge.

Proverbs 15:2 (KJV)
2 The tongue of the wise useth knowledge aright: but the mouth of fools poureth out foolishness.

Proverbs 15:4 (KJV)
4 A wholesome tongue is a tree of life: but perverseness therein is a breach in the spirit.

Proverbs 15:7 (KJV)
7 The lips of the wise disperse knowledge: but the heart of the foolish doeth not so.

Proverbs 15:23 (KJV)
23 A man hath joy by the answer of his mouth: and a word spoken in due season, how good is it!

Proverbs 15:28 (KJV)
28 The heart of the righteous studieth to answer: but the mouth of the wicked poureth out evil things.

Proverbs 16:1 (KJV)
1 The preparations of the heart in man, and the answer of the tongue, is from the Lord.

Proverbs 16:21 (KJV)
21 The wise in heart shall be called prudent: and the sweetness of the lips increaseth learning.

Proverbs 16:23 (KJV)
23 The heart of the wise teacheth his mouth, and addeth learning to his lips.

Proverbs 16:29-30 (KJV)
29 A violent man enticeth his neighbour, and leadeth him into the way that is not good. 30 He shutteth his eyes to devise froward things: moving his lips he bringeth evil to pass.

Proverbs 17:7 (KJV)
7 Excellent speech becometh not a fool: much less do lying lips a prince.

Proverbs 17:20 (KJV)
20 He that hath a froward heart findeth no good: and he that hath a perverse tongue falleth into mischief.

Proverbs 18:4 (KJV)
4 The words of a man's mouth are as deep waters, and the wellspring of wisdom as a flowing brook.

Proverbs 18:6-7 (KJV)
6 A fool's lips enter into contention, and his mouth calleth for strokes. 7 A fool's mouth is his destruction, and his lips are the snare of his soul.

Proverbs 18:20 (KJV)

20 A man's belly shall be satisfied with the fruit of his mouth; and with the increase of his lips shall he be filled.

Proverbs 18:21 (KJV)

21 Death and life are in the power of the tongue: and they that love it shall eat the fruit thereof.

Proverbs 19:1 (KJV)

1 Better is the poor that walketh in his integrity, than he that is perverse in his lips, and is a fool.

Proverbs 20:15 (KJV)

15 There is gold, and a multitude of rubies: but the lips of knowledge are a precious jewel.

Proverbs 20:19 (KJV)

19 He that goeth about as a talebearer revealeth secrets: therefore meddle not with him that flattereth with his lips.

Proverbs 21:23 (KJV)

23 Whoso keepeth his mouth and his tongue keepeth his soul from troubles.

Proverbs 22:11 (KJV)

11 He that loveth pureness of heart, for the grace of his lips the king shall be his friend.

Proverbs 22:14 (KJV)

14 The mouth of strange women is a deep pit: he that is abhorred of the Lord shall fall therein.

Proverbs 23:9 (KJV)

9 Speak not in the ears of a fool: for he will despise the wisdom of thy words.

Proverbs 23:15-16 (KJV)

15 My son, if thine heart be wise, my heart shall rejoice, even mine. 16 Yea, my reins shall rejoice, when thy lips speak right things.

Proverbs 24:26 (KJV)

26 Every man shall kiss his lips that giveth a right answer.

Proverbs 25:23 (KJV)

23 The north wind driveth away rain: so doth an angry countenance a backbiting tongue.

Proverbs 26:24-25 (KJV)

24 He that hateth dissembleth with his lips, and layeth up deceit within him; 25 When he speaketh fair, believe him not: for there are seven abominations in his heart.

Proverbs 26:28 (KJV)

28 A lying tongue hateth those that are afflicted by it; and a flattering mouth worketh ruin.

Proverbs 27:2 (KJV)

2 Let another man praise thee, and not thine own mouth; a stranger, and not thine own lips.

Proverbs 28:23 (KJV)

23 He that rebuketh a man afterwards shall find more favour than he that flattereth with the tongue.

Proverbs 31:9 (KJV)

9 Open thy mouth, judge righteously, and plead the cause of the poor and needy.

I am also including two powerful verses found in the Book of Ecclesiastes. King Solomon revealed deep wisdom from God about the importance of what we speak before God.

Ecclesiastes 5:2 (KJV)

2 Be not rash with thy mouth, and let not thine heart be hasty to utter any thing before God: for God is in Heaven, and thou upon earth: therefore let thy words be few.

Ecclesiastes 5:6 (KJV)

6 Suffer not thy mouth to cause thy flesh to sin; neither say thou before the angel, that it was an error: wherefore should God be angry at thy voice, and destroy the work of thine hands?

In conclusion, we can see the power of the spoken word revealed in the wisdom of King Solomon. God gave King Solomon a deep understanding of the power of speech. King Solomon used his wisdom and the power of the spoken word to influence the world around him. His life is a wonderful example of what can be accomplished with someone who understands the power of words. To win the war of words, we need a Divine impartation of wisdom from God so we can influence the world around us as King Solomon did.

CHAPTER 26

JEZEBELIC HIT

This chapter is named *Jezebelic Hit* because that is exactly what can happen when the spirit of Jezebel attacks someone with her words; they can get *Hit*. Words spoken from a Jezebelic spirit can affect someone to the core of their being. People are often affected by this spirit's words and don't realize they are under attack. This spirit tries to place people under her spell and inject them with the poison of her words. We are going to look at the story of Elijah because he was the main prophet who was attacked by the words of Jezebel. Elijah was one of the most powerful prophets of Israel but was still hit by Jezebel's words. Elijah's words ultimately defeated Jezebel, but he still went through the biggest battle of his life because of her words.

Elijah lived under the apostasy of King Ahab. King Ahab was one of the worst kings of Israel. He did evil in the sight of the Lord, more than all who were before him. Ahab followed in the sins of Jeroboam (the worshipping of the two cows), but one of the worst things he did was he married Jezebel. Jezebel was the daughter of Ethbaal, king of the Zidonians. King Ethbaal worshipped and served the god baal. After King Ahab married Jezebel, he built an altar for baal in the house of baal, in

Samaria. Ahab angered the Lord more than all the kings of Israel before him.

> ### 1 Kings 16:30-33 (KJV)
> *30 And Ahab the son of Omri did evil in the sight of the Lord above all that were before him.* **31 And it came to pass, as if it had been a light thing for him to walk in the sins of Jeroboam the son of Nebat, that he took to wife Jezebel the daughter of Ethbaal king of the Zidonians, and went and served Baal, and worshipped him. 32 And he reared up an altar for Baal in the house of Baal, which he had built in Samaria. 33 And Ahab made a grove; and Ahab did more to provoke the Lord God of Israel to anger than all the kings of Israel that were before him.**

King Ahab did not take heed to himself and greatly disobeyed the Lord. God spoke in the Book of Deuteronomy that if the children of Israel served other gods, His wrath would be kindled against them. God also forewarned that He would shut up the Heavens, and there would be no rain if they served and worshiped other gods.

> ### Deuteronomy 11:16-17 (KJV)
> *16 Take heed to yourselves, that your heart be not deceived, and ye turn aside,* **and serve other gods, and worship them; 17 And then the Lord's wrath be kindled against you, and he shut up the Heaven, that there be no rain,** *and that the land yield not her fruit; and lest ye perish quickly from off the good land which the Lord giveth you.*

God fulfilled His prophetic Word during the time of King Ahab by sending in the great prophet Elijah to stop the rain.

> ### 1 Kings 17:1 (KJV)

*17 And Elijah the Tishbite, who was of the inhabitants of Gilead, said unto Ahab, As the Lord God of Israel liveth, before whom I stand, **there shall not be dew nor rain these years, but according to my word.***

God used His prophetic Word spoken through the mouth of Elijah to shut up the Heavens. Right after Elijah gave this Word, he went into hiding. Finally, after three years of hiding, the Word of the Lord came to Elijah, telling him to show himself to Ahab and that He would send rain again.

1 Kings 18:1 (KJV)

*1 And it came to pass after many days, that the word of the Lord came to Elijah in the third year, saying, Go, shew thyself unto Ahab; **and I will send rain upon the earth.***

Because of the drought for the last three years, there was a great famine in Samaria. Ahab had sent ambassadors to other countries to seek Elijah. He also sent out one of his servants, Obadiah, to go to the fountains and brooks to find grass to feed their livestock so they didn't lose them because of the famine. While Obadiah was looking for grass to feed the animals, Elijah met him. Obadiah tells Elijah that he had hidden one hundred prophets of the Lord because Jezebel had cut off and killed the other prophets of the Lord. Elijah tells Obadiah to get Ahab because he wants to meet with him. When Ahab saw Elijah, Ahab said to him, *Art thou he that troubleth Israel?* Let's read in the Scriptures how Elijah responds to Ahab.

1 Kings 18:18 (KJV)

*18 And he answered, **I have not troubled Israel; but thou, and thy father's house, in that ye have forsaken the Commandments of the Lord, and thou hast followed Baalim.***

Elijah then called for all of the prophets of baal, and the prophets of the grove, which ate at Jezebel's table, to be gathered together at Mount Carmel. When they get there, let's read what Elijah says to them.

1 Kings 18:21 (KJV)
*21 And Elijah came unto all the people, and said, **How long halt ye between two opinions? if the Lord be God, follow him: but if Baal, then follow him.** And the people answered him not a word.*

Elijah ended up having a showdown with these false prophets and set up a challenge that whichever God answered by fire, He was God. Their god baal never answered. When Elijah set up the Altar of the Lord and poured seven barrels of water on the altar three times, God answered by fire. The fire of God fell and burnt up the sacrifice, wood, stones, and dust. The fire of God also licked up the water in the trench. This event proved that the God of Elijah was the true God, and Elijah had all the prophets of baal killed. He then prayed for it to rain again, and it did.

One would have thought that Ahab and Jezebel would have turned to the Lord after this incredible event, but they didn't. Elijah's whole goal was to turn Israel's heart back to God. I am sure Elijah thought when everyone heard that God answered by fire, they would turn to the Lord. However, Jezebel was no ordinary queen. The devil sent Jezebel to hinder the people of God, and she wasn't about to repent of her sins no matter how much God revealed Himself to His people.

1 Kings 18:36-37 (KJV)
*36 And it came to pass at the time of the offering of the evening sacrifice, that Elijah the prophet came near, and said, Lord God of Abraham, Isaac, and of Israel, let it be known this day that thou art God in Israel, and that I am thy servant, and that I have done all these things at thy word. 37 **Hear me, O Lord, hear me,***

that this people may know that thou art the Lord God, and that
thou hast turned their heart back again.

After the fire of God fell, Elijah and Ahab went to Jezreel, where Jezebel was staying. Ahab then tells Jezebel all that had happened. Then, being the wicked Queen that she was, Jezebel sends a messenger to Elijah to pronounce a death sentence upon him.

1 Kings 19:1-2 (KJV)
1 And Ahab told Jezebel all that Elijah had done, and withal how
he had slain all the prophets with the sword. 2 Then Jezebel sent
a messenger unto Elijah, saying, **So let the gods do to me, and**
more also, if I make not thy life as the life of one of them by to
morrow about this time.

Jezebel not only does not repent, but she doubles down by sending a messenger to Elijah to let him know she is going to kill him by the next day. A good question to ask yourself is, why didn't Jezebel just send her guards to have Elijah killed? Jezebel had already killed the prophets of the Lord before. Why did she first have to send a messenger to Elijah with a death sentence? Jezebel understood the war of words and knew she had to send some words of fear before taking Elijah out. She wanted her words to hit Elijah. This is where the title of this chapter comes from, *Jezebelic Hit.*

Lets' read what happens next and see how these words from Jezebel affect the great prophet, Elijah.

1 Kings 19:2-8 (KJV)
2 **Then Jezebel sent a messenger unto Elijah, saying,** *So let the*
gods do to me, and more also, if I make not thy life as the life of
one of them by to morrow about this time. 3 And when he saw

*that, **he arose, and went for his life**, and came to Beersheba, which belongeth to Judah, and left his servant there. 4 But he himself went a day's journey into the wilderness, and came and sat down under a juniper tree: **and he requested for himself that he might die; and said, It is enough; now, O Lord, take away my life;** for I am not better than my fathers. 5 **And as he lay and slept under a juniper tree,** behold, then an angel touched him, and said unto him, Arise and eat. 6 And he looked, and, behold, there was a cake baken on the coals, and a cruse of water at his head. And he did eat and drink, **and laid him down again.** 7 And the angel of the Lord came again the second time, and touched him, and said, Arise and eat; because the journey is too great for thee. 8 And he arose, and did eat and drink, and went in the strength of that meat forty days and forty nights unto Horeb the mount of God.*

Jezebel's words affected Elijah terribly. When someone is under attack from Jezebel, they can have three responses: flight, freeze, or fight. Elijah chose flight. The words of Jezebel hit him at the core of his being. Elijah went from one the most remarkable displays of God's power to running for his life. I am sure he wasn't expecting this evil response from Jezebel. I believe her response caught him off guard. Elijah only ran to Jezreel because he thought they would all get right with God after the fire of God fell from Heaven. Elijah had no idea that Jezebel was going to threaten his life.

Let's look at a few things that happened to Elijah when the words of Jezebel hit him. From studying what happened to Elijah, we can learn a lot about what to look out for if we are ever attacked and hit by the words of a Jezebelic spirit. We know this is a spirit because of what Jesus says in the Book of Revelation. In Revelation, Jesus refers to

Jezebel, the prophetess seducing His servants to commit fornication and eat things sacrificed to idols.

Revelation 2:18-23 (KJV)

*18 And unto the angel of the Church in Thyatira write; These things saith the Son of God, who hath his eyes like unto a flame of fire, and his feet are like fine brass; 19 I know thy works, and charity, and service, and faith, and thy patience, and thy works; and the last to be more than the first. 20 **Notwithstanding I have a few things against thee, because thou sufferest that woman Jezebel, which calleth herself a prophetess, to teach and to seduce my servants to commit fornication, and to eat things sacrificed unto idols. 21 And I gave her space to repent of her fornication; and she repented not. 22 Behold, I will cast her into a bed, and them that commit adultery with her into great tribulation, except they repent of their deeds. 23 And I will kill her children with death; and all the Churches shall know that I am he which searcheth the reins and hearts: and I will give unto every one of you according to your works.***

This same Jezebelic spirit is found in one of the New Testament Churches of God. Remember, Jezebel came to Israel where God's people were and became a queen over them. This spirit likes to infiltrate the people of God and kill the prophetic. This spirit first does this by the war of words. Next, this spirit wants to speak fear into the people of God. When the spirit of fear hits someone, it affects them and tries to stop them. Let's look at the five effects of a *Jezebelic Hit* by studying what happened to Elijah.

1. **FEAR** - It puts a spirit of fear on you and makes you want to run for your life. Some people want to get away and not face this spirit head-on out of fear.

   1 Kings 19:3a (KJV)
   3 And when he saw that, he arose, and went for his life,

2. **ISOLATION** - It makes you want to isolate yourself. It wants to separate you from the very people of God that you need.

   1 Kings 19:3 (KJV)
   *3 And when he saw that, he arose, and went for his life, and came to Beersheba, which belongeth to Judah, **and left his servant there.***

3. **DEATH** – This spirit makes you want to die. Some people hit by this spirit may even want to commit suicide. A spirit of death comes upon the person being *hit* by this Jezebelic spirit.

   1 Kings 19:4b (KJV)
   *4 ...and he requested for himself that he might die; and said, It is enough; now, **O Lord, take away my life**; for I am not better than my fathers.*

4. **SELF-PITY** - Next, when hit by this spirit, it makes you feel sorry for yourself.

   1 Kings 19:4c (KJV)
   4 ...It is enough; now, O Lord, take away my life; for I am not better than my fathers.

5. **NO ENERGY** - Finally, this spirit sucks the life right out of its victims and makes them tired. When hit by this spirit, you want to sleep and have no energy.

1 Kings 19:5 (KJV)
5 And as he lay and slept under a juniper tree, behold, then an
angel touched him, and said unto him, Arise and eat.

If these curses have ever come upon you, then you know the spirit of Jezebel has hit you. These Jezebelic hits are no joke and will aim to take a man or woman of God out. But, do you see how Jezebel had to say something to Elijah first? She didn't just send people to kill him. She knew he was a mighty prophet and that she would have to use her words first. Her words did affect Elijah, and he needed to get alone with God.

An angel of God supernaturally fed Elijah so he could go to Mount Sinai and spend some alone time with God. When Elijah got to the Mountain of God, he was able to talk to God, and God restored his strength. When you spend time waiting on God, you renew your strength.

Isaiah 40:28-31 (KJV)
28 Hast thou not known? hast thou not heard, that the everlasting
God, the Lord, the Creator of the ends of the earth, fainteth not,
neither is weary? there is no searching of his understanding. 29
He giveth power to the faint; and to them that have no might he
increaseth strength. 30 Even the youths shall faint and be weary,
and the young men shall utterly fall: 31 But they that wait upon
the Lord shall renew their strength; they shall mount up with
wings as eagles; they shall run, and not be weary; and they shall
walk, and not faint.

God also spoke to Elijah about whom next to anoint as king of Israel. Ahab ended up dying in a battle. God wanted Jehu to be the next anointed king of Israel. Jehu was used to kill Jezebel after the death of Ahab. Jehu also went on a killing spree and killed anyone who worshipped baal in Israel. God showed Elijah the future. Prophets live and have hope by future prophetic insight from God.

As we can see, a *Jezebelic Hit* can have a terrible impact on a man of God. The words of this spirit are like the poison of a snake going into someone who has been bitten. These words are poison to the soul and spirit.

Romans 3:13-14 (KJV)

13 Their throat is an open sepulchre; **with their tongues they have used deceit; the poison of asps is under their lips:** *14 Whose mouth is full of cursing and bitterness:*

During their ministry, Jesus and John the Baptist had to deal with this spirit. As a result, they both called them out as vipers.

Luke 3:7 (KJV)

7 Then said he to the multitude that came forth to be baptized of him, **O generation of vipers,** *who hath warned you to flee from the wrath to come?*

Matthew 12:34 (KJV)

34 **O generation of vipers,** *how can ye, being evil, speak good things? for out of the abundance of the heart the mouth speaketh.*

Matthew 23:33 (KJV)

33 **Ye serpents, ye generation of vipers,** *how can ye escape the damnation of hell?*

Vipers and poisonous snakes have to inject their poison into their victims just like a demonic spirit of Jezebel has to inject their toxic words into their victim.

Their untamed tongue is full of deadly poison.

James 3:8 (KJV)

8 But the tongue can no man tame; it is an unruly evil, **full of deadly poison.**

God's Word, on the other hand, brings health and life.

Proverbs 4:20-22 (KJV)

*20 My son, **attend to my words;** incline thine ear unto my sayings. 21 Let them not depart from thine eyes; keep them in the midst of thine heart. 22 **For they are life unto those that find them, and health to all their flesh.***

Jesus said the Words He spoke were Spirit and life.

John 6:63 (KJV)

*63 It is the spirit that quickeneth; the flesh profiteth nothing: **the words that I speak unto you, they are spirit, and they are life.***

Looking back at the story of Elijah, he was caught off guard, but he didn't have to run. He was one of the most powerful prophets to ever live in Israel. He was surrounded and protected by God's angels. And, if you get right down to it, Jezebel feared him. He could have still dominated the situation. Elijah had the upper hand because God was with him. Elijah ended up making a prophecy about the death of Jezebel that came to pass by Jehu, the next king of Israel.

2 Kings 9:30-37 (KJV)

*30 And when Jehu was come to Jezreel, Jezebel heard of it; and she painted her face, and tired her head, and looked out at a window. 31 And as Jehu entered in at the gate, she said, Had Zimri peace, who slew his master? 32 And he lifted up his face to the window, and said, Who is on my side? who? And there looked out to him two or three eunuchs. 33 **And he said, Throw her down. So they threw her down: and some of her blood was sprinkled on the wall, and on the horses: and he trode her under foot.** 34 And when he was come in, he did eat and drink, and said, Go, see now this cursed woman, and bury her: for she is a king's* *daughter. 35 And they went to bury her: but they found no more of her than the skull, and the feet, and the palms of her hands. 36 Wherefore they came again, and told him.* **And he said, This is the word of the Lord, which he spake by his servant Elijah the Tishbite, saying, In the portion of Jezreel shall dogs eat the flesh of Jezebel: 37 And the carcase of Jezebel shall be as dung upon the face of the field in the portion of Jezreel; so that they shall not say, This is Jezebel.**

If you ever find yourself in a war of words with a Jezebelic spirit, look for the five signs that we talked about in this chapter that happens to someone when hit by this spirit. This type of Jezebelic spirit still exists today because it is a demonic spirit, and it uses the same evil tactics from generation to generation. If you are fearful, want to isolate yourself, are spiritually tired, have self-pity, and want to die, wake up. The spirit of Jezebel has hit you. Stand up on your feet, spend time with God alone and start declaring the Word of God over your life. Speak to yourself out loud that you are strong in the Lord and the power of His might. Shout your way back into a spirit of victory. You can defeat this spirit just like Jehu did through the prophetic Word of Elijah. You have to connect with and hear the prophetic Word of God to stay strong and win the war of words.

There have been many men and women of God who stood their ground and faced Jezebel head-on. Remember that you do not have to run when Jezebel wants to spue her poison on you. You are called to tread on serpents, and nothing will harm you. This is part of the Great Commission that Jesus pronounced before His ascension into Heaven.

Mark 16:15-18 (KJV)

15 And he said unto them, Go ye into all the world, and preach the gospel to every creature. 16 He that believeth and is baptized shall be saved; but he that believeth not shall be damned. 17 And these signs shall follow them that believe; **In my name shall they cast out devils;** *they shall speak with new tongues; 18* **They shall take up serpents; and if they drink any deadly thing, it shall not hurt them; they shall lay hands on the sick, and they shall recover.**

You are called to defeat the spirit of Jezebel and not run from it. You must learn the devil's tactics and not be ignorant of his devices. You have the victory, and you never have to succumb to this devil. But know you are dealing with a real threat, with real poison and potential to take you out if you don't stand up and fight. One thing to note is these attacks usually come by someone in the body of Christ right after a great victory. Remember Jezebel infiltrated the people of God when she married Ahab, and Jesus said this spirit would be in one of the Churches in the Book of Revelation.

When you are on a high from a great victory from the Lord, and not looking, is when this spirit likes to attack you with her venomous words. You, however, now have insight into this kind of spirit, and by faith, you can win this spiritual battle of the war of words. You have the victory!

In conclusion, we must admit if this wicked spirit has hit us. It is only through faith and prayer you can defeat the spirit of Jezebel. You don't have to run when hit by this spirit. This chapter was written to equip you better to deal with and defeat this spirit. God has given you the victory; you just have to apply that victory with your words. You will win the war of words against this spirit if you stay close to God and understand Jezebel's tactics. God will never leave or forsake His children.

CHAPTER 27

THE LOST ART OF REBUKING

For the most part, today's Church has lost the secret art of rebuking. Rebuking, however, was a big part of Jesus' ministry, and it was also a big part of the early Church. This chapter will reveal how vital *rebuking* is to winning the war of words.

To rebuke means to speak angrily and with authority to someone or something because you disapprove of what they have said or done. It expresses sharp verbal disapproval of something or someone's words and actions. It means to verbally reprimand, scold, or criticize sharply with a verbal confrontation. In today's terms, a rebuke is a verbal smackdown.

When Jesus rebuked something or someone, He did it with authority and urgency. He rebuked demons, people, and things with a firm conviction of His Words when they were not in alignment with the will of God. Many people have painted the picture of Jesus being so friendly, kind, and loving that He wouldn't hurt a fly. Jesus is loving and kind, but when it comes to evil, demons, things, and people out of the will of God, He had no problem speaking with authority to them. God's Holy Spirit anointed Jesus, and when He spoke to something or someone, they had to obey. Disobedience is not an option when God is rebuking you. When Jesus rebuked things, He would tell them to stop talking or, "Hold your peace."

If winning the war of words has everything to do with words, it is easy to understand why Jesus rebuked people, demons, and things. When you rebuke something, you use your words with authority and force. It takes forceful, authoritative, and bold words of reprimand to come against evil utterances that are causing things to come to pass. Even bad people have power with their words, and whatever they have spoken that is causing evil to come to pass must be **REBUKED**.

When you understand the full impact of what rebuking means in the Bible and how much Jesus was going around rebuking, you end up having a different image of Jesus. Jesus is the most influential person ever to live. He is strong in His love for people and His hatred of evil. The Book of Hebrews says that Jesus loved righteousness and hated iniquity, which is why God anointed Him.

> ### Hebrews 1:8-9 (KJV)
> 8 **But unto the Son he saith,** *Thy throne, O God, is for ever and ever: a sceptre of righteousness is the sceptre of thy kingdom.* 9 **Thou hast loved righteousness, and hated iniquity; therefore God, even thy God, hath anointed thee with the oil of gladness above thy fellows.**

Let's look at some Scriptures that show who and what Jesus was rebuking. One of the first places we see Jesus rebuking something was when He was crossing the Sea of Galilee and a great storm came upon Him and His disciples. The storm filled the ship with water while Jesus was asleep on a pillow, and it threatened to drown them. These ships were small, so Jesus had to be sleeping in water before His disciples woke Him up in fear of their lives.

Mark 4:35-41 (KJV)

*35 And the same day, when the even was come, he saith unto them, Let us pass over unto the other side. 36 And when they had sent away the multitude, they took him even as he was in the ship. And there were also with him other little ships. 37 And there arose a great storm of wind, and the waves beat into the ship, so that it was now full. 38 **And he was in the hinder part of the ship, asleep on a pillow:** and they awake him, and say unto him, Master, carest thou not that we perish? 39 **And he arose, and rebuked the wind, and said unto the sea, Peace, be still. And the wind ceased, and there was a great calm.** 40 And he said unto them, Why are ye so fearful? how is it that ye have no faith? 41 And they feared exceedingly, and said one to another, **What manner of man is this, that even the wind and the sea obey him?***

The disciples had never seen anyone rebuke a storm, and the storm obeyed Him. Peter, James, and John were fishermen and had seen many storms. This storm was so dangerous that it could have sunk their ship. This storm was attempting to kill them all. When Jesus was awakened, He immediately rebuked the wind and told the sea to be at *Peace.* This word peace means to muzzle one's mouth. Not only did Jesus rebuke the storm with authority, but He recognized it was talking to Him. Jesus was not going to tolerate a storm speaking to Him and try to stop His mission from God. Jesus was in the perfect will of God and had every right to verbally rebuke this storm.

Now, let's look at the fig tree Jesus rebuked and cursed.

Mark 11:12-14 (KJV)

12 And on the morrow, when they were come from Bethany, he was hungry: 13 And seeing a fig tree afar off having leaves, he came, if haply he might find any thing thereon: and when he came

to it, he found nothing but leaves; for the time of figs was not yet.
*14 **And Jesus answered and said unto it, No man eat fruit of** **thee hereafter for ever.** And his disciples heard it.*

Jesus answered this fig tree. That means the fig tree talked to Him and told Him He couldn't eat from it. You only answer things that are talking to you. Jesus responded by rebuking and cursing the fig tree by saying that no man would eat fruit from it forever. Let's see what happened after Jesus rebuked this fig tree.

Mark 11:20-21 (KJV)

*20 And in the morning, as they passed by, **they saw the fig tree** **dried up from the roots.** 21 And Peter calling to remembrance saith unto him, **Master, behold, the fig tree which thou cursedst** **is withered away.***

This fig tree heard the rebuke of Jesus and died by drying up at the roots. Jesus spoke with authority to this fig tree. Jesus used the example of the fig tree drying up at its roots from His rebuke to teach His disciples about having faith in God or having the faith of God and speaking to mountains, and they will obey you.

Mark 11:22-24 (KJV)

22 And Jesus answering saith unto them, Have faith in God. 23 ***For verily I say unto you, That whosoever shall say unto this*** ***mountain, Be thou removed, and be thou cast into the sea; and*** ***shall not doubt in his heart, but shall believe that those things*** ***which he saith shall come to pass; he shall have whatsoever he*** ***saith.*** *24 Therefore I say unto you, What things soever ye desire, when ye pray, believe that ye receive them, and ye shall have them.*

This passage of Scripture indicates that speaking to mountains involves rebuking them because Jesus tied this in with Him rebuking the fig tree. We not only speak to mountains, but we must rebuke them. A mountain is an impossible thing standing in the way of God's will. Mountains must be rebuked to be moved.

Now let's see how Jesus handled the fever attacking Peter's mother-in-law.

Luke 4:38-39 (KJV)

*38 And he arose out of the synagogue, and entered into Simon's house. And Simon's wife's mother was taken with a great fever; and they besought him for her. 39 **And he stood over her, and rebuked the fever;** and it left her: and immediately she arose and ministered unto them.*

Jesus rebuked the fever! That means He spoke with authority and anger against this fever attacking Peter's mother-in-law and told it to leave her. This fever heard what Jesus said, and it left her immediately.

Now lets' look at how Jesus handled demon-possessed people.

Luke 4:33-35 (KJV)

*33 And in the synagogue there was a man, which had a spirit of an unclean devil, and cried out with a loud voice, 34 Saying, Let us alone; what have we to do with thee, thou Jesus of Nazareth? art thou come to destroy us? I know thee who thou art; the Holy One of God. 35 **And Jesus rebuked him, saying, Hold thy peace, and come out of him.** And when the devil had thrown him in the midst, he came out of him, and hurt him not.*

Jesus rebuked this devil and told him to quit speaking and come out of the man. Jesus did not want to hear what this demon had to say. He rebuked this demon with so much authority it amazed the people who witnessed this event.

> *Luke 4:36 (KJV)*
>
> *36 **And they were all amazed,** and spake among themselves, saying, **What a word is this! for with authority and power he commandeth the unclean spirits, and they come out.***

These people witnessed the Son of God rebuke a demon, and it obeyed Him. We have no record in Biblical history of anyone ever speaking to a demon and telling it what to do up to this point in history, and it obeying them. Most people were afraid of demons. Jesus had no fear and commanded this demon what to do by the rebuke of God.

Let's read another story of Jesus rebuking a demon that His disciples could not cast out.

> *Matthew 17:14-18 (KJV)*
>
> *14 And when they were come to the multitude, there came to him a certain man, kneeling down to him, and saying, 15 Lord, have mercy on my son: for he is lunatick, and sore vexed: for ofttimes he falleth into the fire, and oft into the water. 16 And I brought him to thy disciples, and they could not cure him. 17 Then Jesus answered and said, O faithless and perverse generation, how long shall I be with you? how long shall I suffer you? bring him hither to me. 18 **And Jesus rebuked the devil;** and he departed out of him: and the child was cured from that very hour.*

Jesus spoke to demons with authority. When He rebuked them, they listened and came out of people. Jesus was not soft-spoken when He was rebuking demons. He knew when and how to talk to a demon. Demons try to speak to people and tell them what to do. As a Christian, you must never allow this to happen. You have to rebuke with authority any demon trying to torment someone. You must give demons a verbal smackdown when casting them out.

This next story is interesting because it gets into one of the disciples of Jesus trying to rebuke Jesus. This disciple receives a wake-up call as Jesus rebukes him instead.

Mark 8:31-33 (KJV)
31 And he began to teach them, that the Son of man must suffer many things, and be rejected of the elders, and of the chief priests, and scribes, and be killed, and after three days rise again. 32 And he spake that saying openly. **And Peter took him, and began to rebuke him.** *33* **But when he had turned about and looked on his disciples, he rebuked Peter,** *saying,* **Get thee behind me, Satan**: *for thou savourest not the things that be of God, but the things that be of men.*

Peter tried to rebuke Jesus when Jesus was revealing to them the plan of God about His coming suffering and rejection by the elders. Jesus immediately turned around and rebuked Peter. In this rebuke, He spoke directly to Satan. Jesus recognized that Satan was speaking through Peter and rebuked him. We must be careful never to let the devil talk through us, or we could be the one finding ourselves being rebuked.

Now let's see what some New Testament writers had to say about rebuking. Rebuking played a big part in the early New Testament Church.

Titus 2:15 (KJV)
15 These things speak, and exhort, **and rebuke with all authority.** *Let no man despise thee.*

The Apostle Paul told Titus to rebuke with all authority and to let no one despise him.

1 Timothy 5:1 (KJV)

*1 **Rebuke not an elder,** but intreat him as a father; and the younger men as brethren;*

We are not supposed to rebuke an elder in the Church.

1 Timothy 5:19-20 (KJV)

*19 Against an elder receive not an accusation, but before two or three witnesses. 20 **Them that sin rebuke before all, that others also may fear.***

Those that sin are to be rebuked before everyone that others will fear and not sin. A real rebuke from God is fearful and is meant to get someone to stop sinning. When you are rebuking, you are not putting someone down or cursing them. You are just calling them out on their sin, and telling them with the authority of God to stop sinning.

2 Timothy 4:1-4 (KJV)

*1 I charge thee therefore before God, and the Lord Jesus Christ, who shall judge the quick and the dead at his appearing and his kingdom; 2 Preach the word; be instant in season, out of season; reprove, **rebuke,** exhort with all long suffering and doctrine. 3 For the time will come when they will not endure sound doctrine; but after their own lusts shall they heap to themselves teachers, having itching ears; 4 And they shall turn away their ears from the truth, and shall be turned unto fables.*

Rebuking played a big part in the New Testament minister's ministry, and it went along with the preaching and the teaching of the Gospel. Rebuking is essential because sometimes, the rebuke of God helps people get back on track with God. True ministers of the Gospel are not called to just be your friend. God sends them to prepare the Church for the coming of Christ. This is not always an easy task. There are many voices and demons that ministers have to come against to accomplish their mission, and it is going to get worse in the Last Days.

Now, let's see how Michael the archangel spoke to the devil when disputing about the body of Moses.

> ### Jude 1:9 (KJV)
> *9 Yet Michael the archangel, when contending with the devil he disputed about the body of Moses, durst not bring against him a railing accusation, but said,* **The Lord rebuke thee.**

Michael the archangel rebuked the devil in the name of the Lord. The only way to handle the devil is to rebuke him in Jesus' name. The devil either needs to be behind you or under your feet. You do this by rebuking him in the Name of the Lord when he comes against you.

Let's look at how God handles His true children.

> ### Hebrews 12:5-8 (KJV)
> *5 And ye have forgotten the exhortation which speaketh unto you as unto children, My son, despise not thou the chastening of the Lord,* **nor faint when thou art rebuked of him:** *6 For whom the Lord loveth he chasteneth, and scourgeth every son whom he receiveth. 7 If ye endure chastening, God dealeth with you as with sons; for what son is he whom the father chasteneth not? 8 But if ye be without chastisement, whereof all are partakers, then are ye bastards, and not sons.*

Revelation 3:19 (KJV)

*19 **As many as I love, I rebuke and chasten:** be zealous therefore, and repent.*

God, Himself, rebukes His children. Being rebuked by God proves you are His child and that He loves you. When God is rebuking His children, He does it in love. If you, as a minister, have to rebuke a fellow Christian, do it in love.

God even rebuked the Red Sea when it stood in the way of the children of Israel when Pharaoh was chasing them down. He rebuked the Red Sea out of love for His children. The Red Sea was standing in the way of their deliverance and needed to be rebuked.

Psalm 106:9-10 (KJV)

*9 **He rebuked the Red sea also,** and it was dried up: so he led them through the depths, as through the wilderness. 10 And he saved them from the hand of him that hated them, and redeemed them from the hand of the enemy.*

The Bible also says that God will rebuke the devourer when we tithe.

Malachi 3:8-12 (KJV)

*8 Will a man rob God? Yet ye have robbed me. But ye say, Wherein have we robbed thee? In tithes and offerings. 9 Ye are cursed with a curse: for ye have robbed me, even this whole nation. 10 Bring ye all the tithes into the storehouse, that there may be meat in mine house, and prove me now herewith, saith the Lord of hosts, if I will not open you the windows of Heaven, and pour you out a blessing, that there shall not be room enough to receive it. 11 **And I will rebuke the devourer for your sakes,** and he shall not destroy the fruits of your ground; neither shall your vine cast her fruit before the time in the field, saith the Lord*

*of hosts. 12 And all nations shall call you blessed: for ye shall be
a delightsome land, saith the Lord of hosts.*

If you are going to be blessed financially, you must give your tithe to
God. But, tithing alone will not get you blessed. God must open the
windows of Heaven for you, and He also has to rebuke the devourer for
you. The devourer must be rebuked by God for you to be financially
blessed.

I could go on with many more Scriptures, but you can see how
important rebuking is from the ones mentioned. When a demon, tree,
sea, fever, or mountain is speaking to you and in the way of God, you
must rebuke it. Rebuking is the lost secret of winning the war of words.
If you are going to win a war of words against an evil force, it must be
rebuked. When you rebuke something or a demon with strong words of
authority, the faster it will obey you. You cannot speak softly to a devil
or mountain and think it will move at your command. You must
reprimand it with an authoritative rebuke and give it a verbal
smackdown for it to obey you.

CHAPTER 28

———•◦•———

THE POWER OF PROPHECY

I n this chapter, we will discover what prophecy is and why it is so important to allow God to prophesy through you. God wants to use your mouth to speak His Words, and prophesying is one of the most powerful ways He can do this. Our mouths are in an eternal spiritual battle, and if God can speak through you by way of prophecy, you will win the war of words. The war of words is easy when God speaks through you, because His Word dominates every other word.

To get started, let's define what prophecy is. Prophecy is when the Spirit of God comes upon someone and speaks directly through them. God uses their mouth as His mouth. God is literally speaking through the person prophesying. Prophecy is God speaking in the first person through a person's mouth. This is why prophecy usually starts with, *"Thus says the Lord."*

Here is an example of God speaking directly through Moses. God used Moses' mouth so He could speak directly to Pharaoh.

> *Exodus 4:22-23 (KJV)*
> *22 **And thou shalt say** unto Pharaoh, **Thus saith the Lord,** Israel is my son, even my firstborn: 23 And I say unto thee, Let my son*

go, that he may serve me: and if thou refuse to let him go, behold,
I will slay thy son, even thy firstborn.

In this example, God used prophecy to speak directly to Pharaoh through Moses' mouth. Another form of prophecy is when God foretells the future or wants His thoughts to be known on a subject. Finally, in the New Testament, it was revealed that prophecy was to be used to edify, exhort, and comfort people.

1 Corinthians 14:3 (KJV)
3 But he that prophesieth speaketh unto men to edification, and exhortation, and comfort.

Prophecy is one of God's most powerful gifts to the Church. In the Old Testament, prophecy was spoken through the prophets or when the Spirit of God came upon someone. In some cases, the person prophesying may not have been a prophet, but God still prophesied through them.

In the New Testament, prophecy was a gift given by God to the whole Church and was to help people. God gave nine gifts of the Spirit to the Church. Prophecy is one of those nine gifts any believer can have and should desire to have.

1 Corinthians 12:7-11 (KJV)
7 But the manifestation of the Spirit is given to every man to profit withal. 8 For to one is given by the Spirit the word of wisdom; to another the word of knowledge by the same Spirit; 9 To another faith by the same Spirit; to another the gifts of healing by the same Spirit; 10 To another the working of miracles; to another prophecy; to another discerning of spirits; to another divers kinds of tongues; to another the interpretation of tongues:

11 But all these worketh that one and the selfsame Spirit, dividing
to every man severally as he will.

Prophecy is one of the most powerful gifts of the Spirit, because, as stated before, God would come upon the prophet or believer and communicate directly through their mouth. God, the Creator, who spoke everything into existence, can speak into someone's situation by a prophetic Word of prophecy. When someone receives a prophetic Word from God, it will change their life. This is why the Apostle Paul wrote in 1 Corinthians 14 that we should desire these spiritual gifts that God has given, but, most importantly, we should desire to prophesy.

1 Corinthians 14:1 (KJV)
*1 Follow after charity, **and desire spiritual gifts, but rather that***
ye may prophesy.

When you understand the power of words and their effect on this world, you can see why prophecy is important. Your words have power, but God's Words have more power. Getting God to speak into your situation is more powerful than you speaking into your situation. God loves His people and knows they need help. Prophecy is one way He sends this help. God loves to speak into situations and change them for good. This is why the gift of prophecy is one of the most powerful gifts given to the Church.

To win the war of words, we have to have stronger words than the enemy. God's Word is the most powerful Word in the universe. If you can get God to speak into your situation in your time of need, you will not only be comforted, but you will win the war of words. His prophetic Word is more powerful than all other words. Therefore, we must get God's Word spoken into our lives to win the war of words.

God revealed through Moses that He wanted all His people to be prophets and have God speak through them. Moses needed help, so God said He would take the Spirit on him and put it on seventy elders of Israel. Let's read about this story from the Old Testament.

Numbers 11:14-17 (KJV)

*14 **I am not able to bear all this people alone, because it is too heavy for me.** 15 And if thou deal thus with me, kill me, I pray thee, out of hand, if I have found favour in thy sight; and let me not see my wretchedness. 16 And the Lord said unto Moses, **Gather unto me seventy men of the elders of Israel, whom thou knowest to be the elders of the people, and officers over them; and bring them unto the tabernacle of the congregation, that they may stand there with thee. 17 And I will come down and talk with thee there: and I will take of the spirit which is upon thee, and will put it upon them; and they shall bear the burden of the people with thee, that thou bear it not thyself alone.***

God promised Moses to help him by putting the Spirit of God on these elders. Moses needed more people to help him. The best form of help was God putting His Spirit upon the elders and have them prophesy.

Numbers 11:24-25 (KJV)

*24 And Moses went out, and told the people the words of the Lord, and gathered the seventy men of the elders of the people, and set them round about the tabernacle. 25 **And the Lord came down in a cloud, and spake unto him, and took of the spirit that was upon him, and gave it unto the seventy elders: and it came to pass, that, when the spirit rested upon them, they prophesied, and did not cease.***

When the Spirit of God came upon these seventy elders, they began to prophesy. God helped Moses by the gift of prophecy coming out of their mouths. Also, when this occurred, two people, who were not there, started prophesying. Joshua said to Moses that he should forbid them from prophesying. Let's see how Moses responded to what Joshua said.

> *Numbers 11:26-29 (KJV)*
> *26 **But there remained two of the men in the camp, the name of the one was Eldad, and the name of the other Medad: and the spirit rested upon them;** and they were of them that were written, but went not out unto the tabernacle: **and they prophesied in the camp.** 27 **And there ran a young man, and told Moses, and said, Eldad and Medad do prophesy in the camp.** 28 And Joshua the son of Nun, the servant of Moses, one of his young men, answered and said, **My Lord Moses, forbid them.** 29 And Moses said unto him, Enviest thou for my sake? **would God that all the Lord's people were prophets, and that the Lord would put his spirit upon them!***

Moses said he wanted God's Spirit to come on all of God's people and that they would prophesy. It has always been the will of God for His Spirit to come upon His people that they would prophesy. We can see this in the prophetic Word spoken by the prophet Joel.

> *Joel 2:28-29 (KJV)*
> *28 **And it shall come to pass afterward, that I will pour out my spirit upon all flesh; and your sons and your daughters shall prophesy,** your old men shall dream dreams, your young men shall see visions: 29 **And also upon the servants and upon the handmaids in those days will I pour out my spirit.***

God prophesied that His Spirit would come upon all flesh. We know that this prophecy was fulfilled in the Book of Acts, Chapter 2 when the Holy Spirit was given on the Day of Pentecost. The Apostle Peter spoke the prophecy of Joel when speaking to the Jews who were in wonderment of what was going on by what they were hearing on the Day of Pentecost.

> ### *Acts 2:14-18 (KJV)*
> *14 But Peter, standing up with the eleven, lifted up his voice, and said unto them, Ye men of Judaea, and all ye that dwell at Jerusalem, be this known unto you, and hearken to my words: 15 For these are not drunken, as ye suppose, seeing it is but the third hour of the day. 16 **But this is that which was spoken by the prophet Joel;** 17 And it shall come to pass in the last days, saith God, **I will pour out of my Spirit upon all flesh: and your sons and your daughters shall prophesy,** and your young men shall see visions, and your old men shall dream dreams: 18 And on my servants and on my handmaidens I will pour out in those days of my Spirit; **and they shall prophesy:***

Prophecy has always played an essential role in the Old and New Testaments. This is because God has always been ready to speak His prophetic Word to people. This is why the gift of prophecy is a gift you should ask God to give you if you don't have it already. It is wonderful to be used by God to speak into someone's situation and give a word that helps them in their time of need.

I want to add something important when it comes to prophecy. God's Word will always win, but there are always conditions to prophetic Words. It is critical you hear those prophetic conditions and obey what He tells you to do. Every prophecy will come with a condition. Make sure you listen carefully to what God says and any condition He speaks regarding the prophecy coming to pass. The victory is yours if you obey God. Don't, however, expect a prophetic Word to come to pass if you are living in disobedience to God's Word. I have also listed the sixteen *Laws of Faith* to help you understand your end of the bargain. The *Laws of Faith* will help you receive all of your prophetic Words from God.

It is also vital that you don't despise prophesyings and prove all things. Make sure that when you receive a prophetic word from someone, God is speaking to you and not a false prophecy. Sometimes the enemy will send in false prophets. Therefore, every prophetic word has to be proved.

1 Thessalonians 5:19-21 (KJV)

*19 Quench not the Spirit. 20 **Despise not prophesyings.** 21 **Prove all things;** hold fast that which is good.*

Jesus said we would know a prophet by their fruits. Fruit represents the life and words of the prophet. So we have to look at the lives of prophets to see if they obediently serve God and have good fruit. We also know that all of the words of a true prophet have to come to pass. This is a sign they are true prophets of the Lord. One sign of a false prophet is they will always be after financial gain.

Matthew 7:15-20 (KJV)

*15 **Beware of false prophets,** which come to you in sheep's clothing, but inwardly they are ravening wolves. 16 **Ye shall know them by their fruits.** Do men gather grapes of thorns, or figs of thistles? 17 Even so every good tree bringeth forth good fruit; but a corrupt tree bringeth forth evil fruit. 18 **A good tree cannot bring forth evil fruit, neither can a corrupt tree bring forth good fruit.** 19 Every tree that bringeth not forth good fruit* *is hewn down, and cast into the fire. 20 **Wherefore by their fruits ye shall know them.***

Because words are so powerful and can affect the future outcome of your life, you must make sure you only allow God to speak to you. But you are wise now, and God will help you discern false prophets. If a false word is spoken over you, you must come against those words and send them back to the sender. Also, never be afraid to stop someone from prophesying over you if you feel they are not right, even in a public meeting. The devil likes to use the pressure of people to get you in fear and receive a word that could bring a curse on your life. But God has His true prophets, and the way you discern it is by asking yourself, "Did the prophetic word bring edification, exhortation, and comfort?"

1 Corinthians 14:3 (KJV)
3 But he that prophesieth speaketh unto men to edification, and exhortation, and comfort.

We are in a real fight, and prophetic words play a big part in this battle. This is why the devil tries to come in and speak false words over people. When the Bible talks about the devil coming in like a roaring lion seeking whom he may devour, it is talking about the devil coming in authoritatively speaking life-threatening words. The devil comes in like a roaring lion speaking overwhelming thoughts of death, hell, and destruction. The devil comes to steal, kill, and destroy from whomever he can. He knows if he can get someone to believe what he is speaking to them, he can defeat them, especially if they speak out of their mouth what he threatens them with. Never repeat any thought of destruction the devil says to you out of your mouth.

1 Peter 5:8-9 (KJV)
*8 Be sober, be vigilant; **because your adversary the devil, as a roaring lion, walketh about, seeking whom he may devour:***

*9 **Whom resist stedfast in the faith**, knowing that the same afflictions are accomplished in your brethren that are in the world.*

God's answer to the devil coming in like a roaring lion is to send a prophet or child of God with a prophetic Word that will defeat his roaring. The Lion of the Tribe of Judah's *Roar* will always prevail. Jesus' prophetic roar will send the devil running when you submit to God. The Book of Amos proclaims that when the lion roars, who will not fear, and when God speaks, who can but prophesy. This passage is the link to the roar of a lion and prophecy.

Amos 3:7-8 (KJV)

*7 **Surely the Lord God will do nothing, but he revealeth his secret unto his servants the prophets. 8 The lion hath roared, who will not fear? the Lord God hath spoken, who can but prophesy?***

God's roar is fearful, and He sends in His prophets to prophesy and send the devil running. The true fivefold ministry is put into the Church to help mature the Church, so nobody is deceived or left in fear of the devil.

Ephesians 4:11-14 (KJV)

*11 **And he gave some, apostles; and some, prophets; and some, evangelists; and some, pastors and teachers;** 12 For the perfecting of the saints, for the work of the ministry, for the edifying of the body of Christ: 13 Till we all come in the unity of the faith, and of the knowledge of the Son of God, unto a perfect man, unto the measure of the stature of the fulness of Christ: 14 **That we henceforth be no more children, tossed to and fro, and***

carried about with every wind of doctrine, by the sleight of men,
and cunning craftiness, whereby they lie in wait to deceive;

The testimony of Jesus is the spirit of prophecy. Testimony means to be a witness of someone who speaks with authority. Jesus wants to prophesy through His people by the Spirit of the Lord with authority.

Revelation 19:10 (KJV)
*19 And I fell at his feet to worship him. And he said unto me, See thou do it not: I am thy fellowservant, and of thy brethren that have the testimony of Jesus: worship God: **for the testimony of Jesus is the spirit of prophecy.***

In conclusion, winning the war of words is easy when you have God on your side and have Him speaking into your situation. We don't see God with our natural eyes, but we hear His voice. God has sent His Spirit into the Church so He can speak by the gift of prophecy. This gift is a wonderful operation in the body of Christ. If you do not have the gift of prophecy operating through you, you should ask God for this gift. You will not only help yourself, but you will also help many other people who need to hear from God. The gift of prophecy is priceless when it comes to winning the war of words.

CHAPTER 29

———◦●◦———

PRAISE AND WORSHIP

P raise and worship cannot be underestimated in a believer's life and are foundational to the Christian's faith. Through praise and worship, we declare the goodness and greatness of God as we draw close to Him. God is great and is worthy of all our praise and adoration. In this chapter, we will look at what praise and worship are and their importance to the life of a Christian. We will also see how these two significant aspects of a believer's life can help win the war of words.

To get started, we have to understand the definition of each of these words. First, let's look at the word *Praise* and what it means. The word *Praise* means to bless, exalt, glorify, magnify, confess, and thank God with your mouth in a joyful way. A believer uses their mouth with a shout or song when praising God. When you are praising God, you are using your voice and instruments to proclaim the goodness of God. Praise also includes raising your hands and dancing before the Lord. Praise, in essence, is the victorious song of victory as you dance and proclaim with your mouth the greatness of God and all that He has done.

Psalm 149:1-3 (KJV)

*1 **Praise ye the Lord.** Sing unto the Lord a new song, **and his praise in the congregation of saints.** 2 Let Israel rejoice in him*

357

*that made him: **let the children of Zion be joyful in their King.***
3 Let them praise his name in the dance: let them sing praises
unto him with the timbrel and harp.

Worship, on the other hand, is more personal. The word **Worship** has to do with falling humbly before God with a heart of love. A Christian worships God as an act of reverently honoring and paying homage to God. A true worshipper will fall down or kneel before God in respect of who God is and all that He has done. God is to be worshipped and adored for who He is as God and magnified for the greatness of all of His acts. Christians bow down in love and reverence as they draw closer to God. True worship also has to do with singing intimate songs to the Lord. Songs of intimacy spring out of the heart of one who has been forgiven and redeemed by the blood of the Lamb.

Psalm 95:6 (KJV)
6 O come, let us worship and bow down: let us kneel before the
Lord our maker.

Praise and worship both have to do with singing words from your mouth with bodily displays of affection toward God. With praise, you declare the victorious song of the Lord as you raise your hands and dance before the Lord for all He has done for you. Through worship, you bow yourself in homage before the Lord as you sing love songs from your heart to the Lord because of His Presence, His attributes, and what He means to you. Praise and worship are some of the highest forms of reaching out to God and declaring His greatness on the earth.

We will look at a story where praise played an essential part in a great Jewish victory during one of the kings of Israel reign. A king named Jehoshaphat was faced by a vast army coming to destroy him and his kingdom. Jehoshaphat was a great king over Judah who loved the Lord and did what was right in the sight of God. Not all the kings of Judah feared and served the Lord, but Jehoshaphat was a King of Judah that honored God and His Laws. He served the Lord with all of his heart.

One day Jehoshaphat received an evil report that a vast army was coming to fight against him and his kingdom. However, when God established His law through Moses, He told the children of Israel that He would be with them in war and deliver them if they served Him. Jehoshaphat served the Lord during this time, enabling him to call upon the Lord for help.

Deuteronomy 28:7 (KJV)

7 The Lord shall cause thine enemies that rise up against thee to be smitten before thy face: they shall come out against thee one way, and flee before thee seven ways.

Leviticus 26:7-8 (KJV)

7 And ye shall chase your enemies, and they shall fall before you by the sword. 8 And five of you shall chase an hundred, and an hundred of you shall put ten thousand to flight: and your enemies shall fall before you by the sword.

Jehoshaphat believed in God for the victory because of his obedience to the Lord. So, when this evil report came, Jehoshaphat immediately proclaimed a fast throughout the land of Judah and gathered everyone to ask the help of the Lord. All of the cities of Judah responded and came to Jerusalem to seek the Lord.

While they were seeking the Lord and praying to God, the Hand of the Lord came upon a man named Jahaziel. Jahaziel prophesied that they were not to be afraid or dismayed because the battle was to be God's and not theirs. Let's read what he prophesied together.

2 Chronicles 20:14-17 (KJV)

14 Then upon Jahaziel the son of Zechariah, the son of Benaiah, the son of Jeiel, the son of Mattaniah, a Levite of the sons of Asaph, **came the Spirit of the Lord in the midst of the congregation;** *15 And he said, Hearken ye, all Judah, and ye inhabitants of Jerusalem, and thou king Jehoshaphat, Thus saith the Lord unto you, Be not afraid nor dismayed by reason of this great multitude;* **for the battle is not yours, but God's.** *16 To morrow go ye down against them: behold, they come up by the cliff of Ziz; and ye shall find them at the end of the brook, before the wilderness of Jeruel. 17* **Ye shall not need to fight in this battle: set yourselves, stand ye still, and see the salvation of the Lord with you,** *O Judah and Jerusalem: fear not, nor be dismayed; to morrow go out against them:* **for the Lord will be with you.**

God prophesied that they would not need to fight in this battle, and all they had to do was stand and see the salvation of the Lord. So, Jehoshaphat and all of them responded by bowing down to worship God.

2 Chronicles 20:18 (KJV)

18 **And Jehoshaphat bowed his head with his face to the ground: and all Judah and the inhabitants of Jerusalem fell before the Lord, worshipping the Lord.**

Then they stood up and praised the Lord God of Israel with a loud voice.

2 Chronicles 20:19 (KJV)

19 And the Levites, of the children of the Kohathites, and of the children of the Korhites, **stood up to praise the Lord God of Israel with a loud voice on high.**

The next day, they rose to face this army and what happened in this war was amazing. God did exactly what He said He would do. Jehoshaphat did not need to fight in this battle, but what they did reveals a truth we can live by today. Jehoshaphat appointed singers to go out and praise God ahead of the army. As they sang praises to God, God set ambushes against the enemy and caused them to fight and kill each other. Let's read this incredible story together.

2 Chronicles 20:20-24 (KJV)

20 And they rose early in the morning, and went forth into the wilderness of Tekoa: and as they went forth, Jehoshaphat stood and said, Hear me, O Judah, and ye inhabitants of Jerusalem; **Believe in the Lord your God, so shall ye be established; believe his prophets, so shall ye prosper.** *21 And when he had consulted with the people,* **he appointed singers unto the Lord, and that should praise the beauty of holiness, as they went out before the army, and to say, Praise the Lord; for his mercy endureth for ever. 22 And when they began to sing and to praise, the Lord set ambushments against the children of Ammon, Moab, and mount Seir, which were come against Judah; and they were smitten.** *23 For the children of Ammon and Moab stood up against the inhabitants of mount Seir, utterly to slay and destroy them: and when they had made an end of the inhabitants of Seir, every one helped to destroy another. 24 And when Judah came toward the watch tower in the wilderness, they looked unto the multitude, and, behold, they were dead bodies fallen to the earth, and none escaped.*

This story is one of the most significant recorded victories in the history of the children of Judah. God defeated their enemies while they praised Him. This story reveals the power of the spoken word through the power of praise and worship. Jehoshaphat sought the Lord and worshipped God.

When God prophesied their victory, Jehoshaphat sent out singers to praise God, and God defeated their enemy.

We have been learning a lot in this book about the war of words, and this story reveals this truth in a new light. The war of words is also won when we praise and worship God. God's Word is not only to be spoken but declared through praise and worship. Praise and worship to God takes the war of words to a whole new level.

King David was also known for his Psalms of praise and worship to God. He was very aware of the power of praise and worship. King David wrote 73 of the 150 Psalms to God found in the Bible. These Psalms are prophetic and reveal how to praise and worship God. King David also played the harp, and he demonstrated how to do warfare with a ten-string instrument. King David used the playing of his harp to rid King Saul of the demons that were tormenting him.

1 Samuel 16:23 (KJV)
*23 And it came to pass, when the evil spirit from God was upon Saul, **that David took an harp, and played with his hand:** so Saul was refreshed, and was well, **and the evil spirit departed from him.***

King David was a great warrior and knew how to fight his battles through praise and worship. He won many wars and did great acts before Israel, even defeating the giant Goliath. King David won the war of words in praise and worship. Let's look at some of the Psalms he wrote together.

Psalm 34:1 (KJV)
1 I will bless the Lord at all times: his praise shall continually be in my mouth.

Psalm 40:3 (KJV)

3 And he hath put a new song in my mouth, even praise unto our God: many shall see it, and fear, and shall trust in the Lord.

Psalm 71:8 (KJV)

8 Let my mouth be filled with thy praise and with thy honour all the day.

Psalm 145:21 (KJV)

21 My mouth shall speak the praise of the Lord: and let all flesh bless his holy name for ever and ever.

Psalm 149:6-9 (KJV)

*6 **Let the high praises of God be in their mouth, and a two-edged sword in their hand;** 7 To execute vengeance upon the heathen, and punishments upon the people; 8 To bind their kings with chains, and their nobles with fetters of iron; 9 To execute upon them the judgment written: this honour have all his saints. Praise ye the Lord.*

In the New Testament, the Apostle Paul also revealed the power of praise and worship. Once, he and Silas were thrown into prison, and the power of God was revealed as they worshiped Him in prison.

Acts 16:23-26 (KJV)

*23 And when they had laid many stripes upon them, they cast them into prison, charging the jailor to keep them safely: 24 Who, having received such a charge, thrust them into the inner prison, and made their feet fast in the stocks. 25 **And at midnight Paul and Silas prayed, and sang praises unto God:** and the prisoners heard them. 26 **And suddenly there was a great earthquake, so that the foundations of the prison were shaken: and*** *immediately all the doors were opened, and every one's bands were loosed.*

An earthquake occurred while Paul and Silas prayed and sang praises to God. This supernatural earthquake from God opened the prison doors, and the shackles that bound them were loosed. The prison guard came in, saw what happened, and became a Christian, including his whole household. Praise and worship can help you defeat anything that is coming against you.

When Christians understand the war of words, they will also realize the power of praise and worship. The Bible says that God inhabits the praises of Israel.

Psalm 22:3 (KJV)
*3 But thou art holy, **O thou that inhabitest the praises of Israel.***

When you praise and worship God, you invite God into your situation. Praise and worship are two of the most powerful weapons against the enemy. In the middle of a spiritual attack, the best thing you can do is offer up praise and worship to God. Declare the greatness of God and enter into deep worship, and you will discover that God is there to deliver you. God will give you songs of deliverance.

Psalm 32:7 (KJV)
*7 Thou art my hiding place; thou shalt preserve me from trouble; **thou shalt compass me about with songs of deliverance.** Selah.*

The New Testament has some important things to say about singing to God. Here is one significant verse that reveals the truth of singing and the Words of Christ.

Colossians 3:16 (KJV)
16 Let the word of Christ dwell in you richly in all wisdom; teaching and admonishing one another in psalms and hymns and spiritual songs, singing with grace in your hearts to the Lord.

As Christians, we are called to know and sing the Words of Christ. When the Word of Christ dwells in you richly, you will begin to sing songs to the Lord. You can even get to the place where you can make up new songs to God while you meditate on His Word.

I also want to add the importance of being careful not to let worldly songs get in your head. Sometimes a worldly song might have a great beat, and you can find yourself singing the words to a worldly song but be careful to listen to what you are singing. Many worldly songs have perverted verses or wicked words. You have to be cautious because the devil can use a song with a good beat to get evil words to come out of your mouth. Never let evil songs and perverted worldly words come out of your mouth. As you meditate on God's Words, holy and pure songs will flow out of your mouth. Remember, out of the abundance of the heart, the mouth speaks and sings. What are you filling your heart with, and what songs are you singing?

As you fill your heart and mind with the Word of God, God can create a new song within you. A new song is one you make up based on the Word of God, as He utters this song through you by His Spirit. The Holy Spirit can give you a new spiritual song with a melody never sung before.

Psalm 40:3 (KJV)
3 And he hath put a new song in my mouth, even praise unto our God: many shall see it, and fear, and shall trust in the Lord.

Isaiah 42:9-10 (KJV)

*9 Behold, the former things are come to pass, and new things do I declare: before they spring forth I tell you of them. 10 **Sing unto the Lord a new song, and his praise from the end of the earth,** ye that go down to the sea, and all that is therein; the isles, and the inhabitants thereof.*

Here is another verse that reveals the will of God and us singing. Singing songs before God is a form of sacrifice.

Hebrews 13:15 (KJV)

*15 **By him therefore let us offer the sacrifice of praise to God continually, that is, the fruit of our lips giving thanks to his name.***

Our words, mouth, and lips are powerful sources of speaking God's Word and will into the earth. The power of praise and worship takes the war of words to a new level. When you learn how to praise and worship God in the middle of your toughest battles of life, you will see the Hand of God move. God will defeat armies and open the prison doors as you praise and worship Him.

The number one thing you can do with your mouth is praise and worship before God. God created you and is worthy of all praise and worship for who He is and all He has done. There is a great story where Jesus reveals the heart of God when it comes to worship. Jesus shows who God is and what He wants from His creation.

John 4:19-24 (KJV)

19 The woman saith unto him, Sir, I perceive that thou art a prophet. 20 Our fathers worshipped in this mountain; and ye say, that in Jerusalem is the place where men ought to worship. 21

Jesus saith unto her, **Woman, believe me, the hour cometh, when ye shall neither in this mountain, nor yet at Jerusalem, worship the Father.** *22 Ye worship ye know not what: we know what we worship: for salvation is of the Jews. 23 But the hour cometh, and now is, when the true worshippers shall worship the Father in spirit and in truth: for the Father seeketh such to worship him. 24 God is a Spirit: and they that worship him must worship him in spirit and in truth.*

Throughout all of eternity, we will be given the opportunity to praise and worship God. God has done so much and is so worthy of all our praise and worship. Anyone who has been saved and delivered knows how important it is to worship and praise God. Likewise, people who have been truly saved cannot help but praise and worship God. Jesus said the stones would cry out if we didn't.

Luke 19:37-40 (KJV)

37 And when he was come nigh, even now at the descent of the mount of Olives, **the whole multitude of the disciples began to rejoice and praise God with a loud voice for all the mighty works that they had seen;** *38 Saying, Blessed be the King that cometh in the name of the Lord: peace in Heaven, and glory in the highest. 39 And some of the Pharisees from among the multitude said unto him, Master, rebuke thy disciples. 40* **And he answered and said unto them, I tell you that, if these should hold their peace, the stones would immediately cry out.**

One notable fact is that we are called to praise and worship God, but God also sings over us. God sings songs of joy over His people.

Zephaniah 3:17 (KJV)

*17 The Lord thy God in the midst of thee is mighty; he will save, he will rejoice over thee with joy; he will rest in his love, **he will joy over thee with singing.***

I will end this chapter with the revelation of praise and worship going on in Heaven before the Throne of God.

Revelation 7:9-12 (KJV)

*9 After this I beheld, and, lo, a great multitude, which no man could number, of all nations, and kindreds, and people, and tongues, stood before the throne, and before the Lamb, clothed with white robes, and palms in their hands; 10 **And cried with a loud voice, saying, Salvation to our God which sitteth upon the throne, and unto the Lamb. 11 And all the angels stood round about the throne, and about the elders and the four beasts, and fell before the throne on their faces, and worshipped God, 12 Saying, Amen: Blessing, and glory, and wisdom, and thanksgiving, and honour, and power, and might, be unto our God for ever and ever. Amen.***

CHAPTER 30

SPEAKING THE BLESSING
AND THE BENEDICTION

S peaking a blessing over your children and people plays an integral part in the next generation inheriting the blessings of God. Spoken words have the power to impart a spiritual blessing that can affect the outcome of people's life. God wants His children blessed, and one of the ways He does it is by having someone speak a blessing over them. This chapter will see how God has ordained His blessing to be spoken over people. This blessing can also be called *The Blessing of Abraham.*

As Christians, we should be using our words to bless everyone we come into contact with, even those who curse us.

> **Matthew 5:44 (KJV)**
> *44 But I say unto you, Love your enemies, **bless them that curse you,** do good to them that hate you, and pray for them which despitefully use you, and persecute you;*

However, I will not be discussing this type of blessing in this chapter. Instead, we will be learning about the specific blessing that a parent should speak over children and a spiritual leader over an individual. We will also be talking about a benediction. A benediction is an utterance spoken over a group of people bestowing the blessing and protection of God upon them. A benediction is usually spoken over people at the end of a service or gathering. Blessings and benedictions are meant to invoke God to fulfill what is spoken. God hears these words of blessings and acts according to what is pronounced.

Blessings and benedictions cannot be underestimated or taken for granted. Spoken words have the power to impact people's lives in a meaningful way because God hears everything being spoken and acts on these words. When someone in a spiritual position speaks over someone's life, this pronounced blessing can make a difference in the success of the one being spoken over. The people who have the power to make this declaration are parents, spiritual leaders, or spiritual fathers. They hold the key to speaking a blessing over someone's life that God will honor.

The first blessing in the Bible came from God after He had created Adam and Eve.

> ### Genesis 1:22 (KJV)
> *22 **And God blessed them,** saying, Be fruitful, and multiply, and fill the waters in the seas, and let fowl multiply in the earth.*

God also blessed Abraham and started what is called **The Blessing of Abraham**.

> ### Genesis 12:1-3 (KJV)
> *1 Now the Lord had said unto Abram, Get thee out of thy country, and from thy kindred, and from thy father's house, unto a land that I will shew thee: 2 And I will make of thee a great nation,*

and I will bless thee, and make thy name great; and thou shalt be a blessing: 3 And I will bless them that bless thee, and curse him that curseth thee: and in thee shall all families of the earth be blessed.

God visited Abraham many times during his life and kept speaking powerful words of blessing over him. God also made a covenant with Abraham, which later was revealed to be a covenant between God and Christ. Abraham's life was very blessed because of these blessings being spoken over him by God. However, when Abraham was childless, he knew he needed seed to pass down the blessing of God upon them. Let's read what Abraham said to God regarding his seed and him being childless.

Genesis 15:1-6 (KJV)

*1 After these things the word of the Lord came unto Abram in a vision, saying, Fear not, Abram: I am thy shield, and thy exceeding great reward. 2 **And Abram said, Lord God, what wilt thou give me, seeing I go childless,** and the steward of my house is this Eliezer of Damascus? 3 And Abram said, Behold, to me thou hast given no seed: and, lo, one born in my house is mine heir. 4 And, behold, the word of the Lord came unto him, saying, **This shall not be thine heir; but he that shall come forth out of thine own bowels shall be thine heir. 5 And he brought him forth abroad, and said, Look now toward Heaven, and tell the stars, if thou be able to number them: and he said unto him, So shall thy seed be.** 6 And he believed in the Lord; and he counted it to him for righteousness.*

God promised Abraham that his offspring would be like the stars in Heaven. God kept coming to Abraham and revealing more of His covenant to him little by little. Finally, God changed his name from

Abram to Abraham, which meant father of many nations, and gave him the covenant of circumcision. ***The Blessing of Abraham*** also included the land of Israel. God was speaking words of blessing, and these Words changed the history of the world.

Abraham and Sarah miraculously had a child in their old age and named him Isaac, which means laughter. The promises of God are so wonderful and miraculous that all you can do is believe and laugh at them. Every extraordinary and laughable word that God blessed Abraham with came to pass.

Once Abraham died and had gone to be with the Lord, Isaac, his son, walked in the ***Blessing of Abraham***. Isaac had two sons, Esau, and Jacob. Esau was the eldest son and was supposed to inherit the ***Blessing of Abraham***. Esau, however, despised his birthright and sold his birthright to his younger brother Jacob for a pot of stew. Esau did not value what God promised to Abraham and his seed.

> ### *Genesis 25:29-34 (KJV)*
> *29 And Jacob sod pottage: and Esau came from the field, and he was faint: 30 And Esau said to Jacob, Feed me, I pray thee, with that same red pottage; for I am faint: therefore was his name called Edom. 31 **And Jacob said, Sell me this day thy birthright.** 32 And Esau said, Behold, I am at the point to die: **and what profit shall this birthright do to me? 33 And Jacob said, Swear to me this day; and he sware unto him: and he sold his birthright unto Jacob.** 34 Then Jacob gave Esau bread and pottage of lentiles; and he did eat and drink, and rose up, and went his way: **thus Esau despised his birthright.***

Jacob understood the power of the Covenant God made with his grandfather Abraham, which was passed down to his father, Isaac.

Jacob deceived his father when it came time for Isaac to speak this blessing over Esau. The blessing was supposed to go to Esau because he was the firstborn. However, Isaac couldn't see in his old age, and Jacob and his mother conspired to get Isaac to speak the ***Blessing of Abraham*** over Jacob. Jacob wore clothes that smelled like Esau and made food Esau usually made for Isaac to eat. Let's read the part of the story where Jacob comes in and deceives his father Isaac to get the ***Blessing of Abraham.***

Genesis 27:18-29 (KJV)

18 And he came unto his father, and said, My father: and he said, Here am I; who art thou, my son? 19 And Jacob said unto his father, I am Esau thy first born; I have done according as thou badest me: arise, I pray thee, sit and eat of my venison, that thy soul may bless me. 20 And Isaac said unto his son, How is it that thou hast found it so quickly, my son? And he said, Because the Lord thy God brought it to me. 21 And Isaac said unto Jacob, Come near, I pray thee, that I may feel thee, my son, whether thou be my very son Esau or not. 22 And Jacob went near unto Isaac his father; and he felt him, and said, The voice is Jacob's voice, but the hands are the hands of Esau. 23 And he discerned him not, because his hands were hairy, as his brother Esau's hands: **so he blessed him. 24 And he said, Art thou my very son Esau? And he said, I am. 25 And he said, Bring it near to me, and I will eat of my son's venison, that my soul may bless thee.** *And he brought it near to him, and he did eat: and he brought him wine and he drank. 26 And his father Isaac said unto him, Come near now, and kiss me, my son. 27 And he came near, and kissed him: and he smelled the smell of his raiment,* **and blessed him, and said, See, the smell of my son is as the smell of a field which the Lord hath blessed: 28 Therefore God give thee of the dew of**

Heaven, and the fatness of the earth, and plenty of corn and wine: 29 Let people serve thee, and nations bow down to thee: be lord over thy brethren, and let thy mother's sons bow down to thee: cursed be every one that curseth thee, and blessed be he that blesseth thee.

Isaac spoke this blessing over him but thought Jacob was Esau. I want to point out here that the people in the Old Testament understood the power of words. They knew that once a blessing was spoken, it was done and could not be reversed. They knew the power of the spoken word and the power of the **Blessing of Abraham** being spoken over someone's life. Esau came in later to his father Isaac, but the blessing could not be reversed.

Genesis 27:30-33 (KJV)

*30 And it came to pass, **as soon as Isaac had made an end of blessing Jacob,** and Jacob was yet scarce gone out from the presence of Isaac his father, that Esau his brother came in from his hunting. 31 And he also had made savoury meat, and brought it unto his father, and said unto his father, Let my father arise, and eat of his son's venison, **that thy soul may bless me.** 32 And Isaac his father said unto him, Who art thou? And he said, I am thy son, thy firstborn Esau. 33 And Isaac trembled very exceedingly, and said, Who? where is he that hath taken venison, and brought it me, **and I have eaten of all before thou camest, and have blessed him? yea, and he shall be blessed.***

Isaac could not reverse the blessing spoken over his son Jacob, although he deceived him. Jacob knew the power of the blessing being spoken over him, and that is why he deceived his father to get it. This may look bad to us, but God saw this situation differently. God knew the type of man Esau was and how he didn't value the **Blessing of Abraham**. On the other hand, Jacob understood and valued the **Blessing of Abraham.** God always honors those who honor Him. Once Isaac knew that he had blessed Jacob and not Esau and could not reverse the blessing spoken over Jacob, he said more words of blessing over Jacob. Let's read the added words of blessing he spoke over Jacob.

> ### Genesis 28:1-4 (KJV)
> *1 **And Isaac called Jacob, and blessed him,** and charged him, and said unto him, Thou shalt not take a wife of the daughters of Canaan. 2 Arise, go to Padanaram, to the house of Bethuel thy mother's father; and take thee a wife from thence of the daughters of Laban thy mother's brother. 3 **And God Almighty bless thee, and make thee fruitful, and multiply thee, that thou mayest be a multitude of people; 4 And give thee the blessing of Abraham, to thee, and to thy seed with thee; that thou mayest inherit the land wherein thou art a stranger, which God gave unto Abraham.***

Jacob was blessed because of the spoken blessing over his life from his father, Isaac. Jacob was used to establishing all that God promised to Abraham. As a result, God blessed Jacob abundantly with wealth and children. This story reveals the power of the spoken word through a blessing from a parent to a child. Our spiritual forefathers understood for a blessing to go into effect, it had to be spoken over someone. Once the blessing was spoken, it could not be reversed.

Now let's look at Moses, the Law, and the blessing of God. God gave Moses the Law and established the Levitical priesthood. In the Law of Moses, God commanded Aaron and his sons to speak a blessing over the children of Israel. Today we call this the ***Aaronic Blessing.*** Let's read how God said they should bless the children of Israel.

Numbers 6:22-27 (KJV)
*22 And the Lord spake unto Moses, saying, 23 Speak unto Aaron and unto his sons, saying, **On this wise ye shall bless the children of Israel, saying unto them,** 24 **The Lord bless thee,** and keep thee: 25 The Lord make his face shine upon thee, and be gracious unto thee: 26 The Lord lift up his countenance upon thee, and give thee peace. 27 And they shall put my name upon the children of Israel, **and I will bless them.***

The ***Aaronic Blessing*** had to be spoken over the children of Israel. We can also see the importance of the spoken blessing from this portion of Scripture. God hears these blessings and acts on them. There is something significant about the spoken word needing to be pronounced and heard by others. You can't just think of these blessings in your mind. People and all of creation need to hear the blessing being spoken over someone or a group of people.

Many people don't know this, but Jesus spoke a blessing over the disciples before He was taken up into Heaven.

Luke 24:50-51 (KJV)
*50 And he led them out as far as to Bethany, **and he lifted up his hands, and blessed them.** 51 And it came to pass, **while he blessed them, he was parted from them, and carried up into Heaven.***

As Jesus was speaking a blessing and benediction over His disciples, He was taken up into Heaven. Many people also wanted Jesus to bless their children during His ministry. The apostles tried to stop it, but Jesus said for them not to stop it.

Mark 10:13-16 (KJV)
*13 And they brought young children to him, that he should touch them: **and his disciples rebuked those that brought them.** 14 **But when Jesus saw it, he was much displeased,** and said unto them, Suffer the little children to come unto me, and forbid them not: for of such is the kingdom of God. 15 Verily I say unto you, Whosoever shall not receive the kingdom of God as a little child, he shall not enter therein. 16 **And he took them up in his arms, put his hands upon them, and blessed them.***

The Jewish culture has always understood the power of blessing someone. This understanding came to them from the stories of their forefathers like Isaac, who blessed his son Jacob. The spoken blessing over someone's life is significant. Unfortunately, far too many parents don't bless their children but curse them with hurtful words. You must speak only blessings upon your children. Pastors should also speak a blessing upon their congregation each week before they walk out the Church's door. This blessing is called the *Benediction*.

People face many things in life and have a war raging against them at times. When you speak a word of blessing over your children or someone else, you give them the upper hand at the war of words. Your words impact their life for the better in more ways than you may ever understand. The revelation of speaking the *Blessing* and *Benediction* over people is one of the most important things you can do. Your words of blessing can make the difference between someone succeeding or not succeeding in life.

Unfortunately, many parents in our generation don't understand the power of speaking a blessing over their children. But not all is lost. If you were raised by a parent that did not bless you, you could still get a blessing from a spiritual leader. There are great men and women of God out there who can speak a blessing over you. God wants you to be blessed. If you cannot find a person to speak a blessing over you, then go to God, and you can start speaking blessings over your own life. As a child of God, you have the power to bless and not curse yourself with your own words. You do this by putting God's Words of blessings in your mouth.

We are in a war of words, and when a blessing is spoken over you by someone else, you can fight with greater strength. Maybe a blessing was not spoken over you, but you can be the person God uses to speak over other people's lives and your own life. God wants to use your mouth to speak the *Blessing of Abraham* to others.

I declare and decree a blessing over your life right now by the power of God and in **The Name of the Lord Jesus Christ of Nazareth**! Be blessed with all the *Blessings of Abraham* upon you now and the rest of the days of your life! May you be blessed coming in and going out! May you be the head and not the tail! May you live a long life, fulfill the will of God, and prosper in everything you set your hand to do! I decree and declare a word of blessing to everyone that reads this book! May the God of Abraham bless you and keep you, may His face shine upon you and give you peace! I place **The Name of the Lord Jesus Christ of Nazareth** upon you! Amen and amen!

CHAPTER 31

THE END TIME BATTLE OF WORDS

A s we come near the end of this book on the war of words, I now want to focus on the biggest battle of words found in the Bible between Jesus Christ and the antichrist. This is the epic battle of all ages. The antichrist takes on a war of words against God Almighty and His people in an unprecedented way. This subject is rarely preached but must be understood for those preparing for the final battle between God and the devil. During the Great Tribulation, the devil will use the antichrist's mouth to blaspheme and speak against God. God, however, is going to secretly utilize the body of Christ to prophesy against this attack. This chapter will get into this end-time prophetic war of words and show God's final solution for the devil and his antichrist.

To gain prophetic insight into this war, we will look into the Book of Daniel and the Book of Revelation. These books prophesy about the antichrist and the coming war of words. These books have been around for thousands of years and reveal what will soon occur on earth. Anyone who wants to understand the coming war must have insight into these prophetic books.

Let's start by looking at the Book of Daniel for prophetic clues into the antichrist. The best place to start is in Daniel Chapter 7. Here we find four times the mentioning of the mouth of the antichrist and his use of words against God. Before I get into this chapter, it is crucial to understand who the Bible says the antichrist is. I am not here, however, to give an actual name to the antichrist but rather to reveal what the Bible says about the details of his coming when it comes to the war of words.

> ### *1 John 2:18 (KJV)*
> *18 Little children, it is the last time:* ***and as ye have heard that antichrist shall come, even now are there many antichrists; whereby we know that it is the last time.***

The actual antichrist is one who the Bible prophesies will be a profound wicked leader in the last days. This is a specific man who will be the embodiment of evil. He will be filled and controlled by the devil himself. He is also known as the man of sin or the son of perdition.

> ### *2 Thessalonians 2:3-4 (KJV)*
> *3 Let no man deceive you by any means: for that day shall not come, except there come a falling away first, and that* ***man of sin be revealed, the son of perdition;*** *4 Who opposeth and exalteth himself above all that is called God, or that is worshipped; so that he as God sitteth in the temple of God, shewing himself that he is God.*

In the last days, God's temple will be rebuilt by the Jews, and they are going to set up the sacrifices to God established in the Law of Moses. When they do this, they will be deceived by this man of sin; the antichrist. He will enter into a time of peace with them, but his ultimate goal will be to desecrate the Holy Temple of God by entering into the

Holy of Holies, declaring himself to be God. I am not going to get into all the details of the antichrist, but it is crucial to know his ultimate goal. He wants to be worshiped as God.

As we get into the Book of Daniel, we will see how the antichrist attacks God with his words. The antichrist will use his words to attack God, His people, and everything Holy. During this time, people who do not know God will be deceived by this demonic talker and pulled into his lies. The antichrist is going to deceive the entire world.

Let's now look at the Scriptures found in the Book of Daniel, Chapter 7, and what it has to say about the mouth and words of the antichrist.

Daniel 7:7-8 (KJV)

*7 After this I saw in the night visions, and behold a fourth beast, dreadful and terrible, and strong exceedingly; and it had great iron teeth: it devoured and brake in pieces, and stamped the residue with the feet of it: and it was diverse from all the beasts that were before it; and it had ten horns. 8 I considered the horns, and, behold, there came up among them another little horn, before whom there were three of the first horns plucked up by the roots: **and, behold, in this horn were eyes like the eyes of man, and a mouth speaking great things.***

This passage symbolizes the antichrist as a horn and is the first prophetic revealing of the antichrist in the Bible. This horn has a mouth that speaks great things. The word here for *great* means domineer, boastful, and arrogant. So, the antichrist will be speaking domineering, boastful, and arrogant words.

Let's see more of what is written about the antichrist and his words.

Daniel 7:11 (KJV)
11 I beheld then because of the voice of the great words which
the horn spake: I beheld even till the beast was slain, and his
body destroyed, and given to the burning flame.

Once again, we see the great words coming out of the antichrist. Horns, in the Bible, are symbolic of power and authority.

Daniel 7:20 (KJV)
20 And of the ten horns that were in his head, and of the other
which came up, and before whom three fell; even of that horn that
had eyes, and a mouth that spake very great things, whose look
was more stout than his fellows.

This passage mentions the antichrist having a mouth that speaks *very* great things. This is the third mention of the words coming from the antichrist. So, we see a pattern about the antichrist and his words in just this one chapter. This gives us a prophetic warning to watch what is coming out of the mouth of the antichrist.

Daniel 7:25 (KJV)
25 And he shall speak great words against the most High, and
shall wear out the saints of the most High, and think to change
times and laws: and they shall be given into his hand until a time
and times and the dividing of time.

This antichrist will be speaking great words against the Most High. He will also go after God's saints who must be on the earth during this time. Many people think the Church will be raptured off the earth before the antichrist comes, but too many verses point to the antichrist attacking the saints during the Great Tribulation.

We now see that the Book of Daniel, Chapter 7, mentions the mouth and words of this antichrist *four times.* If something is said once in the Bible, it is important, but mentioning this four times in one chapter tells us God wants us to understand this war of words the antichrist will wage against God and His saints. Daniel also mentions the antichrist and the words coming out of his mouth one more time in Daniel Chapter 11. Let's look at this verse.

Daniel 11:36 (KJV)

*36 And the king shall do according to his will; and he shall exalt himself, and magnify himself above every god, **and shall speak marvellous things against the God of gods,** and shall prosper till the indignation be accomplished: for that that is determined shall be done.*

Daniel prophesies one more time about the antichrist speaking marvelous things against the God of gods. This antichrist is dead set on attacking the Most High God. Up to this point in history, no man on the earth has ever verbally gone after God like this. The antichrist uses his mouth to attack God in such a personal way that it confounds the natural mind. Why is he attacking God? He is attacking God because he is filled with the devil himself. The devil has hated God from the beginning and even tried to take over His throne. Isaiah prophesied about this event in Chapter 14 of the Book of Isaiah. Let's look at this verse.

Isaiah 14:12-15 (KJV)

*12 **How art thou fallen from Heaven, O Lucifer, son of the morning!** how art thou cut down to the ground, which didst weaken the nations! 13 **For thou hast said in thine heart, I will ascend into Heaven, I will exalt my throne above the stars of God: I will sit also upon the mount of the congregation, in the sides of the north: 14 I will ascend above the heights of the*** *clouds; I will be like the most High. 15 Yet thou shalt be brought down to hell, to the sides of the pit.*

The Book of Revelation says that the dragon, which is the devil, gives power to the beast. This beast is the antichrist and has the people of the earth worshipping him. During this time, people living on the earth think that no one can make war with the beast. His words are powerful and audacious.

Revelation 13:4 (KJV)
4 And they worshipped the dragon which gave power unto the beast: and they worshipped the beast, saying, Who is like unto the beast? who is able to make war with him?

The dragon hates God and wants to be worshipped. Because the devil cannot get what he wants in Heaven, he tries to steal it from the kingdom of men. The devil unites with the antichrist as they verbally assault God Almighty and His saints. The antichrist goes into the Temple of God, declares himself to be God, and seeks man's worship. The mouth of the antichrist is used by the devil himself to blaspheme God.

Let's look at more verses in the Book of Revelation about the mouth of the antichrist.

Revelation 13:1-2 (KJV)
*1 And I stood upon the sand of the sea, and saw a beast rise up out of the sea, having seven heads and ten horns, and upon his horns ten crowns, and upon his heads the name of blasphemy 2 And the beast which I saw was like unto a leopard, and his feet were as the feet of a bear, **and his mouth as the mouth of a lion: and the dragon gave him his power**, and his seat, and great authority.*

The antichrist is pictured as a lion because the devil always imitates God. Jesus is called the Lion of the Tribe of Judah. Lions are a representation of kingdom rule. Lions are also known for roaring, and we understand that the roaring of a lion represents God prophesying.

Amos 3:8 (KJV)

8 The lion hath roared, who will not fear? the Lord God hath spoken, who can but prophesy?

Prophecy is God speaking directly through His people. The devil walks about like a roaring lion seeking whom he may destroy with his words. The devil destroys people by prophetically speaking to them like a roaring lion.

Let's see what else the Book of Revelation has to say about the antichrist and his mouth.

Revelation 13:5-9 (KJV)

5 And there was given unto him a mouth speaking great things and blasphemies; and power was given unto him to continue forty and two months. 6 And he opened his mouth in blasphemy against God, to blaspheme his name, and his tabernacle, and them that dwell in Heaven. 7 And it was given unto him to make war with the saints, and to overcome them: and power was given him over all kindreds, and tongues, and nations. 8 And all that dwell upon the earth shall worship him, whose names are not written in the Book of life of the Lamb slain from the foundation of the world. 9 If any man has an ear, let him hear.

This antichrist goes on speaking great things and blasphemies against God. It is also important to note that the antichrist is also making war against the saints. This verse indicates that the saints will be on the earth during this time. The saints come under heavy attacks from the antichrist during the Great Tribulation. Although the saints come under attack, I will show you how God uses the saints during this time. Before I get into the role of the saints in the Tribulation, let's look at what the people of the earth are doing during the Tribulation.

Revelation 16:9 (KJV)

*9 And men were scorched with great heat, **and blasphemed the name of God,** which hath power over these plagues: and they repented not to give him glory.*

Revelation 16:10-11 (KJV)

*10 And the fifth angel poured out his vial upon the seat of the beast; and his kingdom was full of darkness; and they gnawed their tongues for pain, 11 **And blasphemed the God of Heaven because of their pains and their sores, and repented not of their deeds.***

Revelation 16:21 (KJV)

*21 And there fell upon men a great hail out of Heaven, every stone about the weight of a talent: **and men blasphemed God because of the plague of the hail;** for the plague thereof was exceeding great.*

We already know that the antichrist is blaspheming God, but now we see all the people of the earth blaspheming God. They are judged for following the antichrist and not repenting of their sins. Their sins, however, are causing all these torments to come upon them. The word blaspheme means to speak irreverently about God or sacred things. The word blasphemy also means insulting, slandering, speaking evil, or verbally showing contempt for God.

During this same time, the antichrist also sets up a false image that can speak. If someone does not worship the image of the beast, they must be killed.

Revelation 13:15 (KJV)
*15 And he had power to give life unto the image of the beast, **that the image of the beast should both speak, and cause that as many as would not worship the image of the beast should be killed.***

While all of this is occurring on the earth, Jesus Christ is in Heaven preparing for His great promised return. This day will be marvelous as He defeats the devil, and this wicked antichrist. The words of this demonically inspired antichrist must be stopped. We know his words are powerful, and the devil uses the antichrist to destroy the world. During the Tribulation, we see the world is being rocked by natural disasters, cosmic destruction, plagues, and wars. The earth was not created to have this many evil words spoken into it. The earth is the creation of God and was intended to be ruled by the *good* Word of God.

We noted earlier that the saints come under great attack during the Tribulation, but I want to point out a secret mystery of how God uses them during this time. God always wins and outsmarts the devil. We know that prophecy is God speaking through His people. The Book of Revelation reveals God's response to the words of the antichrist. While the antichrist is spewing out blasphemies, God is speaking through the Church by the spirit of prophecy, which is the testimony of Jesus. Let's look at this secret together.

Revelation 19:10 (KJV)
*10 And I fell at his feet to worship him. And he said unto me, See thou do it not: I am thy fellowservant, and of thy brethren **that***

have the testimony of Jesus: worship God: for the testimony of Jesus is the spirit of prophecy.

God uses the Church to prophesy His plan and purpose on the earth. God battles the words of the antichrist through the spirit of prophecy coming out of the mouth of His saints. God speaks on the earth through His saints, while the devil talks through the antichrist and evil people.

Revelation 12:17 (KJV)

*17 And the dragon was wroth with the woman, and went to make war with the remnant of her seed, which keep the Commandments of God, **and have the testimony of Jesus Christ.***

Revelation 12:10-11 (KJV)

*10 And I heard a loud voice saying in Heaven, Now is come salvation, and strength, and the kingdom of our God, and the power of his Christ: for the accuser of our brethren is cast down, which accused them before our God day and night. 11 **And they overcame him by the blood of the Lamb, and by the word of their testimony;** and they loved not their lives unto the death.*

While the antichrist is in high gear speaking against God, God's Church is prophesying. God also sends two witnesses who have the power to call down fire, stop the rains, turn water to blood, and hit the earth with plagues spoken by prophetic words coming out of their mouths. The two witness's time of ministry is called their testimony. Their testimony is the spirit of prophecy.

Revelation 11:3-13 (KJV)

*3 And I will give power unto my two witnesses, **and they shall prophesy a thousand two hundred and threescore days, clothed in sackcloth.** 4 These are the two olive trees, and the two* *candlesticks standing before the God of the Earth. 5 **And if any man will hurt them, fire proceedeth out of their mouth, and devoureth their enemies: and if any man will hurt them, he must in this manner be killed. 6 These have power to shut Heaven, that it rain not in the days of their prophecy: and have power over waters to turn them to blood, and to smite the earth with all plagues, as often as they will. 7 And when they shall have finished their testimony,** the beast that ascendeth out of the bottomless pit shall make war against them, and shall overcome them, and kill them. 8 And their dead bodies shall lie in the street of the great city, which spiritually is called Sodom and Egypt, where also our Lord was crucified. 9 And they of the people and kindreds and tongues and nations shall see their dead bodies three days and an half, and shall not suffer their dead bodies to be put in graves. 10 And they that dwell upon the earth shall rejoice over them, and make merry, and shall send gifts one to another; **because these two prophets tormented them that dwelt on the earth.** 11 And after three days and an half the spirit of life from God entered into them, and they stood upon their feet; and great fear fell upon them which saw them. 12 **And they heard a great voice from Heaven saying unto them, Come up hither. And they ascended up to Heaven in a cloud; and their enemies beheld them.** 13 And the same hour was there a great earthquake, and the tenth part of the city fell, and in the earthquake were slain of men seven thousand: and the remnant were affrighted, and gave glory to the God of Heaven.*

These two witnesses have great power to prophesy on the earth. The antichrist goes to war with these two prophets and kills them; however, God raises them from the dead in front of the entire world. He then calls them up to Heaven before all of His enemies. No matter what the antichrist does, he cannot defeat God or His people. The Bible says there is no wisdom, understanding, or counsel against the Lord.

> **Proverbs 21:30 (KJV)**
> 30 **There is no wisdom nor understanding nor counsel against the Lord.**

The Bible also says that no weapon formed against us shall prosper, and every tongue that rises against us in judgment we shall condemn.

> **Isaiah 54:17 (KJV)**
> 17 *No weapon that is formed against thee shall prosper;* **and every tongue that shall rise against thee in judgment thou shalt condemn.** *This is the heritage of the servants of the Lord, and their righteousness is of me, saith the Lord.*

No one can defeat God or His Word. Although the antichrist comes against God and His people, he is ultimately defeated. God and His Word always prevail. There is no greater honor than to be able to offer your life as a martyr for Christ. This is how we can prove we love God. If you are willing to die for God, you love Him. Death is temporal, and those willing to accept Jesus as their Lord and Savior and love not their lives unto death, will live eternally with God. The war of words will rage violently during the Great Tribulation, but God wins.

When we near the end of the Great Tribulation, a significant event defeats the antichrist. Jesus Christ returns with His saints and defeats the antichrist and the devil with the sword coming out of His mouth. This sword is none other than the Word of God. Jesus will ultimately win the war of words when He returns. Jesus doesn't have a natural sword. His Words are the sword that defeats the devil and the antichrist.

Revelation 19:11-16 (KJV)

11 And I saw Heaven opened, and behold a white horse; and he that sat upon him was called Faithful and True, and in righteousness he doth judge and make war. 12 His eyes were as a flame of fire, and on his head were many crowns; and he had a name written, that no man knew, but he himself. 13 And he was clothed with a vesture dipped in blood: **and his name is called The Word of God.** *14 And the armies which were in Heaven followed him upon white horses, clothed in fine linen, white and clean. 15* **And out of his mouth goeth a sharp sword, that with it he should smite the nations:** *and he shall rule them with a rod of iron: and he treadeth the winepress of the fierceness and wrath of Almighty God. 16 And he hath on his vesture and on his thigh a name written, King Of Kings, And Lord Of Lords.*

Jesus is the Word of God and defeats the devil and the antichrist with His powerful Words. Nothing can withstand Jesus and His Words. His Words created the universe and the earth, and it will be His Words that set everything straight in the earth. The devil, through the mouth of the antichrist, attempts to destroy all that was holy on the earth, but Jesus defeats everything that is spoken by the *Sword* coming out of His mouth, which is the *Word of God.* Jesus uses His Word to defeat every word the antichrist speaks.

It doesn't go well for anyone who speaks against the Lord. The antichrist will be held accountable for every word he spoke against the Lord, and everyone else who blasphemed God will be held accountable for what they spoke against God.

Matthew 12:36-37 (KJV)

36 **But I say unto you, That every idle word that men shall speak, they shall give account thereof in the day of judgment.**

37 For by thy words thou shalt be justified, and by thy words thou shalt be condemned.

The final end time war of words will be raged against Jesus and His saints. When Jesus returns, He will stop the antichrist from speaking completely. The devil will also be bound for 1,000 years and not be allowed to deceive and speak lies to humankind. At the end of the 1,000 years, the devil will be loosed for a time, but he will be defeated again.

Revelation 20:7-10 (KJV)

7 And when the thousand years are expired, Satan shall be loosed out of his prison, 8 And shall go out to deceive the nations which are in the four quarters of the earth, Gog, and Magog, to gather them together to battle: the number of whom is as the sand of the sea. 9 And they went up on the breadth of the earth, and compassed the camp of the saints about, and the beloved city: and fire came down from God out of Heaven, and devoured them. 10 And the devil that deceived them was cast into the lake of fire and brimstone, where the beast and the false prophet are, and shall be tormented day and night for ever and ever.

To conclude this chapter, let's reflect on the fact that God wins every time. No one can defeat God, and every word spoken must be accounted for. God's Word created the world, and God will have the final say at the end of the world. God is good, and He should never be spoken evil of. The world and the antichrist blaspheme God who has done nothing but good by creating the world and sending Jesus to die on the cross when humankind sinned and lost their way. Who would ever want to speak against a Great God as our God? God ultimately wins the war of words and has the final say.

CHAPTER 32

Manifesting God With Your Mouth

God is no farther away from you than the confession of your mouth. Your mouth has the ability to make a confession that God will respond to and show up in whatever way you need Him to. God has chosen to remain invisible during this dispensation of time we live in, but that does not mean He is not here. God is everywhere, and He will always show up and manifest Himself in a special way for those who call upon Him with their mouth. This chapter will reveal how God can and will manifest with the words that come out of your mouth.

To start with, let's define what I mean when I say God will manifest. What is a manifestation of God? A manifestation of God is when He reveals Himself in various ways. God can reveal Himself through miracles, one of the nine gifts of the Holy Spirit, dreams, visions, prophecy, signs and wonders, cosmic events, earthly events, Divine judgments, and His Presence. When God manifests Himself, you will not see Him with your natural eyes, but you will know He is there through the miraculous way He reveals Himself in a supernatural occurrence. You don't have to see God with your naked eye to know that He is there by the signs and wonders He does.

Moses was one of the few men in history to get really close to God. God manifested Himself to Moses in very powerful ways. God also came down on Mount Horeb, The Mountain of God, and revealed Himself through speaking of the Ten Commandments audibly to the children of Israel. During the time of Moses, God was revealing Himself through a visible cloud, signs and wonders, and His audible voice. When the children of Israel heard the audible voice of God, they thought they were going to die.

> ### Deuteronomy 4:32-36 (KJV)
> *32 **For ask now of the days that are past, which were before thee, since the day that God created man upon the earth, and ask from the one side of Heaven unto the other, whether there hath been any such thing as this great thing is, or hath been heard like it? 33 Did ever people hear the voice of God speaking out of the midst of the fire, as thou hast heard, and live?** 34 Or hath God assayed to go and take him a nation from the midst of another nation, by temptations, by signs, and by wonders, and by war, and by a mighty hand, and by a stretched out arm, and by great terrors, according to all that the Lord your God did for you in Egypt before your eyes? 35 Unto thee it was shewed, that thou mightest know that the Lord he is God; there is none else beside him. 36 **Out of Heaven he made thee to hear his voice,** that he might instruct thee: and upon earth he shewed thee his great fire; **and thou heardest His Words out of the midst of the fire.***

The children of Israel were granted an unprecedented number of miracles during their day. God revealed Himself through all the judgments of Egypt, the crossing of the Red Sea, multiple forms of supernatural provision, and so many more miracles performed through His servant Moses. We can say with all certainty that God revealed Himself to this generation in more ways than ever before seen on the earth. Some people have lived and died without ever seeing one miracle from God, let alone all that this generation saw.

Although Moses saw many manifestations of God and His power, Moses was still not able to completely see all of God. Let's read the account where Moses asked to see God's glory and how God responded to him.

> ### *Exodus 33:18-23 (KJV)*
> *18 And he said, I beseech thee, shew me thy glory. 19 And he said, I will make all my goodness pass before thee, and I will proclaim the name of the Lord before thee; and will be gracious to whom I will be gracious, and will shew mercy on whom I will shew mercy. 20 **And he said, Thou canst not see my face: for there shall no man see me, and live.** 21 And the Lord said, Behold, there is a place by me, and thou shalt stand upon a rock: 22 And it shall come to pass, while my glory passeth by, that I will put thee in a clift of the rock, and will cover thee with my hand while I pass by: 23 And I will take away mine hand, and thou shalt see my back parts: **but my face shall not be seen.***

God hid Himself for Moses' protection. If God showed His Face or all that He is in the fullness of His Glory, natural man would die. One reason a man would die is that they are all born into a natural body under Adam's curse. When Adam sinned, he put the whole world, and everyone born in it under a curse.

God lives in what people on the earth call the unseen world. When you die and go to Heaven, you will be able to see God and His Kingdom, but for now, He is hidden from us. The Bible also reveals that the unseen world is more real than the seen world that we live in. The seen world we live in is temporal, but the unseen world is eternal.

> ### 2 Corinthians 4:18 (KJV)
> *18 While we look not at the things which are seen, but at the things which are not seen: for the things which are seen are temporal; but the things which are not seen are eternal.*

While we live in this body, we will not be able to see God completely, but that does not mean He is not here. God is everywhere and can manifest Himself in more ways than one. We can't see Him with our naked eye, but that does not mean we can't see God with the eye of faith. God has revealed in the Holy Scriptures how we can call upon Him and have Him show up in our time of need with a miraculous manifestation.

This chapter is titled **Manifesting God with Your Mouth** for a reason. I am now going to show you from the Scriptures how you can get the invisible God to show up. God will show up by the very words you confess with your mouth. To start with, let's look at how you were saved. We have to go to Romans Chapter 10 to see how someone gets saved.

> ### Romans 10:5-13 (KJV)
> *5 For Moses describeth the righteousness which is of the law, That the man which doeth those things shall live by them. 6 But the righteousness which is of faith speaketh on this wise, **Say not in thine heart, Who shall ascend into Heaven? (that is, to bring Christ down from above:) 7 Or, Who shall descend into the deep? (that is, to bring up Christ again from the dead.) 8 But what saith it? The word is nigh thee, even in thy mouth, and in***

> *thy heart: that is, the word of faith, which we preach; 9 That if thou shalt confess with thy mouth the Lord Jesus, and shalt believe in thine heart that God hath raised him from the dead, thou shalt be saved. 10 For with the heart man believeth unto righteousness; and with the mouth confession is made unto salvation. 11 For the Scripture saith, Whosoever believeth on him shall not be ashamed. 12 For there is no difference between the Jew and the Greek: for the same Lord over all is rich unto all that call upon him. 13 For whosoever shall call upon the name of the Lord shall be saved.*

This is one of the most powerful Scriptures found in the Bible regarding someone getting saved. This passage of Scripture starts by saying, *who shall ascend into Heaven? (That is to bring Christ down from above.) Or, who shall descend into the deep? (That is, to bring up Christ again from the dead.)* This means you do not have to go into Heaven or bring Christ from the dead for you to be saved. Then it goes on to say how you are saved. *But what saith it? The word is nigh thee, even in your mouth, and in your heart: that is the word of faith.* So salvation is found in your heart and by speaking what you believe with your mouth. You don't have to physically see God with your eyes to get saved. You just have to make a confession of faith, and He will show up in your heart. If you confess with your mouth the Lord Jesus and believe in your heart that God raised Him from the dead, you will be saved.

Once someone believes in their heart that God raised Jesus from the dead and confesses with their mouth, He is Lord, Jesus comes to dwell on the inside of them. They immediately are filled with God, or we can say God manifests on the inside of them. Let's look at some Scriptures to prove this point.

Ephesians 3:17 (KJV)
*17 **That Christ may dwell in your hearts by faith;** that ye, being rooted and grounded in love,*

Revelation 3:20 (KJV)
*20 Behold, I stand at the door, and knock: if any man hear my voice, and open the door, **I will come in to him, and will sup with him, and he with me.***

Christ dwells in your heart by faith.

2 Corinthians 6:16 (KJV)
*16 And what agreement hath the temple of God with idols? for ye are the temple of the living God; **as God hath said, I will dwell in them, and walk in them**; and I will be their God, and they shall be my people.*

When you become a child of God, God dwells on the inside of you and walks in you. This is a wonderful truth!

1 Corinthians 3:16 (KJV)
*16 **Know ye not that ye are the temple of God, and that the Spirit of God dwelleth in you?***

The Holy Spirit also comes inside the new believer, and they become the Temple of God.

John 14:21-23 (KJV)
*21 He that hath my Commandments, and keepeth them, he it is that loveth me: and he that loveth me shall be loved of my Father, **and I will love him, and will manifest myself to him.** 22 Judas saith unto him, not Iscariot, **Lord, how is it that thou wilt manifest thyself unto us**, and not unto the world? 23 Jesus answered and said unto him, **If a man love me, he will keep my***

words: and my Father will love him, and we will come unto him, and make our abode with him.

When you love God and keep His Commandments, He promises to manifest Himself to you and not to the world. This means others can't see this manifestation, but you know He is there. God, The Father, and Jesus manifest in a special way to the obedient believer by making their home with them. None of this is seen by the naked eye but is experienced in the person's heart who confesses Jesus as their Lord.

Jesus also taught His disciples that He was sending the Holy Spirit to them after His death and resurrection. However, He revealed that the world would not be able to see the Holy Spirit, but the believer would know that the Holy Spirit was in them.

> **John 14:16-18 (KJV)**
> *16 And I will pray the Father, and he shall give you another Comforter, that he may abide with you for ever; 17 Even the Spirit of truth; whom the world cannot receive, because it seeth him not, neither knoweth him: but ye know him; for he dwelleth with you, and shall be in you. 18 I will not leave you comfortless: I will come to you.*

The Holy Spirit cannot be seen, but true believers know in their hearts when the Holy Spirit comes to dwell on the inside of them. The Holy Spirit is very special and reveals Himself to the Church through the nine gifts of the Spirit, dreams, visions, His Presence, and more. Although we cannot see God with our naked eye, God is here with us, waiting to manifest Himself.

God manifests Himself personally to the person who calls upon the name of the Lord by believing God raised Jesus from the dead and by confessing with their mouth Jesus is Lord. A confession of the mouth brings a manifestation of God. So, God will manifest in someone who believes and confesses Jesus as their Lord. This means it only takes belief in the heart and a confession of faith to get God to show up.

Now I want to show you a powerful Scripture where you can see how God can show up with just faith-filled words. Let's turn to the story of the centurion during the time of Jesus. Jesus marveled at the faith of this centurion and said He had not found such faith in all of Israel. Let's read this amazing story and see how God manifested Himself to this Roman Centurion.

> ### Matthew 8:5-13 (KJV)
>
> *5 And when Jesus was entered into Capernaum, there came unto him a centurion, beseeching him, 6 And saying, Lord, my servant lieth at home sick of the palsy, grievously tormented. 7 **And Jesus saith unto him, I will come and heal him.** 8 The centurion answered and said, Lord, I am not worthy that thou shouldest come under my roof: **but speak the word only, and my servant shall be healed.** 9 For I am a man under authority, having soldiers under me: and I say to this man, Go, and he goeth; and to another, Come, and he cometh; and to my servant, Do this, and he doeth it. 10 **When Jesus heard it, he marvelled, and said to them that followed, Verily I say unto you, I have not found so great faith, no, not in Israel.** 11 And I say unto you, That many shall come from the east and west, and shall sit down with Abraham, and Isaac, and Jacob, in the kingdom of Heaven. 12 But the children of the kingdom shall be cast out into outer darkness: there shall be weeping and gnashing of teeth. 13 **And Jesus said unto the centurion, Go thy way; and as thou hast believed, so be it done unto thee. And his servant was healed in the selfsame hour.***

I want to point out a few facts in this story.

- **FACT NUMBER ONE** - Jesus was going to go to his house.

- **FACT NUMBER TWO** - The centurion stopped the Son of God from coming to his home and believed that Jesus just had to speak the Word for his servant to be healed.

- **FACT NUMBER THREE** - Jesus marveled at his faith and listened to him.

- **FACT NUMBER FOUR** - Jesus did what He asked and just spoke the Word.

- **FACT NUMBER FIVE** - His servant was healed by just the spoken Word of Christ.

So, with all these facts in mind, if Jesus didn't show up to heal his servant, who showed up to heal him? Someone showed up and healed this servant, and we know it was not Jesus. Jesus only spoke the Word. The Holy Spirit showed up and healed the centurion's servant. So, we can see from this amazing story that Jesus revealed that by the spoken Word, the Holy Spirit would show up without being seen by anyone and perform the miracle. The invisible God was made manifest with the confession of Jesus' Words, and a miracle occurred. No one saw God show up, but they knew God was there when the servant was healed.

This story proves the point of this chapter; God can show up and manifest with just a spoken word. The apostles continued the ministry of Jesus and had many miracles occur by just their spoken word. God showed up for them and was revealed in the healing, but someone had to confess something for God to show up.

Acts 3:1-8 (KJV)

1 Now Peter and John went up together into the temple at the hour of prayer, being the ninth hour. 2 And a certain man lame from his mother's womb was carried, whom they laid daily at the gate of the temple which is called Beautiful, to ask alms of them that entered into the temple; 3 Who seeing Peter and John about to go into the temple asked an alms. 4 And Peter, fastening his eyes upon him with John, said, Look on us. 5 And he gave heed unto them, expecting to receive something of them. 6 Then Peter said, Silver and gold have I none; but such as I have give I thee: **In the name of Jesus Christ of Nazareth rise up and walk.** *7 And he took him by the right hand, and lifted him up: and immediately his feet and ankle bones received strength. 8 And he leaping up stood, and walked, and entered with them into the temple, walking, and leaping, and praising God.*

The Apostle Peter confessed **The Name of Jesus Christ of Nazareth** to this man who couldn't walk, and God manifested Himself by healing the man. No one saw God with their naked eye, but it was evident He was there when the man was healed. What made this healing possible? The confession of Peter's mouth made this miracle from God manifest.

In conclusion, God is no farther from manifesting Himself to you than the confession of your mouth. Your confession of Jesus will cause Him to come to dwell on the inside of your heart at salvation, and your confession will get Him to manifest healing or signs and wonders if you need Him to. The words of your mouth can bring a wonderful manifestation of God, if you believe. So, in winning the war of words, there is no better victory than to have God show up when you make a confession of faith. Faith-filled words will cause the invisible God to be seen in our world through miracles, signs, and wonders.

CHAPTER 33

FINAL WORDS

Understanding the power of your words and how they affect the outcome and destiny of your life is a truth that cannot be underestimated. The Bible reveals how God wants to speak through His people and change the world around them. When someone comes into a mature understanding of the power of their words, they are no longer a victim to circumstances but a ruler of their destiny. Coming into the full maturity of being a Christian who knows how to control their tongue is what the Bible calls a *perfect man.*

James 3:2 (KJV)
2 For in many things we offend all. If any man offend not in word, the same is a perfect man, and able also to bridle the whole body.

It is the will of God that we are presented to Jesus as a *perfect man* when He returns. Remember, there is only one gender in Heaven, so the *perfect man* refers to men and women. The word *perfect* in Greek means completely blameless, without transgression, full-grown in mind and understanding, without wavering, and a person obedient to Christ. A *perfect man* will be blameless and without transgression in the words they speak. They will also be full of faith, knowing how to speak to mountains and make them move. To mature to this level, they must be obedient to Christ.

Colossians 1:27-28 (KJV)

27 To whom God would make known what is the riches of the glory of this mystery among the Gentiles; which is Christ in you, the hope of glory: 28 Whom we preach, warning every man, and teaching every man in all wisdom; **that we may present every man perfect in Christ Jesus:**

One of the main functions of the five-fold ministry of the apostles, prophets, evangelists, pastors, and teachers is to help people mature into this **perfect man**.

Ephesians 4:11-13 (KJV)

11 And he gave some, apostles; and some, prophets; and some, evangelists; and some, pastors and teachers; 12 **For the perfecting of the saints,** *for the work of the ministry, for the edifying of the body of Christ: 13 Till we all come in the unity of the faith, and of the knowledge of the Son of God, unto a* **perfect man**, *unto the measure of the stature of the fulness of Christ:*

It is time for Christians to mature and speak with the wisdom of God. The Scriptures were written to help us grow up and learn what we should say and not say. It is astounding how many Scriptures talk about our mouths and the words we speak. The Bible is filled with story after story of the power of the tongue. This is because we were made in God's image, and God does everything by the power of His spoken Word. God communicates, works, and fights with His Words. When your eyes are opened to the reality that you were made in God's image and have power with your words, your life will never be the same.

The extraordinary truth of the responsibility we carry by speaking to things and having them obey us is a privilege beyond all comprehension. God is waiting for the day for His Church to come into this revelation. When the Church fully comes into this revelation and the knowledge of who they are, it will be the day of the manifestation of the sons of God. All of creation is waiting for the sons of God to be manifested.

> **Romans 8:19 (KJV)**
> *19 **For the earnest expectation of the creature waiteth for the manifestation of the sons of God.***

The sons of God know who they are and what they can accomplish with the spoken Word of God. The devil has deceived the Church far too long and tried to keep them from coming into this revelation. Jesus revealed to His generation the truth of His followers being sons of God and the power they have with their tongue. This revelation may have been hidden from other generations, but now is the hour for this revelation to sweep across the earth once again.

The return of Christ is near, and the revelation of the war of words is of high importance if we are to be ready to meet our Maker. The Church of the living God will be ruling and reigning with Christ throughout all the ages with the understanding of the power of the tongue. God has destined you to come into the maturity of a ***perfect man***.

The mysteries, truths, and revelations in this book are life-changing when understood and applied to one's life. God has called you to walk in the wisdom of God, and to understand His wisdom has everything to do with how you speak. You are called to be a *verbal tactician*. A *verbal tactician* carefully plans and strategizes using their words for a desired outcome. You are no longer called to use your tongue to speak foolishly into the air. Every word you utter out of your mouth carries weight and responsibility.

The responsibility God has given us with our tongues is a game-changer when fully understood. Jesus spoke a parable about the sower sowing the Word to help us better understand the responsibility we have to His Word. This parable contains many revelations about the Word of God and how people respond to His Word. Based upon how you respond to the Word of God is the level of Kingdom power and blessings you will walk in. Let's read this parable together.

Matthew 13:18-23 (KJV)

*18 Hear ye therefore the parable of the sower. 19 **When any one heareth the word of the kingdom,** and understandeth it not, then cometh the wicked one, and catcheth away that which was sown in his heart. This is he which received seed by the way side. 20 But he that received the seed into stony places, **the same is he that heareth the word,** and anon with joy receiveth it; 21 Yet hath he not root in himself, but dureth for a while: for when tribulation or persecution ariseth because of the word, by and by he is offended. 22 **He also that received seed among the thorns is he that heareth the word;** and the care of this world, and the deceitfulness of riches, **choke the word,** and he becometh unfruitful. 23 **But he that received seed into the good ground is he that heareth the word, and understandeth it;** which also beareth fruit, and bringeth forth, some an hundredfold, some sixty, some thirty.*

This parable reveals the level of people receiving or not receiving the power of God's spoken Word. Some people hear the Word of God, but the devil steals the Word from them when they don't understand. Others hear the Word but cannot endure any persecution or warfare the Word might bring. Another person hears the Word but gets distracted in life, choking out the Word. Finally, some people hear the Word of God and bring forth fruit in their life.

God has called you to bring forth fruit in your life. To bring forth this fruit, you will have to respond to the Word of God and walk in the wisdom of God. Each chapter in this book contains wisdom from God in the multi-faceted understanding of how our tongues affect every area of our lives. There is heavy warfare when it comes to God's Word and the words we speak. When you fully understand this war, you will obey the Word of God and watch every word that comes out of your mouth. You will also seek God in a very meaningful way to have Him speak through you. Then, when you develop into the mature image of a *perfect man,* you will be a voice for God on the earth, defeat the devil and win the war of words.

A big part of walking in the wisdom of God is knowing how to pray and talk to God. You cannot come before God haphazardly and speak foolish words before His Presence. God does not listen to prayers that are filled with fear, doubt, and unbelief. God responds to sincere faith-filled prayers. Prayers spoken in faith will cause mountains to be moved and give God the opportunity to do miracles. You must be responsible with the words you say before God Almighty. God takes into account everything you communicate.

Ecclesiastes 5:2 (KJV)
2 Be not rash with thy mouth, and let not thine heart be hasty to utter any thing before God: for God is in Heaven, and thou upon earth: therefore let thy words be few.

There are very few revelations that can dramatically change your life, like understanding the power of your words. You can change your life in an instance by just changing how you speak. If you can shift your thinking, speaking, and acting to align with God's Word, you can go from being a victim to a *powerful spiritual warrior*. God is calling you to come up higher with your words. You must allow God to weaponize your words so you will begin to speak like He speaks and defeat the devil in your generation. You were destined before you were born to be like God and to win the war of words.

The Holy Spirit Divinely inspired me through the entire process of writing this book. What has been revealed within the pages of this book can change your life forever. Each chapter of this book plays an essential guide and blueprint on how to win the war of words. When you start to understand who you are called to be as a **perfect man** and **son of God,** you will go through a paradigm shift in your thinking. This new way of thinking will affect every word you speak. Then, your life will never be the same when you fully understand the power of your tongue and how your words can affect the outcome of your life. Your words make all the difference in the world if you are to come into your God-given destiny and win the war of words. God has given you the ability to have power over creation because you were made in His image.

Now is the time for you to win the war of words!

About the Author

Vince Baker was born in Southern California and lived on 17 acres just north of Sacramento. As a child, Vince was raised as a Southern Baptist. Vince was always drawn to the Lord and even said he wanted to be a preacher at a young age.

Vince's life was uneventful until one day he encountered God while driving in his car at the age of 17. God manifested Himself to Vince in such a powerful way that his life would never be the same. After this experience, Vince dedicated his life to the Lord and became a Christian. In that same month, Vince received a book from his Christian Grandma called "Apostle of Faith." This book was about a famous miracle-working Evangelist named Smith Wigglesworth. God used his testimony to prepare Vince for ministry. God also used the testimony of Smith to talk to Vince about things He wanted to do through him in his later years

Vince decided to go to a Christian High School his senior year. He met a seasoned Evangelist at this high school, who took different Churches to feed the poor and evangelize. Vince found out he lived near the Evangelist and started traveling with him. During this time, Vince became his right-hand man and saw many amazing miracles on the streets through this ministry. This ministry was called to train the Church on how to evangelize with power. Vince was able to travel up and down the west coast ministering to the homeless and helpless while equipping the Church. Vince has a big heart when it comes to the poor, homeless, and hurting people.

Within a short time, Vince heard from God to go to Bible College. Through confirmation from God and a miracle of his tuition paid for, Vince started to study the Bible more deeply at this Bible College. The training and foundation in the Scriptures Vince received were priceless. Vince ended up graduating as the Valedictorian from this Bible College.

After Bible College, Vince started ministering to kids at a Christian school, taught Sunday School, and functioned in the local Church. Vince later moved into full-time ministry and was an assistant Pastor at another local Church for five years during the mid-'90s.

As an assistant pastor, Vince visited a Church where the Prophet Kim Clement was ministering. Prophet Kim Clement pulled Vince out of the crowd and prophesied over him. In that prophecy, God spoke to Vince through Kim Clement that he would use him and that he needed to prepare himself.

Vince later worked in the marketplace, where he is the CEO and part-owner of Agora Advantage. God called Vince to the marketplace, but Vince knew that he would be called back into full-time ministry later in life. Agora Advantage has been a fantastic opportunity where Vince grew in many ways. Vince knew that Agora was where he was supposed to be. He was voted in as the CEO of Agora Advantage on the Day of Pentecost as a sign from God.

As Vince started nearing the prophesied time that God would bring him back into full-time ministry, he began seeking the Lord more deeply. During this time, Vince had another unforgettable encounter with God regarding the Ark of the Covenant. God gave Vince a vision of four men carrying the Ark of the Covenant up the steps onto a stage in a large Church. The Holy Spirit spoke to Vince and said, "Wherever you read Ark of the Covenant in the Old Testament think Holy Spirit. Wherever you read Holy Spirit in the New Testament think Ark of the Covenant. Put the two together and you will know Me." Vince went and studied these two subjects everyplace he could find them in the Bible, and he received tremendous insight into understanding the Holy Spirit.

God also revealed to Vince a prophetic way to study the Bible from this experience. Vince went on to spend years in the Word of God, with the Holy Spirit studying different subjects of the Bible. At the leading of the Holy Spirit, Vince researched every place a word or phrase was found, from the Old and New Testaments. Vince has currently done over 400 of these studies, some of which took over a month to complete. The revelations that came out of these studies were life changing. Vince copied all of these teachings and revelations down in Word docs, which make up a lot of the truths he writes about in his books and messages. When you study a subject everywhere it is found in the Bible you can understand the full counsel of God on the subject. Vince also received many dreams and visitations from God during this time.

Vince has a unique calling where he can preach, teach, prophecy, move in the gifts of the Spirit, bring healing, and perform miracles by the power of the Holy Spirit. Vince is called to help the body of Christ come into their destiny and High Calling.

Currently, Vince resides in Northern California with his wife Eunice and their two dogs enjoying the blessings of God.

INVITE VINCE TO SPEAK

VISIT

WWW.VINCEBAKERMINISTRIES.COM

ADDITIONAL BOOK BY
VINCE BAKER

ADDITIONAL BOOK BY
<u>VINCE BAKER</u>

www.amazon.com/author/vincebaker
www.VinceBakerMinistries.com

ADDITIONAL BOOK BY
<u>VINCE BAKER</u>

www.amazon.com/author/vincebaker

www.VinceBakerMinistries.com

ADDITIONAL BOOK BY
VINCE BAKER

www.amazon.com/author/vincebaker

www.VinceBakerMinistries.com

ADDITIONAL BOOK BY
<u>VINCE BAKER</u>

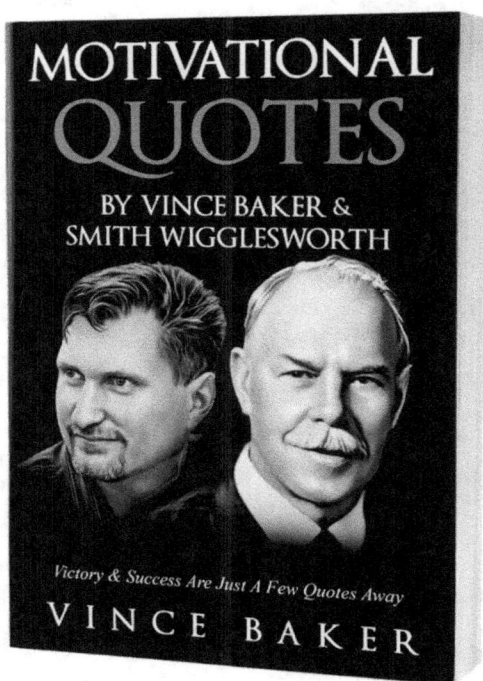

www.amazon.com/author/vincebaker

www.VinceBakerMinistries.com

www.ingramcontent.com/pod-product-compliance
Lightning Source LLC
Chambersburg PA
CBHW071701120626
46550CB00001B/60